"We are not human beings having a spiritual experience.
We are spiritual beings having a human experience."

Pierre Teilhard de Chardin

Untying the Karmic Knot

Healing Through Past-Life Regression Therapy
Knowledge Through Life-Between-Lives Therapy
The Earth's Future Through Progressions

Diane Morrin, M.A.

Cover Image: The Endless Karmic Knot

TO FIND A REGRESSION THERAPIST IN YOUR STATE OR COUNTRY GO TO:
www.newtoninstitute.org

Editor Marty Humphreys
www.coachwrite.com

First published by Dog Ear Publishing
4010 W. 86th Street, Ste H
Indianapolis, IN 46268
www.dogearpublishing.net

ISBN: 978-160844-640-7

This book is printed on acid-free paper.

Printed in the United States of America

DEDICATION

To all of my brave clients who have the strength and courage to step into the unknown and walk the road less traveled.

May their courage, faith, and accomplishments light the way for others who will venture forth on this path of self-discovery and spiritual attainment.

"It takes courage to grow up and become who you really are."

e e cummings 1894-1962

Table of Contents

PART THREE

Life-Between-Lives Regression

PART FOUR

Reflections on Regression Therapy

PART FIVE

Progressions: Enlightened Times to Come

Preface

"We learn the rope of life by untying its knots."
Jean Toomer

The Beginnings

Déjà Vu...

Déjà vu means "Already Seen" in French.

Most of us have experienced recognition or instant awareness in places where we have never been or perhaps have appeared only in our dreams. These flashes appear like a single frame in a film strip: instantaneous, still, and often in full Technicolor.

There are people who enter our lives for whom we have instant rapport, or instant antagonism. Déjà vu is real, because you have been there to those places, and you have a history with those people who evoke emotions when you meet them. Every contact, every life, every location affects us and who we are today...for better or worse.

Consider Steve who cannot drive past the Little Big Horn on US 90 without every hair on his body standing up in fear. The first time Martha went to Munich, Germany, to speak at a Film Festival occurring at theaters all over the city, she never consulted a street map because she already knew where to go and how to get there. Tom, a retired combat pilot and career naval officer, shivered during a drive across Thermopylae in 110 degree heat. He had the same experience on the path taken by the Samurai during a visit to a Shogun's palace in Northern Japan.

Consider Lara who "recognized" her present husband the first time she saw him at the school library. Elizabeth feels very uncomfortable around water, Merrily cannot drive over a suspension bridge because of her fear of heights, and John is afraid of the dark—and he is 52 years old.

Consider Noreen who hates her job and doesn't know why. Wendell, the successful executive, husband, father who senses there is something "missing" in this life. Susannah writes obituaries for a newspaper with a large circulation in a major city, she has no ambition to write anything else, and she has been told she has "healing hands".

My clients come to me with challenges and issues ranging from depression, anger, relationship conflicts, fears, debilitating habits, free-floating anxiety, and chronic apparently incurable pain. After applying traditional talk therapy with little or no success, with the client's permission, we continue our search for a cause and a cure through regression therapy. What is uncovered is the reason for their déjà vu experiences and the origin of their current issues.

Defining the Karmic Knot...

Karma is the law of cause and effect from our thoughts, words, actions, and intentions throughout the totality of our spiritual existence. Karmic Knots are the complex entanglements created between two spirits who have spent multiple lives together. We have free will to select positive or negative choices. These choices either tighten the knot, or loosen the tension of the tangle.

In order to untie the Karmic Knot, first we must locate it. Past-life regression provides access to the source of our emotional, physical, and spiritual problems. Through a hypnotherapeutic journey to an earlier time and place, we experience the inciting event or relationship. That experience releases the tension tightening the Karmic Knot. Comprehension cuts the thread, as it unravels the burden carried by us from the past into the present.

Awareness Brings Healing…

By becoming aware of where we've been over time we begin to understand the reason for our current existence. Our spirit creates the plan for our existence from one life to the next. As we go through each life we are teaching and we are learning; we never rest. There's time to rest *between* lives.

During each life every moment is precious, every moment is special; each inhale, each exhale is purposeful and significant. Throughout history each soul's purpose is to learn and to teach, or do both at differing times in different relationships.

Accidents are not accidents,

Coincidence is not chance,

Synchronicity is not happenstance.

Our spirit's intention is to become aware, aware of when we're learning, when we're teaching, and aware of our progress as we go forward into the future. Past-life regression contributes to our awareness by providing understanding for this life from a former one. Life-between-lives regression provides us with information about the "whys" of our current life. Knowledge is always power, power is always strength, and both our past lives and the spirit world contribute knowledge to our present incarnation.

This is **one instance where it *is* all about us:** our purpose, our challenges, our relationships, and **our progress**. At the same time our actions and reactions affect all those we contact, engage, or ignore. There is no "for better or worse", there is no "good vs. evil", there are no "saints" and there are no "sinners". These are value judgments created by man to elevate or denigrate other men and women. They are earth-bound, human made, and irrelevant to your soul's purpose. Rewards and punishments, assets and liabilities, benefits and detriments are all words, just words. Hot air if spoken, dried ink on paper, dots on tape, chiseled in marble, smoke in the sky, neon lights illuminating the night—transient, temporary, mortal.

Spiritual Imperative...

As human beings on earth, we can discover, accept, and untie our personal Karmic Knots. When we undertake this task collectively, all negative agendas surrounding our intentions will be released. Positive, loving energy will transform the earth for the betterment of all living things. We can learn, teach, and practice loving kindness to all.

As spiritual beings, our responsibility is acceptance of our soul's identity, living our soul's purpose during this lifetime, and lastly, fulfilling our spiritual contracts with others during this incarnation. As we progress through successive lifetimes, learning and teaching, loving and understanding…and always without judgment of self or others, we elevate the energy of the planet.

You Are Not Alone…

Take a moment and digest that statement.

Whether you are physically present on the earth, or in the spirit world between lives, you are surrounded by love and loving spirits…and in turn, when you are between lives you become one of those loving spirits.

We are universal and eternal.

Universal love is the spiritual imperative of our planet.

What is your part in the creation of this love?

Part One

Introducing...
Hope through Healing

"Imagine all the people living life in peace.
You may say I'm a dreamer, but I'm not the only one.
I hope someday you'll join us, and the world will be as one."

John Lennon

Many think there is no heaven, no hell.
That hell is here on earth.
And heaven?

We are spirits, spiritual energy, unique and individual souls who happen to be wrapped in this material physical package, the body, with the assets and liabilities of all things present in a material world; we existed prior to this package and we will survive after the package decays, deteriorates, and eventually dies.

Energy is immortal. Energy cannot be destroyed. Rather it transitions into another form and continues to exist throughout time and space. You are energy.

ENERGETIC QUANTITY

Can we quantify energy?

Can we measure energy?

What units apply to spiritual energy?

Weight, volume?

How much spiritual energy is available to us on a daily basis? Over a lifetime?

Is the spiritual energy a constant, or does it vary, and do we have control over the amount available to us in any given situation?

Through regression therapy we can validate our spiritual energy and that of others around us. We can validate the amorphous quality of that energy, and that it exists and co-exists in more than one place and time. We bring some of our total spiritual energy with us when we come to earth and assume material form. The exact amount or percentage is less important than the location of the majority of our spiritual energy. As we enter and explore the afterlife during a life-between-lives regression experience, we come to accept the truth of the existence of that world and that we exist simultaneously as energy here and now, and there and now.

ENERGETIC QUALITY

Can we qualify energy?

Is there "good" energy?

Is there "bad" energy?

As human beings in this earthly package, are we supposed to know the difference between the two?

How?

Does it matter?

Why?

If it doesn't matter, why do we care?

Why do we spend our lives seeking our purpose, our life's work, our reason to live, our passion or instinct to survive?

Why do we try to understand the meaning of what often seems meaningless?

All of these questions have answers. Across the world, cultures and societies answer these questions for the group. Throughout history, men have answered these questions in order to assume power over other men. Leaders dictated the answers, and the followers turned over their responsibility to come up with their own answers to these leaders. Religions, political systems, philosophies, social and cultural structures rise and fall based on their answers to those questions.

"Untying the Karmic Knot" returns the responsibility for answering those questions to the individual spirit whose purpose is to provide those answers for themselves. Through hypnotic regressions the spirit reunites with its essence and discovers the truth about this life, previous lives, and their life-between-lives in the spirit world. Some will refer to that place as heaven, others as the "hereafter" or "afterlife", all very accurate words describing the place of its existence.

Hope through Healing…

Our survival instinct is evidence of the power of our spiritual energy. Intangible, variable, and immaterial, our survival instinct persists fueled by "hope"— another intangible, variable, and immaterial energy we know exists. Even though we can't see it, touch it, taste it; we can and do "feel" it.

When we are open to the acceptance of our spiritual energy, we can "feel" it, too. During prayer, meditation, in the peak performance zone, watching a sunset, experiencing birth; our spiritual energy takes its rightful space in our daily lives.

Where there is hope, there is spiritual energy.

Where there is spiritual energy, there is hope—*and there is healing.*

Chapter One

A New Perspective on Healing

"Healing yourself is connected with healing others."
Yoko Ono

Through the ages humankind has used various methods to heal the body, mind and spirit. External and internal treatments include herbs, medicines, surgeries, faith-based methods of prayer and laying on of hands, application of various elements of minerals, oils, plants, animal parts, leeches, blood-letting, sweat lodges, ice packs, freezing and sacrifices to the gods. As medicine progressed, treatment replaced banishment and isolation for mental illness. Electroshock, drug therapy, talk therapy, self help, group therapy, drama therapy, cognitive and behavior therapy entered the system for treatment of mental disorders, from depression to total breaks from reality—or the reality as it was defined by the society in charge.

Some treatments healed the person, others simply placed the problem in "remission", and still others actually killed the patient. Accidents, confusion, and miscommunication continue to be responsible for medical failures in traditional hospital settings.

The objective of healing is to improve the patient's physical, mental and emotional health. Ideally, healing cures the patient. If the patient is only a physical, material being, then the word "healing" applies only to the body. If the body is cured, the patient continues to live—unless, of course, he or she died during the treatment. Correction: his or her *body* expired.

Dr. Bernie Siegel, M.D., in his attitude-changing book, "Love, Medicine and Miracles" (Harper Collins, New York, 1982), altered all patients' perspective on treatment. It was no longer just about science and the body parts; it was about attitude, emotions, perspective, and imagery. After years of observation, Dr. Siegel concluded that the mind and the spirit contributed as much, or more, to the curative process as all the drugs, radiation, or chemotherapy in the doctor's little black bag. Those patients, who put forward mental and spiritual energy to support their hope for a positive outcome, a survival script, or a peaceful passing, achieved their purpose. In fact, quantifiable survival rates depended upon the patient's attitude toward his illness and hope for his outcome.

Regardless of your illness, or the quality of the medical care you can afford, some issues are not resolved through traditional methods. Traditional psychotherapy, with or without pharmacological support, can continue for months, or years, without any measurable improvement. When all of the accepted methods fail the client, they often turn to non-traditional therapies in the hope of a cure, or at least an improvement in their condition. Some of those have proved to be quackery, some result in the "halo" effect seen when placebos work even without the designated drug in the pill, and others are a temporary fix for a long term issue.

Hypnotherapeutic regression offers hope for all who suffer from mental, emotional, or physical challenges. Regression therapy is not a cure in the traditional sense; rather it is a return to the source of the problem. Through past-life regression, the client observes the causal factors involved in the current issue during a past incarnation. Knowledge is power. Hypnotism allows the client to observe, re-experience, and understand prior events in their spirit's history in a safe, secure environment.

Childhood regressions go to the traumatic events in this life; past-life regressions go to the source of the problem; and life-between-lives regression takes the client to the spirit world to ask questions, receive meaningful answers, and obtain proof of their continuous and continuing purposeful existence. In my work, I combine past-life regression and life-between-lives regression. The past-life regression releases the negative energy involved with the issue the client has chosen to heal. When we die in the past life, the client moves into the life-between-lives portion of the regression session where knowledge and information are received in the spirit world. Part of the information provided is rediscovery of the lessons we are working on, our purpose for coming to earth at this time, and where we will find meaning.

After we become aware of our purpose, and realize the truth of our immortality in a loving environment, hope is found and therefore healing comes to all who have experienced this process.

Chapter Two

Hypnosis
Entering the Experience

"Only hypnosis is capable of opening up amnesia."

Betty Hill

U nlike most popular misconceptions, hypnosis does not render us unconscious. It is a wakeful state of relaxed attention focused on the voice of the facilitator. It is not possible for us to do anything that we don't want to do, as our ego is always in control. Rather, hypnosis uses relaxing imagery that enables us to access information that is stored in the unconscious mind.

Hypnosis allows our mind to relax, which creates what is called a "trance state". We can access our past lives when we are in a trance state. A trance state is an altered state of mind that can be naturally created in several different ways. People who meditate may experience an altered state similar to a hypnotic trance. Native Americans drum, Buddhists chant, Dervishes whirl, and artists slip into a trance-like zone when their creations are "inspired".

Through this hypnotherapy we are able to see the path our spirit has traveled throughout time. We learn the lessons we have chosen, the purpose behind our traumas, and the reason for our relationships, then and now.

Re-experiencing our past lives shows us where our current problems began, how and why we created them, and with whom. No man is an island, even though there are times in our lives when we feel isolated, abandoned and so alone. As we encounter the origin of our issue in a past life the negative energy within it is released and the hurt healed.

The first step in regression therapy is to share one's life story. While sharing the entire life story, from birth to the present, details emerge of relationships; supportive, abusive, confusing, and loving. Happy times, traumatic events, choices and consequences are shared and discussed in a supportive atmosphere of acceptance. Phobias, fears, and awkward uncomfortable feelings emerge hand in hand with the warm emotions that lie within all of us.

Currently, clients may struggle with anger, depression, resentment or anxiety produced by events resulting from their choices, or their reactions to the actions of others. Or those same emotions can come from taking what they considered wrong turns at the forks in their path. Or perhaps they were simply "at the wrong place at the wrong time" when an event occurred that radically altered the direction of their lives.

Their history, those details they share, reveals the clients' most pressing problems. From their revelations, we focus the past life portion of the regression on their most significant issue, and go back to the lifetime holding the secret to resolving that problem.

The Karmic Knot...

Karma is the relationship between our actions and the natural consequences that follow them. Our actions include all of our thoughts, words, and deeds. These can be with loving intention or harmful intention. Those with loving intention cause positive results to come to us and those with harmful intentions cause us to suffer negative consequences. Karma basically is the law of cause and effect. The actions we choose have shaped our past, continue to shape our present, and will determine our future experiences. It's the old saying, "what goes around comes around". The individual is the sole doer of his actions and is also the sole enjoyer of the fruits of his actions or the sole sufferer of them. Our actions and reactions form the quality of our life. We have free will to choose in every situation that arises in our lives.

In regression therapy I see karma playing out continuously. It is important to note, however, that before we incarnate into our next life we do write our script. We are in no way coerced into experiencing negative happenings in our life because of our poor choices in past lives. Rather, we are lovingly guided to learn lessons that will help us understand that loving choices promote our spiritual growth. If we have harmed someone in a past life, we will want to write adversity into our life script so that we will have the opportunity to learn the lesson from the other side of a similar experience. Therefore, adversity is not punitive; we have chosen it to learn.

The Karmic Knot, then, is a term used to describe the complex web of karmic entanglements created between two spirits who have spent multiple lives together. Through time, our relationships combine the entire range of emotions, thoughts, and deeds, and the energy expressed weaves strands of karma together in loops, bows, and circles culminating in a knot of complexity. Sometimes the knot strangles the individuals, sometimes the knot is the source of present day pain, and yet sometimes the knot represents the intimate connection between two loving soul mates. Regression therapy frequently untangles the Karmic Knot when one of the two in a relationship returns to the origin of the knot in a past life. Re-experiencing the original drama releases the negative energy held between the two, enabling both to move forward in their current life unencumbered by hostile energy toward the other.

Therefore, regression therapy leads clients to the Karmic Knot that is the source of their pain in this lifetime. They will re-experience the actions in a former life that created their current adversity.

The first portion of the regression leads the client to the past life that illuminates the origin of the chosen issue or difficult relationship that brought them to my office. Re-experiencing the beginning of a problem can resolve the issue, whether it is a phobia, a difficult relationship, or a painful emotion. Because the purpose of this therapy is to heal today's issue or problem, the process of taking the client back to its origin releases the negative karmic energy.

Consider the issue a blister with fresh clean skin beneath the translucent bubble of fluid covering it. Constant painful friction has resulted in the blister, and then ignoring the pressure on that area of skin increased the swelling and the pain. Lancing the blister is dangerous as it lets bacteria and infection into the vulnerable area. The recommended remedy is to simply allow the body to absorb the fluid. That takes time, patience, and assumes we can ignore the pain and inconvenience of the blister. The blister becomes a constant reminder of our suffering.

Past-life regression accelerates the cure by observing the area *as* it became damaged. Observing what caused the blister allows the sufferer to understand that the pain was the direct result of their actions and/or reactions, and what motivated them at that time.

Our assumption is that we do not hurt ourselves on purpose. That makes sense. If we learn that all harm, all pain, and all suffering have reasons in the universal order of things, does that reduce the harm, lessen the pain, or eliminate the suffering? As human beings we seek order in our universe.

We need balance, justification, and reason in order to achieve understanding. We seek these elements throughout our lives believing our discoveries will ease our pain, stop our suffering, and guarantee salvation, happiness and finally, contentment. By turning outward instead of inward, we believe the answers are just beyond our reach. Past-life regression encourages us to turn inward and beyond to discover the source of this life's challenges.

So Many Lives, So Much to Learn...

Like restoring your computer to an earlier time and date to recover a lost file full of essential data, how do you know which point to specify for recovery? The client answers that question during the session.

At the beginning of the regression, some clients describe seeing a card file in a recipe box in their mind's eye. Each file represents a past life, and they go through the series of past lives until they drop into the "right" one. In actuality it is our spirit guide who selects the particular past life that will help us find the Karmic Knot that needs untying. This spirit guide is with us always, both during this life and for many past lives. They help us through difficult times on earth, trying to keep us out of harm's way and on the path we chose before incarnating. Our spirit guide also accompanies us into the afterlife to help us learn from our experiences on earth.

The Trance…

Relaxation techniques provide the stimulus to ease the body and the mind into a passive, receptive state. This enables the brain waves to change from the alpha waves of the aroused, alert, conscious mind to the theta waves present in periods of deep relaxation. Should you relax even further you will fall asleep. Relaxation does not mean you are powerless. During the entire process you are totally in control.

You are aware of being in the counseling room. Your internal censor is in charge of what information you choose to share with the counselor. Even though my clients close their eyes, they can, and sometimes do, open their eyes and are fully back in the counseling room. This trance state allows the conscious mind access to the unconscious mind where all memories are stored from our past lives. It is impossible to do or say anything you do not want to do or say while in a trance state.

You are always in control.

The Experience…

During the experience of a past life, the client relives the events emotionally. For example, when you experience a marriage, you feel the joy of that event…if the event was joyful. When a loved one passes, you feel the grief of the loss. During each past life you recognize some of the important people as being the same spirit that currently occupies the body of an important person in your present life.

There is truth to the statement: "The eyes are the windows to the soul." Regardless of the period in history, recognition happens when you look into the eyes of the person in your past life. Their essence is familiar to you. Gender is irrelevant, as we incarnate as both women and men. Physical attributes vary from lifetime to lifetime, so recognition is not based on the package, but the "person" within.

After experiencing a few past lives you realize certain people in your current life have been with you in many of your past lives. These spirits are a group of beings that incarnate throughout time together.

They teach, and they learn.

They help each other work on issues. Each spirit chooses lessons to learn or to teach another spirit in the group. On the stage of time, the group sets the scene, writes the script, and casts the roles in an effort to push, pull, or coerce one another to grow, to learn, and to heal. The individual souls in the group change roles, sometimes victim, sometimes rescuer, sometimes persecutor in life after life supporting the spiritual growth of each other.

When we look at the total of our past lives we see various themes play out over time. We see issues, problems, challenges, assets, gifts, use and abuse of advantages or disadvantages. It is a process inevitably filled with pain, but also with learning and hope as we progress in our spiritual awareness over time.

We experience either a positive or negative connection to a specific spirit, activity, or emotion. Regardless, when we are born into our current life the veil of forgetfulness falls to conceal the plan we have for this new life. If we knew the end of the story, there would be no point in living it.

We have planned to be attracted to whom and what we have connected to in past lives so that we can work through past difficult situations and grow. In some cases we bring forward aversion and fear toward certain people and situations. These become the issues that we have the opportunity to resolve in this life. For example, if a person has harmed us in a prior life we may be either attracted to him or afraid of him in this life. The relationship we choose to develop in this life depends on what provides the best opportunity to resolve the past situation. In addition, we are attracted to some people in order to form a positive relationship because he or she is playing a supportive role in this life during our times of difficulty.

The Duet, The Dance, The Do-over...

In past-life regressions I have seen two spirits who are partners in the dance of life. In one life, he leads. In the next life, she leads. In the next life they vie for leadership. In one life one will be the villain, in the next life he or she will be the victim. It's about the experience of living on both sides of the equation, the feelings associated with each role. Often, the villain learns more than the victim.

Sometimes two spirits will keep the same role life after life. He or she is always the villain, or always the victim, regardless of the gender.

Even though we are all heroes in our own drama, my clients know they should not be surprised to discover dishonorable deeds in their past lives. Many clients come into counseling believing that they have been wronged; rarely do they come to find help processing responsibility for harming others. As true as their victimization may be in this lifetime, there is always the possibility—perhaps the probability—that they have wronged others in previous lifetimes.

Villain or victim, until they see it for themselves, many clients have a hard time accepting responsibility for causing someone else's pain. The villain incarnation is rarely, if ever, all bad. As the victim incarnation is rarely all good.

We teach or we learn.
We instruct or we observe.
We accept or we deny.
We love or we fear.
There is nothing else.

Consistent Comfort...

Emotions we think of as painful or negative are often comfortable to some individuals because of their familiarity. If a person lives through periods of high anxiety and fear, when the source of those feelings is gone, often the intensity lingers on beyond the existence of what provoked them in the first place.

Spirits reincarnate in groups with relationships juggled to accomplish the education for every member of the group. In addition, intense emotions such as anger, jealousy, grief, and depression can continue throughout many lifetimes.

Clients come for regression work because they cannot determine the source of the emotional pain in this lifetime. Even though the client will tell me the reasons she is depressed or angry – usually very valid reasons – it has always been true that these emotions did not begin in this life. Because these feelings are familiar from past lives, we turn to them naturally, like a favorite old sweater that we pull on and instantly feel comfortable.

In many cases, discovering the origin of these feelings in past lives causes them to disappear in this life. Watching or re-experiencing the decision or the incident is enough to dispel the negative energy associated with the event. Taking this to the extreme, I have had clients come into their first session suicidaly depressed. In most of these situations the clients have committed suicide in a former life, often their most recent past life. They are attracted to this exit route because it is familiar. Uncovering this truth in a past life cuts off the need for suicidal thinking in this life as the client sees from the past life that this is a bad choice. Of all choices available to the spirit, suicide is never in the script.

Another familiar carry-over from a past life is anger. Even though human beings have good reasons for anger in this life, the tendency of an individual to react (or over-react) to a situation with anger is often a carryover from past lives. It is important to remember that what is familiar to us from past lives will *attract* us in this life. This makes past-life regression work critical to the resolution of our attraction to these harmful emotions, people and actions.

Physical Pain...

If you have a body pain that has no explanation in your present life, it could have come forward from a past life. The good news is that if it is a residual past life body pain, and you re-experience that past life episode, that pain probably will go away. In my regression work I have seen pains in the neck, back, and knees totally vanish after my client goes back to the past life where these originated. I'm sure any area of the body could hold this type of past life pain.

"Why Me?"

We have all asked that question when faced with life's challenges. Some of us turn to the Bible for answers, others consult therapists, and still others disappear into their despair. Past-life regression is the technique we have to answer that question, whether the clients seek answers for their challenges or reasons for their blessings.

A valuable method without judgment, past-life regression can solve problems, clarify issues, and help us to understand the circumstances that cause us pain. Past-life regression releases the negative karmic energy within the knot and therefore changes the energy in one's present life.

But, is it true?

Clients often ask me if I believe in past lives.

My answer is always the same: It doesn't matter if either of us "believe" in past lives, reincarnation, or spirit guides. Access to past lives through hypnotherapy opens the window into a place where the answers to that eternal question, "Why me?" may be. If the information is available, whether it's physically located in our own brain or in a nonphysical form in another dimension, we benefit from the light shed on the issue.

My research indicates that our most difficult problems rarely originate in this life. Therefore the resolution of these problems lies at the root of them, where and when they occurred. It is critically important to go to the root of the problem to discover the answer to "Why me?"

The answer is *not*:

"Why NOT you?"

Chapter Three

The Therapeutic Process

"…there is no difference between large and small problems,
for issues concerning the treatment of
people are all the same."

Albert Einstein

My clients come to me with an issue, challenge, or problem that has become so troublesome it interferes with living their lives. They are in enough pain to make the effort to contact a therapist to help them ease or eliminate it altogether. Traditional talk therapy involves active listening on the part of the therapist, a gift for some of us, but an essential part of our training for all of us.

The skills I apply in traditional psychotherapy are the same ones I use in past-life and life-between-lives regression therapies. In both models, there is no judgment, no criticism, and no control of the client. The process is the same until my clients cross the threshold into the other dimension, the spirit world.

When a client comes to me to do regression therapy (which combines both past-life and life-between-lives regressions), he or she spends the first session of approximately two hours telling his or her life story. Many are familiar with the therapeutic process because of treatment from different therapists, for them this session looks like the "Cliff Notes" of a life. They've related the story so often that it comes out almost as if they are talking about their best friend, worst enemy, or a perfect stranger who happened to share their skin. For others, their survival instinct kicks in as soon as they sit down in the chair and they hide behind their masks, roles, or sense of humor.

In traditional psychotherapy, the therapist pays as much or more attention to the body language coming from the client as to the words flowing or stumbling from his or her mouth. What is said, or what is left unsaid, must be heard by the therapist in order to be successful in helping the client.

When the client tells his life story, I offer suggestions for information he might be able to learn in the spirit world based on details from his autobiography. If the client has a particular request to question someone who has passed; or if the client's issues are with someone still living and wants to know what that someone needs from him now; or perhaps the client has "why" or "why me" questions he seeks answers to help him with his struggle; my purpose is to help him ask the significant questions in order to get the most helpful answers.

At the end of her life story, we discuss her top issue, problem, or relationship that she wants to focus on during the past life portion of the regression. I give her an assignment to make up a list of about 12 questions she would like answered in the spirit world during the life-between-lives portion of the regression. The goal of the past life portion of the regression is to heal the chosen issue, while the goal of the life-between-lives portion of the regression is to gather information and knowledge. The regression itself takes between three and five hours, and is done in the second session. I have found that it is important to put a space between the life story and the regression as most clients remember significant happenings or feelings after telling their story. This information is important to include.

Acknowledging everyone's need for assurance when entering any unknown territory, the first half hour of the regression session is designed to relax the client and provide information about the experience and what to expect. I take great pains to reassure my clients that this is not "judgment day", nor will their cruel parent continue the pattern of abuse that may have brought them to me in the first place. Our mission is healing and fact finding, not justice on either side of the spiritual curtain.

As the facilitator, I have a script designed to induce relaxation in order to gently access the former lives and then gain entry into the spirit world. With the eyes closed and the body reclined in an extended chair in my office, the client relaxes into a trance state.

As I recite the script, I notice the tension leave the body as the facial muscles go slack, and the client leaves the cognitive state. The forehead smoothes, the lines around the mouth fill out, and the shoulders sink into the upholstery supporting the client. Limbs stretch, feet and ankles create arcs, and deep thoughtful sighs escape the lips. When rapid eye movement appears behind the eyelids, the client experiences a past life.

Once there, emotions surface; at times confusion at what is seen, some clients talk with their hands in their efforts to describe the setting, and sometimes those gestures become defensive movements as if to ward off an attacker.

It's important to finish the precipitating episode in order to cover all aspects of the issue chosen to release the karmic energy and heal. When the past life has been fully experienced, then the client moves into the spirit world to obtain knowledge and information, asking her questions with my prompting.

In all of the literature on this therapeutic technique and my personal experience as a therapist there is no record of any harm occurring to the client. It has been my experience that all the past life memories have a positive impact on the quality of this current life.

Issues Responding to Regression Therapy:

Abandonment and rejection

Addiction

Trauma

Victims of abuse or crimes

Grief and loss

Anger

Major illness

Chronic illness

Depression

Difficult relationships

Issues with difficult children

Issues with difficult parents

Fears and phobias

Body pains that have no explanation in this life

Perpetrators of abuse or crimes

Truly – any issue a person brings with them to heal.

"We may define therapy as a search for value."
Abraham Maslow

Part Two

Past-Life Regression
...moving forward by looking backward.

*"God generates beings, and sends them back over
and over again, till they return to Him."*

Koran

*"Souls are poured from one into another of different kinds
of bodies of the world."*

Jesus Christ, in Gnostic Gospels: Pistis Sophia

*"All pure and holy spirits live on in heavenly places,
and in course of time they are again sent down
to inhabit righteous bodies."*

Josephus, Jewish Historian

A Start to Healing, Not a Short Cut...

In addition to talk therapy, psychotherapists who are trained in hypnosis use this tool to regress their clients into their early childhoods to discover the source of their physical, emotional, or psychological pain. This is called "age regression". All children have traumatic events in their childhoods. Some parents are aware of them and provide the appropriate supportive responses, and some are incapable of the appropriate response to their child.

The therapist is more interested in the emotional effect the event has had on the client rather than the details. For that reason, regression to an early age can often provide significant information to *shorten* the healing process.

Shorten, Not Heal, the Trauma.

Lengthening the process ...

The objective is to heal. Today, people are committed to their therapy sessions, their medications, and their comfort levels. Many are reluctant to heal, because that forces change...and human beings resist change.

It takes courage to heal.

In the following chapters, you will read about people in pain who have the courage and the commitment to face the source of their suffering in order to heal. Traditional talk therapy may identify the issue, age regression may isolate the initiating event in this life, and drugs may relieve the symptoms —temporarily. Only through discovering and re-experiencing the adversity when it first occurred, can the individual heal.

Past-life regressions reveal the totality of our experience over time and throughout space. We see our entire history and those with whom we have shared it. We are able to see the path our spirit has traveled, our lessons learned, our lessons taught, and the entangled relationships we have created with other spirits. Some of these spirits share our present life.

Our past lives show us the source of our current problems, how and why we created them, and with whom we learn and teach.

Experiencing the beginning of a problem resolves the issue as the negative karmic energy that has been held over time is released, whether it is a phobia, a difficult relationship, or a painful emotion.

The healing occurs there, in that time and space.

It does so on many levels:

1)   Mental:

By re-experiencing the original event objectively, logically and emotionally detached, you watch your earlier self relate to the other players in the drama. Gender, age, and roles differ, and are less important to the event than who is the actor and who is the re-actor, the villain and the victim, the rescuer and the rescued, the black hat and the white hat in the drama. Debts, obligations, and paybacks, the relevant ones play out before your eyes. Through observation of the past situation, you understand on an intellectual level the reasons behind any relationship challenges in this incarnation.

2)   Psychological:

Your personality is intact regardless of the era, the culture, the society or your role in it. Your personality is part of your essence that is re-born life after life. That's who you were then, that's who you will be in the spirit world, and in future lives. Extroverts will be extroverts, introverts are still introverts, intuitives intuit their knowledge, helpers will help, leaders will lead, and perfectionists will try to be perfect. Some things never change, because the universal purpose is to work with your gifts and work to change your liabilities.

3)   Emotional:

We experience appropriate feelings when in a past life. For example, when you see yourself getting married you feel the joy of that event. Or when a loved one passes you grieve the loss. During each past life you recognize some of the important people as being the same spirit that currently occupies the body of an important person in your present life.

4)   Spiritual:

Regardless of the horror of the events you experience during the past life, it is your spirit who is present in the scene. The spiritual energy that by definition is positive, loving, and safe is therefore protected from harm occurring in the event. As you discover at the moment of your passing in the former life, your spirit exits prior to the "death" of your body. It is that spirit, that energy, whole, light and loving that continues on eternally through time and space.

We have free will, we always have choices, and when there are choices there are also consequences. Some of the events that play out in our former lives are a function of when and where we are at that time. For example, if someone born into slavery because his parents were slaves, and therefore his children will also be slaves, his life choices will be restricted. Regardless of what happened then, we cannot avoid the responsibility of being there and in charge of our choices.

At that time, our spirit's progression was appropriate for that time and place, and our choices reflected not only our station in life at that time, but the spiritual development of people at that time. Centuries later, we carry the burden of the choices we made then into our current life. Though given the same situation today, our choice would be different because we have progressed through many lives and much spiritual development. Through past-life regression, we are able to return to that earlier life, that earlier choice and through that re-experience, the negative energy disperses, is released and we heal. The evidence of the healing occurs in unusual and amazing ways.

We are always in charge of our lives, regardless of the lessons we chose to learn and/or teach.

In our soul's progress we encounter several connections to a specific spirit, activity, or emotion. We fulfill our contracts to learn and to teach, or we don't, and the contracts become re-negotiated. In both cases when we are born into our current life the veil of forgetfulness falls. We do not remember the plan that we have made for this new life, or the contractual agreements we willingly made with other spirits before incarnating. Foreknowledge would reduce the impact of the lessons and influence the outcomes.

Our growth depends on fulfilling these mutually beneficial contracts with other spirits. Whether positive or negative energy exists in our relationships, the dynamic is always beneficial to both parties, because we are working on specific lessons that require spirit in human roles. As long as you have fulfilled your part of the contract, you have accomplished your part of the agreement.

In some cases, we bring forward aversion and fear toward certain people and situations. In other cases, it's attraction and loving support. Whichever it is, we have the opportunity to undo the negative karma carried forward from a past life.

If a person harmed us in a prior life, we will fear them or be attracted to them in this life. We've set up the drama in this current life for the best opportunity to resolve the conflict in the past life. Our challenge in this life is to heal the past life issue without creating further negative karma. Unfortunately, our human nature frequently overrides our spiritual intentions. We cave into the temptation to be hurtful, in speech or actions, thereby extending the drama and creating more negativity.

The current relationship in this life depends on what provides the spirits with the best opportunity to resolve the situation from the past life and undo the Karmic Knot. That is the challenge, and the resolution depends on the decisions, choices and actions of each spirit.

Through the use of past-life regression therapy, the facilitator and the client, with the help of their spirit guides, return to the originating incident for recognition, understanding, and acceptance of the conflict between the current incarnations. The re-experience of the original issue relaxes the tension in the Karmic Knot. This releases the negative energy and unties the knot as it heals the relationship…then, and now.

Chapter Four

Lust, Love & Loss

"...how utterly we are two, the light and the darkness, and how infinitely and eternally not-to-be-comprehended by either of us is the surpassing One we make."

D. H. Lawrence

In the beginning there is lust, and sometimes that's the ending as well. If lust continues into love, then the sexual contact becomes something more than two bodies united in pleasure. The act itself can be creative, taking the participants out of their physical reality into another space in time. Two separate selves create one experience and sometimes another life from their union.

> Every action creates.
>
> When we create positively, we inspire.
>
> Inspiration touches the spiritual aspects of our experience.
>
> Lust is energy, love is energy; and loss is the transformation of energy.
>
> Love is warm, loss is cold.
>
> Loss does not feel good.

When we lose something, even temporarily, we struggle to restore the balance that was there prior to the withdrawal of the energy. Loss hurts. Anticipation of loss creates a negative energy that expresses itself in many destructive ways: anger, paralyzing fear, sadness, worry, anxiety.

When we commit attention to the here and now, there is no anxiety, worry, or fear for whatever loss *may occur* at some later date. Experience the love you have when you have it. Resist the urge to look into the future and create fearful story lines about your tomorrows.

Resolving Real Life Relationships with Past-Life Regressions
COUPLES IN CONFLICT

With the divorce rate exceeding 50%, perhaps more couples should try counseling before going to court. For those who do, traditional therapy usually begins with learning communication skills. Healthy conflict resolution and anger management are two prominent issues discussed in couples' therapy.

With the addition of children to the couple's relationship, the added elements often inflame unresolved relationship issues. In addition, disagreements on how to parent their children, how to rediscover the romance among wet diapers, exhaustion, and incessant demands on parents' time and energy bring couples into counseling. Others have experienced infidelity and want to heal the wounds. Many have financial problems due to differences in spending habits. Some struggle with addiction in one or both partners.

After some traditional counseling, it is not uncommon that the two want to use regression therapy to look at the history of the relationship over time. It becomes clearer that the source of the current conflict lies somewhere before the birth of the partners. One or the other, sometimes both, want to be regressed to heal the current stress in the relationship.

The Root of All Evil...and the Cause of Most Divorce...

"It's the money, honey." Travis reached across the couch in my office to grasp Heather's knee in an apparent effort to cut off Heather's assessment of their problems. She glared at him, and then rolled her eyes before falling into a sullen silence.

Two young people dressed in t-shirts and jeans, fashionably tousled streaked hair, and cross trainers sat across from me. Heather still carried some of the pregnancy weight from her recent delivery four months ago.

The size of her nursing breasts stretched the thin cotton of her rock concert t-shirt to the limits. Clearly, Travis was convinced of his own charm and attractiveness by the way he carried himself with his hours-in-the-gym physique. He had the confidence of the successful young man who had proved his manhood through reproducing a smaller version of himself—only without hair. Apparently, no one had told him that the person who carries the baby within her body takes a few more days, weeks, months to fully recover from the experience of bringing another human being into the world.

"Money has *nothing* to do with you and me..." Heather's voice betrayed her anger and resentment in addition to the hours spent caring for their child.

Travis withdrew his possessive hand from her knee, folded his arms across his chest, and turned to look out of the window next to him.

After working through several communication skills, it became apparent that it would take more than talk to heal the differences between these two. In spite of Heather's protestations, it *was* about the money as far as Travis was concerned. From young DINKs (Double Income No Kids) to the credit card shuffle in a few short months, this couple voted most likely to stay married appeared unable to survive the birth of their first child.

Heather's pregnancy had been tough on both of them, as she had to quit her well-paying job after being confined to bed rest during her fifth month. The loss of her income placed additional stress on Travis to make up the difference by taking on extra jobs on nights and weekends. After talking this out successfully, I thought things were improving. Then Travis shared that he had lost his "loving feelings" toward Heather…which may or may not have had anything to do with her lost income, or her baby weight, or the drain of more money going out with less coming in.

I suggested regression therapy to see if we could get some history of their spiritual union over time. Travis suggested Heather be regressed as "I can't be hypnotized," he announced with pride.

I resisted the urge to ask him if anyone had ever tried, because I already knew the answer: "no".

Heather arrived a little late and flustered, "Sorry, but Travis didn't get home to take care of the baby when he promised…"

After giving her some time to settle down and relax into the process, we went over the questions she and Travis had to explore their past lives together. The questions pointed to what had made them happy in previous relationships in past lives they were certain they had shared….and what might have happened to ruin the relationship.

Diane: Where are you now?
Heather : In the country…on a small farm.
Diane: Tell me more about it.

Heather went on to describe an English countryside sometime during the 19th century. She and Travis worked the land, raised crops and cared for animals. They were happy. But they were unable to have children of their own. When Heather's sister was widowed, Heather and Travis welcomed her family to live with them. There was plenty of love between the couple to enhance the good times and to sustain them through the crop failures and other adversities that were part of that modest life. As far as Heather could see, that marriage was happy throughout that lifetime.

When she returned to the present, Heather's eyes clouded in confusion. "I thought this would help me figure out what went wrong then, so we could avoid it now."

"And?"

"Did I miss something? Nothing went wrong..." she answered, still puzzled.

We talked more about the experience, and her face glowed remembering how wonderful their marriage was, their partnership, and their mutual support. Clearly, Travis and Heather were gifted with the love they have for each other.

"Is it about the baby?" she asked, almost afraid to hear the answer.

"I don't think so," I replied. "What are you feeling, right now?"

Wrapping her arms around herself in an enthusiastic self hug, she grinned. "I'm in love with my husband!"

After further discussion about their former circumstances, she acknowledged that losing her financial support had a more profound effect on Travis than either of them realized. Heather went home determined to increase her attention toward Travis and to praise him for his extra efforts to support the family, rather than complain about his attitude.

In addition to dissolving the negative energy in difficult relationships, past-life regressions can rekindle the positive energy present in an earlier life together. Apparently, even though Travis was not present for the regression, he was affected by it. When Heather arrived home that evening, Travis welcomed her with open arms and apologies for his apparent lack of interest in her or their marriage since their son's birth.

These two continued couples counseling with the resentment and anger dissolved in their renewed commitment to each other and their marriage. The ease with which they spoke kindly to each other and the dramatic increase in loving feeling in both directions was obvious. Years and two more children later, Heather and Travis are still the "happily married couple" on the corner.

Traditional talk therapy might have gotten there eventually, but regression therapy revealed the underlying issue quickly in dramatic clarity. There were no lectures, advice, directions, or behavior modification assignments to manipulate the relationship to a higher level. Rather, the solution came from *within* the relationship and was therefore more apt to be successfully resolved by the participants, rather than directed by an external influence.

Infidelity...

The phone rang in Nancy's country kitchen as she was cleaning up the breakfast dishes and pulling out two frozen Omaha steaks for tonight's dinner. Since both of the girls were in college, Nancy felt relieved of the obligation to fix a three-course meal every night. Bob usually worked late anyway...just as he had always done in the twenty-five years of their marriage, whether their daughters were home or at a school event.

"I'm coming…"she called out to the wall phone as it rang for the third and final time before going to voice mail. For a split second she thought about letting the machine take the message, but something made her dive for the receiver and snatched it out of the charger. "Hello…"

"Nancy?" Bob's voice, thick and more aloof than usual.

"Bob?! What's wrong? You never call me during the day…" Their daughters' faces flashed in the forefront of her mind. "Is it…?"

"No." A flat response, even though he had apparently read her mind about her immediate concern for their children. "Nancy—I want a divorce."

She wasn't sure she had heard him correctly. A divorce? From what? His job?

Divorce…that word didn't apply to her, to them. They did everything right: met in college, married after graduation, she worked to save money for a down payment on a house and then they had children, exactly two years apart. He worked, she stayed at home to raise the children…all the time looking forward, always looking forward to their life together as a couple again.

"A divorce?" she whispered into a dial tone, as Bob had hung up as soon as he delivered the message.

It wasn't long before Nancy learned of Bob's affair and gave him what he wanted: a divorce.

A year later, the phone rang in Nancy's country kitchen but this time Nancy did not answer it. She was at the community college teaching an art appreciation course.

A few hours later, she saw the red light blinking on the receiver indicating a message.

Punching in the code, *98, she waited to hear the phone number, a local number which she didn't recognize. The sound of Bob's baritone brought the sharp intake of breath she was so familiar with since the first time she heard it so many years ago.

Damn! She thought she was over him, over it.

She had moved on, she reassured herself…hadn't she?

She almost deleted his voice. The voice that had seduced her, the voice that had told her he loved her, the voice that soothed her, comforted her, and eventually betrayed her, and inflicted more pain than she thought she could bear.

"Nancy? It's Bob, and I've made a terrible mistake…" that familiar voice shook with emotion as he cleared his throat. "Uh, I uh, don't know what to say, how to say…"

When he asked to come home and try again, her first reaction was anger, resentment, and refusal. Then she remembered how she felt with him, and how little she felt without him. She agreed to give it a try.

And try they did, for two long years. Two long years of Nancy's futile attempts to release the resentment over Bob's affair. For six months in counseling, this couple worked on improving their communication skills and trying to heal the wound of the affair. There didn't seem to be enough pay-backs to equal the pain Nancy felt at Bob's dumping her for another woman.

When I welcomed them into my office, their body language indicated that all of our attempts at reconciliation were not working well for this couple. Nancy announced she was ready to throw Bob out of their new home. Bob looked like a whipped puppy as he took his seat as far away from Nancy as he could get and still be in the same room.

I suggested regression therapy and explained that the purpose of this methodology was to reveal underlying causes of current events. A glance of hope from Bob, skepticism from Nancy, but agreement from both that it was worth it, as they had run out of other options.

(*Although I do not think of this as a last option to treatment, many of my clients are reluctant to try a method that is not mainstream. Unlike traditional talk therapy, the results from regression therapy are always positive and almost always immediate. Perhaps with more independent, recorded and verified research, in addition to my work, this alternative therapy will assume its rightful place among therapeutic choices.*)

We identified two issues: getting past her resentment toward Bob for dumping her, and her apparent inability to forgive him. Her spirit's desire to do both was evidenced by her willingness to do the past-life regression in order to heal these very human emotions. She went into trance easily and went back to her most recent past life with Bob.

In that life she had been Bob's mother. After her husband, Bob's father, died, Bob chose not to marry and instead remain on the family farm to help his mother with the property. Bob was a workaholic who was devoted to his mother and the ranch. When she died, he felt abandoned. Soon his grief was replaced by resentment at living his entire life for his mother and the ranch. Eventually, he died a bitter old man.

As I brought Nancy back to the consultation room she was amazed at how they had traded roles in their current life. It was clear to her that they were close spiritually – after all, she had never stopped loving him. She realized that their spirits were working on the issues of abandonment and forgiveness. Bob had not forgiven her for his mother's abandonment in their past life. It seemed clear to her that they changed roles so that their spirits could learn that lesson from the other side: he was now the abandoner and she the unforgiving abandoned.

Remember, we are either teaching or learning, sometimes at the same time, throughout all of our lifetimes.

And who better to learn from than a kindred spirit who has chosen to experience adversity with you?

The smile that softened Nancy's face indicated her understanding of the experience. Her ability to see the connection between the two lives enabled her to move forward in this life and release her anger at Bob. With amazing speed she dropped her anger and forgave Bob for the abandonment. The regression enabled the release of the negative energy held by Bob, not only in the past life, but in the present one as well. That regression was five years ago and they remain happily married today.

Past-life regression gets to the core of the problem. The origin of the couple's problem is specific to the couple working on a particular issue. Infidelity is a huge problem in our culture. Many may still feel it is unforgivable regardless of the past life karma involved. And for some this is true. But for others, when the karma is uncovered, it is immediately healing. The negative energy is released and they move forward with their life. That issue is resolved, the Karmic Knot untied.

Regression therapy allows understanding of the meaning of events and adversity in one's life. This knowledge is enough to heal the client. Many clients come to counseling because they do not understand why their life is the way it is. Regression removes the "why" from the equation and motivates us to move forward with faith in our path.

Uncoupled Couples, Parted Parents

"I thought when I divorced John the abuse would be over…" My client Susan said, as she stared down at her lap where her thin fingers twisted a wrinkled tissue. Glancing up at me, her blue eyes red from her tears, she forced a smile. "What can I do to make it stop?!"

She said this more as a statement than a question. "Why won't he leave me alone?"

Now *that* was a question we could answer with the healing available in a past-life regression.

Susan had been my client for several years, during and after her divorce from a physically and emotionally abusive husband. Their only child, an eight year old daughter, was being affected by the continuous negativity coming from her father about her mother. Susan was a strong, capable, well educated woman, and yet she carried residual fear from the relationship with her former husband. "I can't get past the dread, the fear, and the distrust that John will do something, or say something truly horrible!"

She was aware that I did regression therapy, but her religious beliefs prevented her from deviating from traditional therapy for relief. I explained to her that the process heals, even though it may not fit with her religious beliefs. I suggested that she could assume that the past life images were fictional, if this would help her get through the process.

After observing outward signs of Susan's physical relaxation, I suggested Susan return to a past life she had shared with John, her former husband in her current life.

Diane: What are you aware of?
Susan: I'm wearing sandals and am walking on a dry sand path. I'm wearing a blue robe and have a laurel wreath on my head.
D: Are you male or female?
S: I'm a man of about 30. Over the hill is the ocean – there are ships there without their sails up. Sea gulls are flying overhead.

There's a very steep ledge on the right of me that has craggy rocks way down over the edge, and the ocean is far down the cliff. There's some grass in the sand, the wind is blowing, and there are trees farther up the path.

D: Where are you heading?

S: There's a town ahead on the path.

D: When you get to the town please describe it to me.

S: Yes, the streets are full of children. There are canvas awnings over tables where people are selling baskets, bowls, and grains. There're big buckets of water being collected from the roofs. I come to my house, it's white washed rock. There's no glass in the windows. I go inside – my wife is there. She's kind and loving.

D: Look into her eyes. Do you recognize her spirit? Is she familiar to you?

S: Yes, she is my best friend, Betty. There's a table and chairs. There's a hole in the roof over the kitchen area, above where we cook. The roof is thatched. I have a son who is four years old.

D: Look into your son's eyes, and see if his spirit is familiar. Is he in your current life?

S: Yes, he's my brother, Steve. I also have a daughter who is eight. She's helping her mother cook.

D: Look into your daughter's eyes. Do you recognize her spirit?

S: No – I don't know her. She is kind like her mother.

D: How big is the village?

S: It has a lot of rock houses up and down the dirt road. There are carts drawn by horses and oxen. There are stables with oxen and horses. Life is good here. But the ruler is not a good man. He lets the Roman soldiers that come through the village do whatever they want. I hear lots of noise outside now. I'm going to the window to see what is going on.

D: Let me know what you see.

S: Roman soldiers are marching into town. They're on foot, not harming anyone. They're in uniform and carry spears. They have metal armor on. They are going to the ruler's palace. The ruler's palace is up the street. They leave some guards outside of the palace. Now more soldiers are coming up the street, knocking over things. They have swords; they do not care about the people that live here. Their leader stops outside my house. I'm going outside to see what he wants.

D: Is he there in front of you?

Susan's brow furrows slightly, her fists clench at her side.

S: Yes, he's on his horse, demanding my wife.

D: Look into his eyes and see if you recognize his spirit. Is his spirit familiar to you?

S: Yes, it's John (her ex-husband in her current life). He yells for my wife. She comes outside. He gets off his horse and is moving toward her. My son comes out and gets between his mother and this mean soldier. He pushes my son down and grabs my wife. I can't fight back, I have no weapons. The ruler does not let us protect ourselves.

Susan's voice rises with urgency.

S.   I talk to him, I tell him to move on and find another woman. The soldier says he can take whoever he wants. Other soldiers take other people. No one stops them. The soldier drags my wife off. She is screaming. My son is crying, so is my daughter.

Susan's hands twitch in her lap.

The soldiers tie the people they have gathered up together with rope – tying their hands together. I feel so powerless, I can't fight back. If I do I'll be killed and my children will be orphans. Noooo….

The Roman soldier rapes my wife in front of me, in front of everyone. I'm so powerless. The soldiers do not speak to any of the people; they just take whoever they want. They leave the village the way they came – leading away all of the people they took.

D: Do you ever see your wife again?

S: No. Life just goes on. I work in the fields with my son. I take the oxen to work with us. My daughter takes care of the home. We are all sad.

D: Move forward in time now to the next important event in this life – one – two – three – be there – the next important event in that life. What are you aware of now?

S: It's night. The Roman soldiers are coming up the street with torches in their hands, throwing them inside the houses and onto the thatched roofs. All the people are running, scared, and screaming. They run on foot into soldiers on horses. The soldiers kill some of the people, and take others.

D: What do you do?

S: I pick up my son, and then my daughter and I run up a side street and into the trees in the dark toward the ocean – away from it all. There is a building there that the fishermen use when they work. It has an open fire pit to smoke and dry fish.

Susan's breathing quickens.

We continue to go up the beach. We see more soldiers coming toward us. We turn around and go in another direction – we can't escape. We climb up a cliff with others. When we get to the top of the cliff there are more soldiers there. Those soldiers push some of the people off the cliff – they hit the rocks below. I hold the kids so they don't see the people land on the rocks. There is nowhere to go. We're trapped. Then the head Roman soldier rides up on his horse. It's John. He laughs at us – me and my two children. He thinks this is great sport. He pulls my son from my arms. He has a sword.

Susan releases a low moan before continuing.

Another soldier takes my daughter. John stabs me in the stomach. He doesn't care; he has the right to kill me. I fall off the cliff onto the rocks far below.

D: What are you aware of now?

S: I'm floating above the scene, I see all of the bodies on the rocks below, mine too.

After bringing Susan's awareness back into my consultation room, I sat quietly watching her digest what she had just seen. "Well, he's not much more civilized in this life!" Susan was in a state of shock at John's violence in that past life. Commenting on Roman John's lack of respect for life, she spoke of his violent behavior in their marriage. "He felt he had a right to hurt me. I was his wife, I was his property," said Susan. "Now I know why I let him get away with so much, why I stayed in the marriage as long as I did—I felt powerless, just like before..."

That regression took place 19 months ago. Since that time John has not demeaned Susan nor called her any names. He has made no scenes in front of their daughter, with Susan alone, or over the phone. He has not been nice, but he has been courteous. The two have been able to co-parent their daughter in a productive way – putting the child's needs first. They have been able to make decisions together regarding their daughter without getting upset or angry. Susan is still afraid that one day John will become the "evil person he was". We'll see. I have a feeling he won't.

Susan and John's post-divorce relationship was typical of many I see in my practice. Even though the marital relationship is over, the contractual part resolved, the negative energy between them persists. Children are the ties that bind, and are often the pawns between both sides of the chess board. It's not about winning; it's about putting the pieces back in place. By restoring the balance between the opposing teams, the pawns are spared the warfare, the negative energy is released, and life goes on.

Healing the relationship takes place even if only one party participates in a past-life regression, because the negative energy expressed in the past life is released in the reliving of it...and changes the quality of the relationship today as the Karmic Knot is untied.

Chapter Five

Parenting: Both Sides, Now.

"Psychiatry enables us to correct our faults by confessing our parents' shortcomings."

Laurence J. Peter

Mammals are often divided into two categories: prey or predators. Human beings can experience both sides of the equation at various times in the same life time, or over the course of several lifetimes. Similarly, humans experience both sides of the victim and villain equation. Both roles are part of the totality of the human experience. Through living each role the soul learns, and teaches the other soul in the dynamic the meaning of their role in both souls' progression toward increasing their level of spiritual enlightenment.

The distinction begins at birth: prey animals are capable of standing and moving shortly after birth, because their survival depends on it; predators are born blind, deaf and dependent because their survival depends on their parents' ability to support, protect and nurture them.

Even though human babies are neither blind nor deaf at birth, they are incapable of moving and surviving without caretakers assuming responsibility for their basic needs— not for days, weeks or months, but for years. The maternal and paternal instinct occurs in vastly varying degrees among human beings. It is not a toss of the dice, rather its part of a plan set up prior to birth in order for the soul to learn, to teach, and to progress.

After experiencing past-life regressions, the client understands the reasons behind abusive parents, ungrateful children, neglect and entitlement. Much as we wonder why we chose these relatives, the fact remains that we did, indeed, choose our parents, our siblings, and our children—who also chose us. Whether it is an act of generosity and self-sacrifice to be the villain or the victim in this lifetime is a value judgment that becomes irrelevant with further understanding of the purpose and process of life.

When we consult with our spirit guide to determine the lessons we chose to learn and how we intend to learn them, we need volunteer spirits to play roles in order for us to experience the lessons we need to learn to progress. Keep in mind our soul always has the option of learning in the spirit world, a place of peace, acceptance, warmth and love. The decision to reincarnate comes from many sources, motivations, and reasons which we are not fully aware of—yet.

The relationship between mother and child is primal, instinctive and the first example of unconditional love in our human experience, unless of course it isn't…and that is the lesson. If a baby is born and immediately abused or neglected, the first experience of love is thwarted, corrupted, distorted and it's up to the soul to overcome this adversity to understand the essence of compassion without knowing it from the one person in the world who is the designated role model. Now *that* is a steep learning curve…

Rage, Resentment or Retribution?

Her voice shook over the phone during her initial contact, "I-I uh…" a pause as she swallowed her grief. "I don't know what to do…I-I don't understand…"

Barbara, a statuesque brunette with broad shoulders and a broad smile, came into my office in a crouch. She extended her hand to shake mine, and her grip was firm, confident…quite a contrast to her entrance.

She folded into the client chair and seemed to disappear into the upholstery. Grabbing a handful of tissues, she wadded them up in her fist and then began pounding her fist onto her knee. Apparently, she had controlled herself and not shed a tear, sighed, or uttered a word of doubt, regret, or resentment until this moment.

"What happened?!" Barbara directed the question to the space between us. "I did everything I could for her…"

The "her" referred to Karen, her 22 year old daughter.

Karen's five year old daughter, Breanne, had been raised by Barbara since her birth to her teenage mother.

According to Barbara, mother and daughter had been very close until Karen's 12th birthday at which time she started to resent everything Barabara attempted to do for her or with her. Prior to her puberty, mother and daughter worked around the family ranch, gardening, haying, and trail riding. Barbara enjoyed sharing her knowledge about ranching, gardening, and home-making with her only daughter.

Suddenly, the sweet 4-H blue ribbon winner turned into a sullen angry teenager. This is not an unusual occurrence between mothers and daughters when the younger female hits puberty. Arguments, disobedience, and talking back are the norm; ignoring curfews, smoking, drinking, drug use, and skipping school are not the norm.

From oppositional behavior to running with the "wrong crowd", Karen went from typical obnoxious teenager to disobedient, disrespectful, drug using party girl. Every attempt Barbara made to rein in her daughter's behavior failed. Karen persisted in her self-destruction and never missed an opportunity to blame Barbara for everything that went wrong in her downward spiraling life. Feeling like a moving target for her daughter's rage, Barbara had consulted counselors along the way—sometimes dragging a sulking child along, and other times going it alone in a futile attempt to understand.

The turning point came when Karen broke another promise to stay home and study, but instead snuck out to a party where she was raped and impregnated. A chastened daughter returned to the ranch promising to clean up her act and have a healthy baby.

Lasting until shortly after her daughter Breanne's birth, Karen temporarily returned to the girl Barbara remembered. The transition was short lived, as Karen left Breanne with her parents and resumed her life on the wild side. This lasted for several years until Karen met a man, then married and wanted her daughter back. By this time, Breanne was relating to Barbara as her mother, and didn't depend on Karen for anything. In fact, the little girl preferred spending time with her grandmother, because "Mommy yells a lot."

Throughout this relationship, as Karen acted out her rage, her mother's initial reaction of trying to appease her began to shift into her own anger at this ungrateful, demanding, selfish daughter. The energy between them crystallized.

When Karen approached Barbara for money, her mother turned her down. So, Karen refused to let Breanne see her grandmother. After months of not seeing her granddaughter even though they lived in the same town, Barbara went to court to gain visitation rights. The case was enriching the attorneys involved, creating more and more anger at Karen, while she became more and more determined to prevent her mother's access to Breanne.

Stalemate.

At the start of Barbara's therapy, it had been eight months since she had seen her granddaughter, and there was no reasonable explanation for Karen's ongoing rage or resentment. No amount of counseling could heal the heartache my client experienced from this loss, and any attempt to dissolve the anger at her daughter was met with a cold stare from Barbara's brown eyes.

I recommended a past-life regression to see if we could find a past life that these two had shared together that would account for and help explain her daughter's current anger toward her. We set an appointment for the following week.

Barbara arrived early for our appointment. She was dressed in a fashionable warm-up suit, and well-worn tennis shoes with grass stains on the toes. "Good, she's been gardening," I thought as I settled into my chair.

Diane: Share with me what you are experiencing?

Barbara: I'm in my home with my mother. It's not a very large home. It's made of something like stucco. My mother is upset.

D: How old are you?

B: I'm 15 years old.

D: Are you a boy or a girl?

B: I'm a boy. It's a long time ago. The Romans are persecuting the Christians. My mother is a Christian and has taught me her beliefs. My father does not believe as my mother. But he's okay with her beliefs. He's a Roman. My mother has also taught me to read and write. I'm educated. We have many books.

D: Look into your mother's eyes. Do you recognize her spirit?

B: (pause) No, I don't.

D: Why is your mother upset?

B: The soldiers are coming. They're knocking on doors. They're looking for Christians and arresting them. They're killing them. My mother says I must go. Leave immediately. But I'm so sad. I love her and do not want to go. If I go I will never see her again. She says she will be safe because of my father. They will not know she is a Christian. But she says I'm not safe, that I must go. She is crying and embracing me. I hear them coming, pounding on doors. I run out of the house and into the street. I run down the street away from the soldiers. I'm running toward the edge of the city.

D: What does the city look like?

B: The streets are dirt. The houses are built one next to the other. Attached. They're whitish. Two story houses. The streets are narrow with houses on either side. When I look back I can see the soldiers. They're not running after me, but pounding on a door a few houses before mine. I hope my mother is safe. I know I must leave the city. I'm very sad.

D: What happens next?

B: I'm at the edge of town, at the outskirts of the town. I'm taking the road that goes up into the foothills. Up there are farms. I'll find a farmer that needs a hand. I'm a good worker.

D: Go to the next significant event in this life.

B: I'm working on a farm. I do many things to help with all the animals. The man I work for is not very nice. I've been here for a few months. I miss my home, my mother and father. I know I can't go back. Word has come that many Christians are being killed in the arena. I don't tell anyone that I'm a Christian. I keep my beliefs to myself. But this man is mean. I need to move on. Tonight I will go.

D: Move forward in time in that life as the young man who is a Christian. What happens next?

B: I'm working on another farm. This man is much nicer.

D: How old are you now?

B: I'm 17. I've been here for awhile. He's good to me. He lets me read his books. But I'm getting restless. I'm a long way from Rome. But it's time to go even further. I want to be safer. The stories about Christians being arrested are getting worse. I need to move farther away from the persecutions. This time I'll tell the man I'm leaving. I'm telling the man I need to go. He wants me to stay. He says I'm a good hand. But I still say I'm leaving. I leave the next morning. He lets me take some food, and a blanket. I think this time I'll go much further into the hills.

D: Move forward in time to the next important event in this life.

B: I'm working for a very wealthy farmer. It's a large farm. He has many animals. He treats me well, but watches me closely because he has a daughter. She's very beautiful. She knows

I'm educated. But I'm a poor farm hand, and she's the daughter of a wealthy farmer. We become friends. I read to her. I begin to teach her to read and write. Her father likes my teaching her. He asks me where I learned to read. I don't tell him about where I'm from. I'm afraid. He's not a Christian. He's a Roman citizen.

D: Move forward in time to the next significant event in this life.

B: I'm still at the same farm.

D: How old are you?

B: I'm 20 now. The girl and I have become good friends. The father lets us spend time together because I'm teaching her to read and write. She's a good student. She reads well now. I've fallen in love with her, and she is in love with me. We don't know what to do as her father would never allow us to marry. She knows I am a Christian. I have told her my beliefs. She now secretly believes as I do. We keep this from her father. I'm a good hand and her father treats me well.

D: Is she there with you now?

B: Yes.

D: Look into her eyes and see if you recognize her spirit?

B: (pause)   No.

D: So go forward in time to the next significant event in this life.

B: I'm still on the same farm. I'm now 22. I must go! Her father will be very angry with me.

D: Why will her father be angry?

B: She is carrying my child. She and I have talked about what to do. She is afraid her father will kill me when he finds out. We've decided I must go soon. I'll go in the morning. We are both sad. I'll just leave and not tell him. She will say she does not know why I left when he sees I'm gone. I plan to go a long way from here, but I tell her where I'm going so she can get word to me if she needs to. It's now the next morning. I leave before light with great sadness. I head further down the road, further away from Rome and the persecutions that I hear are still going on there.

D: Go to the next important event of this life.

B: Its many years later, I'm older now. I live in a small town where I teach reading and writing. I'm respected as a teacher. I'm far from Rome. I tell only my close friends that I'm a Christian. They are, too. We share and talk about our beliefs. I like my work. I've not married. I wear long robes with a tie around my waist.

D: How old are you?

B: I'm 36. My life is good. I have many friends. I've been here for a long time.

D: Move forward in time to the next significant event in that life.

B: I'm in the same town. I'm 38. A young man has come to the town looking for me by name from a long distance. He finds me. He hands me a letter which is sealed and tells me his mother sent him to me to learn to read and write. He tells me the letter will tell me more about him. He says his mother wrote the letter. He says he does not know what she has told me about him in the letter. I open the letter. It's from her. She writes that this young man is my son. That he is 16 and it is time for him to know me and for me to teach him to read and write, and also to learn Christian beliefs. She says that she has not told the boy that I'm his father. That, the letter says, is for me to do.

D: Is the boy there before you?

B: Yes.

D: Look into his eyes and see if you recognize his spirit.

B: (pause) Yes. It is my daughter, Karen.

D: What do you do next?

B: I take the boy over to a garden area. It has a huge tree in one corner. It's where I frequently teach. I motion him to sit on the rock below the tree. I tell him that I'm his father; that his mother has sent him to me so we can get to know each other. And so I can teach him.

D: How does the boy respond to this information?

B: He looks amazed, and then his face darkens. He's angry. He asks why I left his mother. He asks why I left him. He says he has wanted to know his father all these years. That he has been sad having no father. He's angry and does not understand. I try to help him understand why. About his grandfather, his wealth, that his mother and I together made the choice, that I loved his mother, and still do.

D: How does he react to this information?

B: He doesn't understand. He says he would not have made that choice. He's angry, but he says he will stay and let me teach him as his mother wishes.

D: Go forward in time to the next important event in this life.

B: I'm much older. The boy is now a man. He has stayed with me all these years. His anger has gone, but he never understood. We've become close, but more like friends, not like father and son. He's a good student and has learned well. He's now also a Christian. We spend much time together, but I still feel his hurt at my leaving him so many years ago. He's also quick to argue with me about philosophies.

D:	How old are you?

B:	I'm very old, I'm 53. I don't have much time left here.

D:	Go to the next significant event of that life.

B:	I'm in my bed, dying. My son is here with me. I can feel it is time to go. The scene is fading out.

D:	Are you dying?

B:	Yes. I'm floating above my body. My son is sad. We had become good friends.

She sighs, swallows, and whispers, "I know he never forgave me."

Upon Barbara's return from that past life back into my consultation room and her current life, she immediately felt the impact of her choice in that former life on the relationship in her current life with her daughter. Barbara felt that her son in that past life was correct: that the choice made by the two young people had a serious effect on the child of that union.

Barbara immediately recognized that the anger she had seen in her son's eyes in that past life had resurfaced in her daughter's eyes in this life. Barbara saw too clearly how she had hurt Karen in that previous incarnation. She, as the man in that life, had deprived her child of knowing his father for 16 years. Her son in that past life had been the 'innocent victim.' Now, her daughter, as Karen, was trying to deprive her of knowing her granddaughter in this life. Karen had been born with that anger toward Barbara, but it took time to surface.

Barbara spent the next two sessions processing her feelings that had come out of the regression. She felt very guilty about her choice in that past life. She had no more anger toward her daughter. She came to understand completely why her daughter felt the way she did toward her. She also understood why her daughter was unconsciously using her granddaughter to even the score.

Barbara's guilt made her consider dropping the case and letting Karen prevent any further contact with Breanne.

However this was not in the best interest of her granddaughter because the two had developed such a close bond. Now the child was distraught and had no idea why her mother and her grandmother were so angry at each other. The granddaughter was now set up to be the innocent victim.

She left my office deep in thought, feeling conflicted, confused and frustrated. I called her a few days later to follow up and suggested she get back to her gardening and make no decisions for a few days.

Two weeks after the regression Karen called Barbara "out of the blue" and told her mother that Breanne really missed her, so couldn't they work something out themselves rather than through lawyers? Barbara was so stunned she almost dropped the phone before her voice returned and she invited Karen and Breanne over for lunch the next day.

That telephone call was the beginning of the rest of the story. The two met for lunch. Karen threw her arms around her mom and cried, telling her how much she had missed her. They wrote out a mutually agreeable visitation plan for the court. Barbara was amazed at the shift in her daughter's attitude toward her. It seemed miraculous. The court accepted the plan and the case was dropped.

The two began to see each other regularly. Barbara visited her daughter's home frequently, always in response to an invitation from Karen. The two resumed their relationship from their present life feelings, not from the unconscious emotions that had them both bound to that past life.

They were freed to live in the present time. They both unconsciously began to go back to the beautiful loving rituals they had established before the anger began. This change seemingly came out of nowhere.

Traditional therapy would assign the blame onto the daughter's behavior for the difficult relationship. However, Karen was not there seeking counseling, and unconsciously considered herself the "innocent victim". An Oppositional Defiant Disorder diagnosis does not correct the problem. Past-life regression, however, goes to the root of the problem.

The daughter brought her past life anger into this life to act it out toward her mother. We can assume this Karmic Knot would continue to pass from life to life, role to role, until one or the other spirit examined the originating event enough to release the negative energy tightening the knot. As this situation illustrates, it doesn't require both parties in the relationship to engage in regression therapy and untie the Karmic Knot. When one returns and re-experiences the origin of the problem the negative energy is released, and both mother and daughter are freed.

Chapter Six
Professional Relationships

"Most are engaged in business the greater part of their lives, because the soul abhors a vacuum and they have not discovered any continuous employment for man's nobler faculties."

Henry David Thoreau

Occasionally, we meet people we have an instant attraction to as if we've known them forever—and perhaps we have. On the other hand, the other end of that spectrum happens, too. There are instances when a new person raises the hair on the back of our neck and we sense ourselves reacting intensely to them and not in a good way. In both instances, we usually have a choice whether to continue the relationship or to walk away.

These reactions occur in other situations that are not as easy to negotiate. On the job, in a volunteer association that means a lot to us, in class, in a club or other social group, these people are not as easy to avoid, ignore, or dismiss.

Rarely do clients come for past-life regressions to learn more about their professional relationships, because if the problem becomes too unbearable a job change occurs. One person or the other usually changes locations, companies or employment. Problem solved. That is not to say there are no Karmic Knots among these on the job associations. If the relationships work, there's no reason to look any further. It's when the atmosphere becomes toxic in the work place for no apparent reason that past-life regression will benefit all those involved: employer and all of the employees.

Turning Distrust into Trust...

The first instance of a professional past-life regression occurred with a client I had known for over three years. In her early forties, Michele was an attractive, highly educated, single mother of two who was very good at whatever she did—on and off the job. Recently, company reorganization sent her to manage another office at a different location and under a new boss.

The management method remained the same: Michele worked independently and communicated with her boss through brief phone contact and emails during the week. Once a week, all of the satellite office managers met with the new boss to provide data, feedback, and support to each other.

When she arrived for her session, I noticed her usual welcome smile was less radiant than the last time we met, and she brought with her some nervous mannerisms that she had left behind after completing her last round of therapy six month earlier.

Dressed in her power suit and off-white silk blouse, her shoulder length highlighted dark blonde hair gathered in a large clip at the base of her neck, Michele looked every inch the successful executive on her way through the glass ceiling to the inner sanctum of upper man-agement....except for the faraway look in her clear blue eyes.

"What's wrong with me?" she laughed, taking back any sugges-tion that she thought the problem was hers.

"Absolutely nothing," I answered.

"Then why does my new boss loathe me?" She was still smiling even though she shook her head back and forth in disbelief.

"Huh?" Now, it was my turn to shake my head.

She continued to tell me about the first weekly meeting between the satellite managers and their boss from the home office. "I know most of my colleagues, and we are a great group of employees! Well, in walks Nancy, our boss, who walks around the room shaking hands with us until she got to me," Michele paused. "I, uh, had my hand out to shake and waited for her to take it—but she didn't, in fact, she didn't even say a word to me, but turned away and returned to the podium. To this day, she has never initiated a conversation with me and only responds when I ask a direct question or make a request." Another bitter laugh. "Which she routinely denies—even if it benefits the com-pany."

"Are you sure you've never met her before?" I asked, clearly stunned that anyone could take such an instant dislike to this very charming, intelligent woman who was clearly an asset to any organiza-tion.

"My friend asked me if I had slept with her husband—in front of her!" Michele laughed at the memory. "Nancy isn't even married...I don't think."

"How does she treat the others?" I asked, sensing the answer before I heard it.

"That's the oddest part of all. Nancy is generous with her praise of anyone else's suggestions, yet puts mine down almost before I can get them out of my mouth. And when I asked for further training in a new software application, she turned me down flat—but signed everyone else in the room up for the classes. When she looks at me, it's a glare...and it lasts for hours."

"How long have you been putting up with this?" I asked.

"Way too long," she replied. "I know I should find another job—but that means moving and the kids are just settled and love their new school and friends. And I'm really good at this job—why should I start all over again, somewhere else?"

At my suggestion of a past-life regression to see if there was a history between them that both were unaware of, Michele adamantly refused to consider it. "There is no possible way this woman has been anywhere in my past without me knowing it—instinctively."

She had been regressed successfully to deal with other trouble-some relationships and was pleased with the results. "You have had no reaction to her at all?" I asked.

"I have heard only good things about her, and she is a very capable executive with good ideas, and if she didn't already hate me, we could work very well together."

Frankly at a loss as to how to help Michele, I shrugged and waited for her to tell me what she needed from our time together. Sometimes it's difficult to remain silent in order to force the client to fill the space between us with their words; but in this case, I had nothing else to contribute to our conversation.

Michele stood up and walked to the bookcase in my office and apparently scanned the titles while she thought about what she wanted to say. I have all of Brian Weiss, M.D.'s works on past-life regression and

Michael Newton, Ph.D.'s books on life-between-lives regressions. Newton is the pioneer in the field of life-between-lives regression, and I received my certification to do regression therapy from his institute. I lend these books out to my clients who are interested in pursuing regressions to further understand their issues and heal their suffering.

She paused, then turned and shrugged at me. "Okay, please schedule an appointment for a past-life regression to see if there is any prior association with Nancy." She shuddered, then smiled and continued. "Maybe I'm afraid to find out..."

The next week, Michele appeared in designer jeans, silk t-shirt, hair in a pony tail and not a trace of makeup on her pretty face. We spent about 20 minutes talking about her difficulties with her boss to provide time for her spirit guide to choose the past life for her to experience. I am only the facilitator. My spirit guide works with my client's guide for a better understanding and full awareness of what is on Michele's mind.

Michele was already familiar with the process and I watched the muscles in her brow smooth, the tightness around her mouth relax, her shoulders sink, her legs flop open, and her hands unknot from the fists they were in when she first reclined in the chair.

Diane: What are you aware of?
Michele: I'm on a flat boat, a raft with logs tied by a rope. They're no sides. It's a very wide river, I can't see any banks. There's nothing on the boat. The river is moving very slowly.
D: Are you a man or a woman?
M: I'm a man. I'm wearing trousers and a rough burlap coat. I have no food. It's late spring. I'm barefoot. The water is calm. I have a long pole to pull the raft forward as I push the

bottom of the river. I'm standing and moving the raft forward, slowly.

Michele raised her hands in front of her to pole her way down the river.

D: Can you see the water's edge yet?

M: Yes. The banks are green and lush. Rolling hills behind the banks. It's the English countryside.

D: How old are you?

M: I'm in my early 20's. I'm going into a narrow stream. It's sunny. I have long dark hair and white skin. I'm rugged but not big. I'm strong, lean, and about 6 feet tall. The fields are alfalfa and mustard. I'm going around a bend. I see smoke and a hut. I'm off the raft now and walking toward the hut.

D: Is this your hut?

M: No. I'm going to see someone for work. The hut is made of branches and the fire is outside of the hut. I see wood cut next to the fire. There's fish frying on the fire, on a flat group of rocks put together—stones. The man's coming toward me. He's old, round and bald. Greasy looking, and not friendly. Mean. I don't trust him. I ask him for work — I offer to do farming, any labor. I'm willing to do anything.

D: Look into this man's eyes and see if you recognize his spirit.

M: (pause) No.

D: What do you do next?

M: The man tells me to come back during the harvest season. I have a very uneasy feeling as I walk away. I'm walking toward the forest, toward my home. I see my home.

D: What does your home look like?

M: It's a hut made of logs, very sloppy, small. There're more huts nearby. A woman comes out, my wife. She's wearing a long skirt and wool top. She's very lean.

D: Look into your wife's eyes and see if you recognize her spirit.

M: (pause) Yes. She's my brother, Ron. We're married because we want kids to help us. There's no love. We're all serfs who work and live together in sort of a village. The village is part of a kingdom. There's a lord - part of a manor. I have two kids. The mean man was the steward of the manor - the lord's assistant who takes care of that manor. I want to break away from the manor. I hope to become part of the mean man's manor. I want to move up so we can have more food.

D: Are your children there with you now?

M: Yes.

D: Look into their eyes and see if you recognize their spirits. Are they familiar to you?

M: The boy is four years old. I'm not close to him, he's Bill (Michele's ex-husband). The girl is two years old. I'm very close to her. She's my daughter, Kylie (in her current life).

D: Go to the next important event in that life.

M: I'm out talking to a group of men. They are part of our village of serfs. They want to know how my talk with the steward went. There're four men including me. We're trying to better ourselves and our families. We're talking about breaking away from the manor. But we are property of the manor and can't leave by law. But the manor is being managed poorly so there is not enough work and not enough food for us. Our families are hungry.

D: Look into these men's eyes and see if you recognize their spirits.

M: (pause) Yes. The one closest to me is John (Michele's fiancé). This man is my best friend here. He's wearing a robe and is a preacher of some sort. He wants the four families to move to a new area because things are not growing well here. The ground is fallow - the lord of the manor is off fighting wars. So the serfs can't produce crops like they did before. There's also a very young looking man that looks to me for help. I'm the leader of this group. This young one is my dad (in her present life). The third one is mean, sour. I don't trust him. I think he is a spy for the manor-lord.

D: Do you recognize the spirit of this mean one?

M: (pause) Yes. He is Nancy. (Remember that Nancy is Michele's current boss. When in a deep trance, Michele shows no reaction to this information of seeing the spirit of her present-life boss in this past life. She is being matter-of-fact.) He does not trust me. He is harsh. I don't trust him either. I think he's a spy and getting some reward to spy on us. I'm the leader of our village. The others look up to me. This mean one does not. He's jealous of me. He's also a quiet, slimy guy. His hut is next to mine. There's conflict between my family and his. He wants to be the leader instead of me. His wife is fat and older and likes me, not her husband. There's competition between us. The mean one wants to be liked like me. The mean one is very unhappy.

D: What else is being said?

M: The young one is an intelligent, forward thinker. He can see a better life for us. The mean one is only part of the group so he can report back to the steward of the manor.

D: Go forward in time to the next important event in this life.

M: The lord comes back from battle. It's fall. The lord sees the steward. Soldiers are here now, in armor to get the three of us. We've been caught because of the slimy one. We three are tied together by rope and marched into town and put in prison. There's a castle wall around the town. The ground is dirt. It's 1380.

D: What happens after you are put in prison?

M: We're not in prison for very long. I'm brought to the lord of the manor. He's not mean, just detached.

D: Look into the lord's eyes. Do you recognize his spirit? Is he familiar to you?

M: (pause) Yes. He's my sister, Susan. He asks why their land isn't fertile. I tell him our problems. That the serfs want to be productive. That they're not planting the fields. That we need more food for our families. He understands. He gives me a sack of gold and tells me to take two families of my choice in addition to mine and he sets us free. The lord also gives us one horse per family and a wagon. I leave him and go.

D: What happens next?

M: I choose to take the minister and the young man. I leave the mean spy behind. He's very angry. I gather up the three families and we go off with our horses and the wagon. We are in South England. Now we are heading north to Wales. We were also given some food. My wife is pregnant with our third child.

D: Move forward in time to the next important event in this life.

M: We're in a small village in Wales. The minister is running a church. The younger one becomes leader of the group. I'm content to raise my family. We used the gold to buy a farm. The younger one is more ambitious than me. So I turned the leadership of the group over to him. The third child is a girl.

D: Is your third child there with you?

M: Yes.

D: Look into her eyes and see if you recognize her spirit.

M: (pause) Yes. She is my best friend, Karen. She is easy going; we have lots of fun together. We're very close. But I'm still distant with my son who is now six. But he works hard, he is not a problem, he is a good kid. We grow vegetables and alfalfa. We work very hard, and are very productive. It's a good life. I have a nice relationship with my wife. She's a good mother. She's closest to our son – they're alike. My best friend, the minister, is gentle, good, and we do lots together.

D: Go forward in time in that life to the next important event.

M: I'm sick. I'm in my thirties. I'm in my home. It's a cottage of clay, white, with a straw roof. It's much bigger than the hut in England. It's wood inside and has several rooms. Our third child is now ten years old. We live in Claire County in Wales. I recover.

D: Go forward in time to the next important event in that life.

M: It is now 1400. I'm asked to go to London on horseback by myself. When I arrive, I find that London is big. The King lives here. I'm in the market place, trading. I see the mean one, the one we left behind (whose spirit is Michele's boss Nancy in her current life), on a wagon with our old lord. He's still a serf and has aged two times what is normal. I go over to greet them. I look prosperous. The mean one just glares at me and looks like he wants to spit at me, so I leave. I laugh because the mean one could not let go of his anger and jealousy. I'm happy and content. Life is good.

D: Move forward in time to the next important event of that life.

M: I'm at my home. Much older now. The minister and the young man educated my children. They started a church and a school together. I'm sitting in my chair by the fire. My kids are now 18, 20, and 22. The oldest has his own home and is married. I have several dogs. I feel tired. Life is good. I fall asleep in my chair by the fire. I don't wake up.

Upon Michele's return from that past life into my consultation room and to her current life, her first reaction was amazement that she had a past life connection with her current boss. After she sat up, she pulled the rubber band from her pony tail and shook her hair out so it returned to framing her face. I watched her brow furrow again as she tried to understand why Nancy felt the way she did toward her. "They look nothing like each other…nothing. But his attitude, his energy was exactly the same…easy to recognize." Her voice softened, "Ha! She hasn't changed a bit!"

Michele accepted the validity of her experience, but wondered why Nancy hated her since Nancy had betrayed the village, and had done the "bad thing", so why is *she* acting the victim? Michele could have been killed instead of set free by the lord. From Nancy's point of view, she was only doing her duty by informing the lord and she should have been rewarded with her freedom, or at the very least accompanied

Michele to Wales. Nancy rationalized her actions as correct, and she deserved to share the benefits with Michele. Nancy's point of view did not include her being abandoned to a lifetime of serfdom by the person who could have freed her, too.

Because of the impact of that past life on her current life, Michele took several days to process all of the information she received. At my suggestion, she wrote her impressions in her journal, as the totality of the messages trickled into her consciousness. The regression took place a week prior to the next business meeting with Nancy.

When the time came to leave for the meeting, Michele was startled to realize she wasn't dreading it; and, in fact, was almost looking forward to it after her awareness of both sides of the relationship. This regression illustrates that the roles of villain and victim are not cast in stone throughout time. It is not always black and white; there are often shades of grey.

We are always heroes in our own drama.

That statement applies today, and all of our yesterdays.

When Michele walked into the conference room, Nancy was already there. For the first time since taking this job two years before, her boss looked up at Michele, made eye contact, said hello, and asked how she was doing. Michele was stunned, then recovered and responded pleasantly.

She noticed that not only was her boss's behavior completely different, but so was hers. The meeting went well. Nancy made no derogatory comments to Michele or about her to the group. When the meeting adjourned for the lunch break, Michele and another woman were going to lunch together. As they passed by Nancy's closed office door, Michele stopped, knocked, and asked her if they could pick her up something for lunch.

Instead of ignoring or dismissing Michele, Nancy replied, "Please wait just a minute, I'd love to go with you." The three women went to lunch, where Nancy shared a difficult personal situation.

Michele remained cautious in her encounters with Nancy for over a year after that first meeting since the past-life regression. Nancy's behavior remained caring and became more so over the months that followed. As time passed Michele slowly became Nancy's most prized employee – she received any training she wanted and Nancy promoted any program Michele wanted to put in motion. In addition, if Nancy needed advice on something she would call Michele. Three years after the regression their relationship is excellent – Michele is now Nancy's confidant and the person she looks to when she needs help - personally or professionally.

This past-life regression involving a difficult relationship between a boss and an employee illustrates the power of this kind of therapy to go to the origin of today's problem between the two people. The goal is always to understand, and through understanding seek a solution.

When the root of the problem is found in the past life and the story is re-experienced, the emotions that have been brought forward from the past life dissolve. The Karmic Knot is untied, and there is no more need to re-run them in this present life.

And, those strong feelings in the past life dissolve through this experience for both the client and the other person in the relationship who is not present.

Why?

I don't know.

The first time I saw strong feelings dissolve between two people who had been locked in a negative emotional grip because the regression took the two back to a past life together, I was truly surprised. It was not only a shock to my client, but a shock to me, the therapist. I had no expectation that this undoing of the negative emotions would occur. I just wanted to find the origin of the problem – because most of the time it is impossible to understand why two people in this life are so strongly locked in conflict or hatred. At first, I thought that understanding where these emotions came from would be helpful to my client, so the goal was to understand, not to dissolve the emotions. I didn't realize dissolving them would be possible, particularly because the other person was not in my office.

Consciousness Cords across Time and Space

As I began to see this undoing of the difficult emotions for client after client, it became obvious that there was some unseen connection between these two people. An invisible "cord" connects the two; a sort of energetic wave-link in which both souls, on a spiritual/energetic level, feel the energy of the past-life regression. Even though my client was the only one to re-experience the event, both souls have the same understanding and response.

This happens on an unconscious level.

Not one of my clients consciously released their dislike or distrust of the problem person in the relationship. It just happened, and I might add, immediately. That is, immediately for the person *not* in my office. My clients would proceed toward the other person with caution and with their guard still up. With the passage of time, my clients always realized that the issue had disappeared for the other person, and keeping their own barriers in place was a waste of time, energy and effort.

The Matrix of Consciousness: Cords Tying the Karmic Knot

This energetic connection exists between all people on our planet. As energy cannot be destroyed, it simply transforms. These energetic strands connect our spirits, our personalities, our selves throughout time and space. When a relationship exists there is a quality affecting the energetic cord, either positive from love, or negative from fear.

When one person in the relationship re-experiences the tension between both spirits, the negative energy can transition to neutral energy and both parties are positively affected. With neutral energy now in place, each of the two within the relationship can choose to keep it neutral or move the energy toward a positive energetic connection. Positive energy can also transition into negative energy. If it is not resolved, it carries forward into following times and lives.

When we pluck one cord between two spirits by exploring their relationship in a past-life regression, it sets off an energetic ripple that moves outward and toward the other person. This enables an unconscious energetic shift within his or her energy field, changing the energy between the two forever.

Chapter Seven

Body Pain: A Spiritual Solution

"Pain is inevitable; suffering is optional."

Anonymous

Why would a spirit choose to bring past life body injuries forward to their present life and experience ongoing pain from the prior life injury?

What possible purpose can it serve the spirit during this life time?

Will the addition of pain, a physical distraction, create increased adversity for the spirit to overcome in order to learn the chosen lessons more effectively or more efficiently?

Regardless of the answers to those questions, while working with body pains *without apparent medical explanation*, I have observed that the pain vanished after a past-life regression during which the client witnessed an injury to the affected body part. I have seen examples pertaining to injuries involving the back, neck and knees. Once the past life is re-visited, the client becomes symptom free immediately or within a few days. These examples would indicate that this process should work with any part of the body.

Evidence indicates physical pain that lacks medical explanation may be associated with a past life event, and therefore is treatable with past-life regression. My clients come to me after exhausting every other medical, traditional, and holistic treatment available to them. There were no remedies, no cures, and no alleviation of the suffering. After past-life regressions, my clients successfully eliminated their body pains of past life origins.

Oh, My Aching Back...

The Reluctant Regression

Sarah, in her early forties and married with teenaged children, came to me for general counseling as she felt she was missing out on life. She was not experiencing clinical depression so much as "Is this all there is?" dissatisfaction.

After a few sessions, I suggested a past-life regression as a possibility to discover the source of her malaise.

"First, let me say, I don't believe in past lives, or reincarnation, or any of that. Okay?" Her statement was accompanied by a stiff smile, which was her way of hiding the adult braces straightening her teeth.

"Soooo?" I asked, waiting for her reasoning.

"I'm just curious. What people see is what they want to believe about themselves. You know, pretending to be someone special." She covered her mouth with her hand and looked down into her lap.

"Most of my clients do not see any famous historical figures, or see themselves in important roles in the past," I replied.

"Oh. Then it's scenes from a book or movie they enjoyed," she said, matter-of-factly.

I shrugged because the "belief" issue is always discussed whenever we mention past lives. The purpose of therapy is to heal by whatever safe means available to the therapist. "Do no harm" is our motto. "Acceptance or belief is not necessary to benefit from the experience," I said.

"Great!" Her head came up to face me, and this time her smile was broad and sincere. "I just want to check it out…no agenda, no intention, okay?"

She shared her life story and her history was as close to a "normal" middle class, middle-aged woman as anyone I knew. She had no questions, no concerns, no intentions, and so we began the induction process.

Diane: What are you aware of?

Sarah: I'm standing on a dock, a large boat dock. It's raining and very foggy.

D: Do you have any footwear on?

S: Yes, I have boots on, high boots that lace up. I am wearing a uniform, some sort of military uniform.

D: Are you male or female?

S: I am a man, about 25. I am staring at a very large sailing ship. I think I am going away on it.

D: What continent are you on?

S: Europe.

D: What city are you in?

S: London. I am in the British Navy. We are about to leave for the Americas. There are other sailors around me. They are talking about the war with the American colonies, who want their freedom. We are sailing there to let them know who they belong to: us.

D: How do you feel about the war?

S: They should be given their freedom – they are so far away from us.

Sarah said this with conviction. Her smooth brow knotted with her concern about what she was about to do, where she was about to go, and why.

S: We are boarding the ship now. It is huge, with sails and cannons. I do not like this at all. (Sarah shook her head back and forth to confirm her feelings.)

D: Move forward in time to the next important event in this life. What is happening now?

S: We are off the coast of the Americas. Not far off the coast. There is an American ship next to us; the side of our ship is facing the side of their ship. We are about to engage in battle. It is dusk, just about dark.

D: How do you feel about going into battle with the Americans?

S: I don't like it at all – not because I am afraid – but because I do not believe in this war. I do not believe my country is doing the right thing. We are close enough to the shore that I could jump ship and swim. I feel like leaving this situation.

D: Let's see what happens next.

S: Cannon fire is beginning. Everyone's attention is on their job. I am sneaking off to the end of the ship – the one closest to the shore. No one is paying attention. I think I can leave without anyone noticing.

D: What do you do next?

S: I climb over the edge, letting myself down into the water on some ropes that are hanging there. No one sees me. I begin swimming to shore. It seems farther than I thought. I get to the shore. It is dark, but there is moonlight. There is a rocky cliff that I am going to climb up. It looks like it is grassy at the top. Huge boulders, sharp. I am climbing up them – they are wet. The cliff is almost straight up, but I am making progress. No one seems to notice I'm gone – that's good. I am struggling to get to the top. I'm getting closer. (pause)

D: What is happening now?

S: I slipped. I fell. I have fallen way down the cliff. I landed on my back and hit a very sharp rock in the middle of my back. I am losing consciousness. It's all dark. (pause)

D: Let me know what you are aware of now.

S: I am floating above my body. Looking down, I see my body on the rocks. I think I must be dead.

I brought Sarah out of trance and that past life, and back into my office. She was dismayed that she had died that quickly. She felt cheated. She felt it was a good story line – unfolding as she would have liked. But the sudden death made her wonder. She said, "Well, I would never have ended the story that way. Maybe it really was a past life." We processed her feelings about that life as a British Navy man.

"Whoa! You know, I have had a pain in my back in the same place I hit that rock. For as long as I can remember, even when I was a kid, a sharp pain right here." She leaned forward and reached behind her to rub the place on her lower back. "That is strange." Her voice drifted into silence.

"Is there any explanation for the pain in your back? A fall off of a horse, or a ladder? Lifting heavy stuff?" I asked.

"No. It's always been there…sometimes it hurts more than others. I've had x-rays taken, muscle relaxants, cold and hot alternating treatments, and nothing works for very long."

"Pay attention over the next week and see if the pain changes in any way," I suggested as she left my office.

Sarah returned the following week for her counseling session. When I asked her how the pain in her back was doing she replied that it was gone. She had never told me about the pain before. When I told her that past-life regression often gets rid of pains in this life that have no medical explanation, she was astounded. After that first regression she moved forward to experience many past-life regressions, looking to 'fix' all sorts of issues, with very positive results. Sarah became a true believer in the healing power of regression work and its ability to transform and heal a wide variety of problems. The quality of her life improved dramatically over the next twelve months. She currently is living a very happy life filled with meaning and personal growth.

Sandra's Solution

Sandra, in her mid-thirties, had been in counseling with me for over a year for anxiety issues. After a few successful past-life regressions she decided she wanted to see if we could find a past life to explain her back pain. The pain was in the center of her back, not so much in the spine, but a circular area about ten inches in diameter. She had had this pain for as long as she could remember. We had a clear intention in this regression: to return to a past life to explain the pain in the middle of her back.

Diane: What are you aware of?
Sandra: I am in some sort of room with other people.

D: What kind of footwear, if any, do you have on?

S: I am barefoot. I have a long white robe on, tied at the waist. I have long blonde hair.

D: Are you male or female?

S: I am a woman, about 20 years old. There are lots of other people with me and I don't think we can get out of this room.

D: What does the room look like?

S: It is square with rock walls. The floor has straw and sand on it. It smells like animals. There is a large door with a square hole sort of in the middle but up at eye level. There is a man looking in at us through bars. He is a soldier with armor on.

D: What are the rest of the people in the room wearing?

S: The same kind of clothes I am, even the men. Everyone looks really scared. I have no idea why we are here.

D: Look around at the people who are in there with you. Look into their eyes. Do you recognize any of their spirits – are any familiar to you?

S: (pause) Yes, there is a young woman next to me. She is my friend now. She is my mother in my present life. She is very scared. We are Christians. The men outside the door are Roman guards. It is dark in this room. They are opening the door.

D: Tell me what happens next.

S: The Roman guards are leading us out into a hallway. We do not know where we are going or why. It is a wide hallway with rock walls and sand on the floor. We are all being lead down the hallway toward a much bigger double doorway. There are guards in front of us and behind us. Now the guards are opening the big doorway. The light coming in is blinding. The door leads to the outside. It is daylight out there and there is lots of noise coming from there. No one is struggling, just scared. I am at the front of the group. We are led out into the sunlight. It is a very hot summer day, and dry. As the guard leads us out I realize we are being lead into the coliseum. There are hundreds, maybe thousands of people, jeering at us. Screaming, yelling about us being dirty Christians.

D: What happens next?

S: I have slowed down. And the guard is now pushing me out into the lead; the others follow me and are being pushed by other Roman guards. We are a group of maybe thirty people of all ages. We are almost to the center of the coliseum. The guards are leaving us and going back through the doors we came out of. At the far end huge doors are opening.

Sandra lifts the back of her hand to her mouth in horror.

S: Oh no! Lions are coming out of the doors. They are moving slowly toward us. I'm scared. I don't know what to do. I am at the front of the group – closest to the lions. They are nearing us. I turn away and run in the other direction. I am running as fast as I can – I don't want to look back! Something hits me from behind, I fall down into the sand, and everything is getting dark.

D: What happens next?

S: I have left my body. I am floating above the scene. A lion is eating my body lying face down in the sand. The people are cheering. I begin to see other spirits leaving their bodies as the lions kill them. I am moving toward these spirits – we are forming a group above the coliseum, looking down at the horror.

After bringing Sandra back from that past life into my consultation room, we sat in silence for a few moments. She was stunned by the horror of that scene. "What kind of people would do something like that? Sick people."

"Yes," I replied. We talked for awhile in general terms about human history and some of the horrors that had been perpetrated by people onto other people for all the wrong reasons. Once she was grounded back into her current life, I suggested she see how her back pain was over the next week.

When Sandra returned for her session the following week her back pain was gone. She was grateful, but wondered about the human race. She brought a new appreciation for being able to freely practice her Christian beliefs without fear in this life.

With respect to regression therapy and body pain, I have never had a client come into therapy with a body pain as their primary complaint. I am sure this is because I am a psychotherapist and these people have gone to medical doctors, chiropractors and massage therapists for treatment for their physical complaint. Body pain has thus far been outside of the realm of psychotherapy, where it should remain unless the individual has no explanation for his or her body pain.

Hangman's Pain....

Resolution of neck pain occurs commonly as a result of past-life regression work...even though my clients never mention the pain when detailing their life history. Even if the pain was not mentioned during the intake interview, my clients concur that they were taken to the past life where the pain originated. After the regression, the pain disappeared.

Cheryl's face reflected years of tension. She had pale skin, and metal rimmed glasses magnified her grey eyes to give her the appearance of a woman who blinked rarely, if at all. She made her appointment specifically to do a past-life regression to work on her relationship with her adult son, who turned out to be her father in a former life. She omitted any mention of neck pain in her life history, even though she had spent thousands of dollars in cures for this chronic condition without a cent's worth of relief.

As I relaxed Cheryl into a trance state, I noticed the color return to her cheeks and the tension drain from the lines on her face. Her intention was to return to a past life she shared with her son.

Diane: What are you aware of?

Cheryl: I am standing on grass.

D: Look at your feet, what kind of footwear are you wearing?

C: I have hand-made shoes on – leather – I am wearing a blue dress with an apron. It is a flower print.

D: Are you a male or female?

C: I am a girl.

D: How old are you?

C: Seven. I am playing outside of my house waiting for my parents to come outside. We are going somewhere.

D: What does your house look like?

C: It is very simple, made of wood, one large room, we cook over a fire. It is dark and smoky inside – I like to be outside.

It is drab and dreary inside. My parents have come out of the house. I guess we are going now.

D: Tell me what you see and what you are doing.

C: We are walking to town to trade. I am skipping along the path, picking flowers, smelling them, running this way and that. I love it when we go to town. My parents are conservative and don't smile or laugh much. They are old. I am too active for them. While we are walking they are trying to get me to just walk alongside of them, but I don't want too. How boring. We are going across a bridge – it is wooden with railings that you can hold onto. They are calling to me to be careful. I just skip over the bridge.

D: What kind of clothes are your parents wearing?

C: Mom has on a long dress with an apron. She's wearing a bonnet. Dad has on overalls with suspenders that button. Drab colors. All of the clothes are made by mom. Dad is in black clothes. Mom is carrying a basket full of eggs. I can see the town ahead.

D: Look into your parent's eyes. Do you recognize their spirits?

C: I don't know my mother, but my dad is my son, Tom.

D: As you get near the town please describe it to me.

C: It is small. Wood buildings with sidewalks. Dirt streets. Most of the people are walking. There are a few buggies with horses pulling them. The people are all dressed like my parents. We are all part of a religious sect of some sort. All the women are in long dresses with aprons and bonnets; all the men are wearing black pants with suspenders that button. The women carry baskets with things they have grown like vegetables or eggs. There is a store where trading is going on. I am an irritant to my parents. They keep trying to make me behave properly – I am an embarrassment to them because I want to do something other than stay by their side.

D: What happens next?

C: We have finished trading and are headed home. My parents are scolding me for my behavior in town. They say I embarrassed them and am not supposed to do this and that. I think I am supposed to do nothing!

D: Okay, now I want you to move forward in time to the next significant event in that life. What is happening?

C: I am thirteen years old. My parents are taking me to the convent. This is what has been expected of me for years. We are very poor. My parents are old. Our religion is very conservative. I do not want to go, but they are taking me. We arrive at the convent – it is just outside of the town – a big building with huge wooden doors. I am scared.

D: What happens next?

C: The head of our church opens the door and greets us. He is very tall and stern looking; he does not smile. He wears all black and has a hat on. He has a beard as all the men have. We go inside. My parents put down my few bags that contain all my belongings. They turn to me and say good-bye. They are cold and do not hug me. They turn and leave me alone with this stern man.

D: What happens next?

C: The man leads me to a room. It is very sparse. There is a cot for a bed and a small dresser. That is it. He tells me to put my belongings away in the small dresser. He says he will return.

D: What do you do?

C: After he leaves, I listen to his foot steps – all is quiet out there. I put some of my clothing into one of my bags and I quietly sneak down the hallway to the front door. I very quietly open the door. I leave.

D: Let's see what happens to you. Move forward in time and let's see what becomes of you. What are you aware of?

C: I am in a garden gardening. It is my garden. I am weeding my beets and squash – my favorite foods. I can see my house – it is right here. It is very tiny – just cobbled together boards – sort of a shack – but it is mine. I am happy.

D: How old are you?

C: I am seventeen. I live by myself. It is a beautiful sunny day. I love to garden. After I left the convent, my parents ostracized me because I shamed them. It was expected that I would go to the convent and stay. I could not do that. I have been taking care of myself since then. I built my house. I grow vegetables and trade. The people of our sect do not like me because I did what I wanted to; I disobeyed my parents. That is not tolerated by our religion. I have been banished by the elders. I have been harassed by some of the men when I go to town – taunted. One day two of them tried to get me to get on a horse that was not safe – I think they wanted me to get hurt. They think I am a very bad example for the children. So no one visits me. But I am happy being alone here.

D: What are you wearing?

C: I am wearing a brown dress that is raggedy and made of jute or rough burlap.

D: Let's see what happens next. Go to the next significant event in that life. What is happening?

C: I am still 17 and am in my garden gardening – so happy. I hear a noise. There are horses coming. They are coming to my house. They stop by the garden where I am. There are three men. They do not look friendly. They get off their horses and come into the garden. They are telling me to come with them. I tell them I will not. They are grabbing me – tying my hands behind my back! I am struggling. There is no use. They blindfold me with some kind of fabric; they grab me and put me on back of one of the horses behind one of the men. I am scared – I do not understand. They say I am bad.

D: What is happening now?

C: We are riding off to somewhere. I can't see so I don't know where they are taking me. We ride for awhile. (pause) We stop. I do not know where we are. I feel them put something around my neck. I don't know what it is. Oh! Everything is getting black.

D: Tell me what you are aware of now?

C: I am floating above my body, looking down. The men hung me from a tree! I am dead. They are laughing.

D: What do they do with your body?

C: They put my body over the back of the horse. They are riding to my parents' house. They're at the front yard..and they throw my body in front of their door.

I slowly brought Cheryl back into the room and her present life. She was quiet for awhile and I let her digest that past life and the way she was treated. Her first words were, "I forgot to tell you about my neck and that I have had pain in my neck all of my life. I think I have had that pain because of those men hanging me in that past life." How true these words turned out to be. We continued to process the rest of that past life and the impact it has had on her present life and her relationship with her son. Before she left, I asked her to call me and let me know how the neck pain was doing. She agreed.

Two weeks later Cheryl called. She said that the neck pain was essentially gone. She said that prior to the regression the pain had been almost intolerable, that she was constantly going to various kinds of doctors. She went on to say that there was occasional residual discomfort now but that it did not bother her – just a lingering awareness of the prior pain. She went on to say, "It is truly miraculous! When I think of all of the years that I have put up with that pain, all of the doctors I have gone to in order to have it fixed, and all of the money I have spent on it, I would never have thought of doing a past-life regression to fix it!"

Six months later I called Cheryl to inquire about her neck pain.

"Gone, gone, gone!" she replied with enthusiasm. "Not a twinge since the regression, wow!"

Body pain that originated in a past life trauma is curious. The sufferer assimilates the pain into this life from a very early age. The pain is simply a part of reality in this life, today's person accepts the pain as if it were hair or eye color. This pain creates daily suffering, but does not seem to hinder the person's life, the direction or the purpose. The pain becomes a part of the whole picture of this lifetime.

Washer Woman Knees...

A county clerical worker in her forties, Stacey's traditional therapy was focused on various difficult relationships throughout her lifetime. She was aware of the regression work that I did, but was not interested. She said she was afraid of the traumas she might encounter and of what she might learn about herself and the people in her current life.

After two years of talk therapy, Stacey's progress with her coping strategies and the results as reflected in her relationships pleased both of us. Toward the end of one particularly enlightening session dealing with her early childhood, she began rubbing her legs in an area two inches below her knee.

"Did you fall on the ice?" I asked.

"What?" Stacey replied. "Oh, no. I've had pain in my knees as long as I can remember. The doctors have no idea, and neither do I, why I hurt there."

"Perhaps a past-life regression will discover the source of your pain," I suggested with a smile.

She paused in her knee massage and looked up at me, her green eyes smiling behind her dark frames. "Okay. About my knees only, right?" I nodded and we set up the appointment for the following week.

When Stacey arrived for her past-life regression she was smiling in anticipation of the process and ridding herself of this chronic pain.

Followed by a large yawn, Stacey eased into a trance state. I invited her to go back to a past life where the pain in both of her knees originated.

Diane: What are you aware of?

Stacey: I am standing on a wooden sidewalk.

D: What kind of footwear, if any, do you have on?

S: Boots that lace up. Very worn out. I need new boots. I have long pants on that have holes in them.

D: Are you a male or female?

S: I am a man, about twenty-five. I am standing in front of my two room house. It is wood. It's sort of like a shack – we are poor. I am going inside – my wife is here. I have a daughter who is six years old. My wife is pregnant with five months left. Over in the corner is her mother sitting in an old broken down chair.

D: Which continent are you on?

S: The United States – Virginia. We are poor and going nowhere. I have no education and no trade.

D: Let's move forward a little in time and see what happens next. What is happening now?

S: I am with some other men. We are talking about going west in wagons. Winter is just ending. We want to leave soon. We are talking about what we need for supplies. There will be six families. There is nothing here for us – we want to strike out on our own.

D: So let's move forward in time to the next significant event in that life. What is going on?

S: We are all just outside of town – all of the families that will be heading west. Our wagons are loaded to the brim. My wife's mom is bringing her piano! My wife, daughter, and grandma are in our wagon. We are happy to be leaving Virginia and heading west – it is a real adventure – someplace new for us to start over. Everyone here is excited to be going. My wife is now very big.

D: So let's move forward in time again to the next significant event in that life.

S: We have been moving west now for two months. We are headed to Wyoming. It's hard on everyone, it is hot and dry.

My wife had the baby, but it died at birth. She is sad. My daughter is trying to cheer her up. I see something ahead – it looks like the fort that we were told was out here somewhere. Yes! Cheers are going up from the people. We need to re-supply and talk to these people about what's out here – like Indians. We're getting closer. It is a military fort. It has a high wooden wall around it. They are opening their large gate for us to enter.

D: So what happens next?

S: We are all inside. It is a large fort with lots of cavalry men here. They begin to tell us about the Indians. How they have been killing settlers like us. We ask which way is the safest for us to head. They say it is three more days to Wyoming. They say there are people there we can join. We begin to re-supply our wagons.

D: Let's move forward in time again. What is happening?

S: We have arrived in Wyoming – to the settlement we were told about. But we do not like it because there are no trees. We decide to go north to the Montana territories where they say the Indians are friendly. The settlement in Wyoming is hot and dry but the people are nice. Grandma does not want to go on. She decides to stay with a nice family. Two of the other families decide to stay so we are only four wagons left to head north.

D: Okay. So let's move forward in time again to the next important event in that life.

S: We get to a beautiful place on the east side of the mountains. The Indians here are friendly. We are building shelters. They are large cabins that we need to finish before winter comes.

We are four families. They tell us there are bands of outlaws – white men that steal. We have chosen a site not too close to the Indians, but we can still trade with them. We are also building corrals for the horses. We spend time hunting. Life is good. We are all happy.

D: Did you get the cabins done before winter?

S: Yes, we are set for winter.

D: So let's move forward in time again to the next important event in that life. What is happening?

S: Sarah, my daughter, is older now, seventeen. Life has been good to us. She is lonely and wants to go to the white settlement that is a three day journey from us. We go there sometimes for supplies. This settlement has two or three shops. She wants to meet a man; there are none among us for her. We are making plans to go, the three of us. We will take the wagon and two horses. We can see the blacksmith when we are there.

D: What happens next?

S: We are in the settlement. There is a fever here and people are dying. We stay just as long as we need to get our supplies and visit the blacksmith. Then we head home.

D: What happens next?

S: We are on the way home. Sarah and my wife get the fever. They both die. I'm so sad. I am burying both. Why not me – I want to go with them. (pause).

D: How tragic. Remember this is a past life. Let's move on now and see what becomes of you. Moving forward in time now to the next important event of that life....

S: Many years have passed. I was so sad after they died that I took some of my guns and a horse and went into the hills to live by myself. I live in a small log cabin that I made with a fire to cook on. I hunt for food. I have learned the mountains and hills well. There are lots of wild animals. They leave me alone - I have a gun – they respect that. For sixteen years I have lived alone here – wandering the mountains.

D: Let's move forward now to the next important event in that life. What is happening?

S: I am walking through the woods hunting. It is a warm sunny day. Beautiful. I am missing my wife and daughter. Wishing they were here to see this wonderful place. Day dreaming. I'm walking along a ledge looking down at the area below, hoping to see a deer. It's dusk, perfect time for deer. Oops! Oh no!

D: What happened?

S: I slipped off of the rock ledge, and fell about 15 feet down onto the forest floor below. I can't move.

D: Why can't you move?

S: I think I broke both of my legs just below the knees. Hurts really bad.

D: What can you do?

S: Not much. I have my gun, though. I hear a wolf howling in the distance. Lots of timber wolves in this area. I'm also bleeding on my arm. If they smell the blood…. (her voice rises in an odd mixture of fear and acceptance).

D: So let's see what you do next.

S: It's dark now, I can't move and the wolves are howling closer. Sounds like a pack is moving in. They're getting closer. I need to put myself out of my misery. I'm going to shoot myself.

D: Let me know what happens.

S: I shot myself. I am floating out of my body. I can see the wolves moving in on the body I left behind.

I suspended the past life experience prior to the inevitable horror she was about to witness. I returned her to the room with gentle reassurance that she was safe here, in the present.

Stacey came back quickly, relieved to be free from the final trauma of that past life in the Rocky Mountains. She was particularly amazed at that past life as she had always been interested in the history of how the west was settled. She has also loved Montana for a long time. That past life helped her to understand many of her spiritual roots and why she is attracted to some of the activities that she enjoys, like riding horses. In addition, of course, she had found the origin of the pain in her knees. Two legs broken at once! Time would tell if the regression would help alleviate that life long pain. In a state of awe, she left my office, having made an appointment to return the following week to do more processing of the many events of that past life.

"No more knee pain!" Stacey announced as soon as she entered my office. "And, I am no longer afraid of my past lives and what they mean in my present life. Maybe that process could get me to the source of my relationship challenges…"

"That's why I incorporate it as part of my work," I said. "It tends to short-cut the therapy process without inflicting any further pain on the client."

"How?" Stacey said, taking her seat in the overstuffed chair next to mine. This time she crossed one leg over the other without the wince of pain I had seen every time she performed this act in the past.

"By going to the originating incident, the source of the physical, emotional or psychological pain in a past life; we are able to heal it then and there. The negative energy surrounding the event or relationship is released and transformed in our present life into neutral energy. This allows us the freedom to leave the energy as neutral or create positive energy within the relationship. We can also find pleasure in situations that before would have been fearful." I replied.

Pain is energy, too. If we can bring fears, anxieties, love and hatred through time and space to reappear in life after life, we can also bring the energy causing the unexplained physical pain as well.

We hold the physical residue of that energy in our body in the form of pain. Now we have an alternative treatment: return to the original source of the pain and untie the Karmic Knot. We always have the power of choice, and one significant action is to explore all the possibilities to ease our suffering "now" by re-visiting "then".

This choice is better than living with pain and suffering unnecessarily. It is also important to realize that certain problems cannot be corrected on a cognitive level; rather they must be dealt with on a spiritual level. Past-life regression therapy is effective with our current issues that have been brought forward from a past life situation.

Chapter Eight

Escaping Emotional Excess

*"If you are distressed by anything external,
the pain is not due to the thing itself,
but to your estimate of it; and this you have the power
to revoke at any moment."*

Marcus Aurelius Antoninus

In Chapter Six, we looked at negative energy from a past life relationship that is now creating difficult dynamics in a relationship between the same two spirits in their present life. When revisiting the relationship on a spiritual level using past-life regression, and when we re-experience the difficult relationship dynamic, we are able to release the negative energy and transform it into neutral or even positive energy in the current situation.

In Chapter Seven, we explored unexplained physical pain and how it can be released on a spiritual level when returning to the past life to re-experience the event that created the pain then and release it now.

Evidence indicates that emotional pain can also be released when re-experiencing its origin in a past life. During a past-life regression, which moves us directly into the fabric of consciousness, we are able to rid ourselves of painful emotional residues that have been brought forward into our current life. Emotional injuries do not heal without an effort to transform the negative energy into a peaceful acceptance. This happens efficiently and effectively on a spiritual level during a past-life regression.

We are now free to live more fully in our present life.

Anger Mismanagement

Emotions are energy. When that emotion is a negative one, like anger, then the effect on our lives is also negative. Whether literally, as in our physical reactions that are detrimental to our overall well-being; or figuratively, as in the consequences of our actions motivated by anger; the results are the same, we suffer.

Anger creates strong reactions to events, situations, and even conversations. Inappropriately expressed or misdirected, anger can cause problems in our relationships both at home and in the work place. Anger, expressed or swallowed, tends to escape over things that, upon retrospect, are not that important, then or now. Anger turned inward results in physical and psychological damage on a physical cellular level.

Anger can destroy our relationships. We hurt people we care about. Although anger is a normal human emotion, how we manage it is critical. When we get angry at another person, whether an intimate or an associate or a complete stranger, if we can pause long enough to work through the energy behind our anger, and then respond calmly to the person who triggered it, the outcome usually benefits both parties. With the negative energy behind us, we can then work on changing, if possible, the situation that upset us. If we can't change it, we need to either accept it, or leave the situation, if possible. It is *never* appropriate to attack, either verbally or physically, the person who triggered our anger.

My clients are familiar with my mantra around anger: "No one can make you angry. Personal anger is your response to an event, situation, or conversation." This is a horse pill, and hard to swallow. People want to blame what is wrong on someone or something else, thereby relieving them of responsibility for the situation. If we are not responsible, then we are unable to fix it, change it, or improve it. When we blame, we vote for the status quo. When we blame another person, a situation, the economy, or the weather, we are saying we are powerless over the circumstance and do not need to change anything about ourselves.

Traditional therapy and age regression therapy will seek the source of this negative energetic response in the client's childhood. Perhaps neglect, abuse, or abandonment in their childhood manifests itself as out of control anger or seething resentment in adulthood. Through re-experiencing the anger in childhood in the safety of a hypnotic state, the client can release the negative energy motivating the anger in adulthood. In addition to that treatment or instead of that treatment, the therapist teaches anger management skills for the client to modify, and eventually, eliminate the client's angry harmful responses.

When these methods fail the client, he continues to over-react to events others let roll off their backs. He will punish his loved ones with destructive outbursts, or harm himself with self-destructive reactions. Then, it is time to seek help elsewhere. Past-life regression returns to the origin of the anger and allows the client to undo the rage that caused their out of control behavior triggered by something in this life. In my practice, I have added past-life regression to all of the approaches listed above to achieve the maximum resolution possible in a client's current life. Exploring the origin of negative emotions in past lives is both exciting and rewarding work. When my clients release the rage in a past life, they continue to experience normal feelings of anger, but they no longer experience the destruction this emotion had in their lives.

Adolescent Anger from Cannon Fodder...

"I don't believe in past lives," said the good mother and committed Christian as she handed the copy of "Many Lives, Many Masters," by Brian Weiss, M.D., back to me. "And I don't care what you do, just fix my son!" Her teenage son looked every inch the 15 year old in his high water worn jeans, rock star t-shirt, Denver Broncos baseball cap with the bill over his neck, and a slight scattering of acne on his handsome face.

He extended his hand to shake and looked me directly in the eye as he introduced himself. Who wouldn't be charmed by this kid? Apparently every authority figure since kindergarten.

From four years old, Steven's anger exploded in violence toward people and objects. His mother reported that his stepfather's abuse started at the same time and she divorced him as soon as possible after she became aware of it. The divorce failed to change his behavior, as Steven continued to lose his temper and inflict damage on anyone or anything in his environment. Even his mother was an occasional target for his rage. By the 7th grade, he had attacked two teachers.

When I spoke to Steven's teachers and principal they told me Steven was the most violent child they had ever seen. He flew into unpredictable rages which he took out on whatever was available in his environment. However, he was not a bully, and was accepted by his peers, priding himself in defending the weaker, unpopular kids from the school bullies. He was considered a loyal friend and an asset to any group most of the time.

It was that small percentage of time that brought his mother in to see me. "He's ready to take driver's ed, and I cannot in good conscience let him behind the wheel of a car with his unpredictable outbursts."

"And I want to finish school, here, at this school," he grinned at me.

When counseling began we worked on the violence. We worked on anger management skills weekly, which included his choices: walking away from a situation rather than a confrontational episode. When discussing his stepfather, he admitted to his powerlessness because of the difference in size between a four year old boy and an adult male. We did age regression to release his negative feelings about the stepfather and heal the hurt it had caused him physically, emotionally, and psychologically.

Every client is unique. Circumstances, backgrounds, assets and liabilities define their choices. Steven was an intelligent young man, with an isolating issue. If we didn't find a solution to his violent outbursts, this young man was going to join the others with violent outbursts in the state penitentiary.

When backed into a corner, most do not choose violence to solve the situation. Steven's first response to solving a problem was always violence.

After a year of weekly therapy Steven had improved but was not considered healthy yet. He was able to walk away from about 70% of the situations that before would have provoked anger followed by violence. He accepted responsibility for all of his actions. Even though the frequency of his violent outbursts was still unacceptable in a zero tolerance environment, the school supported his progress thus far and continued to support his therapy in the hope of a positive outcome.

It was time for a past-life regression, so after obtaining a signed authorization from his mother, and approaching Steven for his opinion on the process, we made an appointment for the following week. His smile indicated his excitement at the prospect of the experience.

Steven went into a hypnotic trance easily. I directed him to go back in time to a past life that would help him understand his violence in his current life. He dropped into a life as a 17 year old boy in mid-twentieth century Chicago. Pearl Harbor's recent attack motivated many to volunteer, and Steven and his best friend were in line to join the Army.

Diane: What are you aware of?

Steven: I am standing in line to join the Army.

D: Where are you?

S: Chicago. Pearl Harbor has just been attacked. I want to fight for our freedom.

D: Is anyone you know there with you?

S: (pause) Yes, my best friend. We want to do the buddy system and fight together.

D: Look into his eyes. Do you recognize his spirit?

S: Yes, it's John (his best friend in school).

D: Okay. Let's move forward in time in that life to the next important event. What is happening?

S: I am in an airplane, in a very small area, kind of on the bottom of the plane. It is a military plane. We are flying a mission over Germany. I'm the gunner. We are on a bombing raid.

D: How do you feel?

S: It is exciting – an adrenaline rush. I am glad to be fighting for my country. It is scary, but I don't mind dying for my country. Hitler is bad. We are nearing our target. I see the bombs falling from our plane. The plane is now banking up and away from the city – I see the bombs explode. WOW!

D: Is this your first mission?

S: No. We have done many. I'll be going home soon.

D: Let's move forward in time to the next significant event in that life. What are you aware of?

S: We are on another mission. There are many planes; we are over a big city moving toward our target. I am in my gunner area. There are German planes in the air, many of them. It does not look good. I can tell our pilot is struggling – he is flying all over the place, but trying to move toward the target. I see enemy planes heading toward us and the other planes in our group. I am firing at them – I hit one – it is going down. Oh no, there is one to the right – I am firing in that direction. We are hit – we're going down – fast. It is all over. Everything is black.

D: Rise above your body. Let me know when you are aware of being out of your body.

S: Okay – I am looking around at the debris of the plane. It crashed in a field. Everyone is dead.

D: How do you feel?

S: I'm really angry – I can't believe I am dead – I am so young. I want to fight for my country – it is not fair that it has ended this way – I have so much more to give. I want to kill Hitler's men – they are evil!

When I brought Steven back to the counseling room his anger showed in his tightly clinched fists and the pinched expression on his young face. He talked about how it was not supposed to end that way, he felt cheated, because he felt he was invincible in that past life. He was trained to kill, but died before he could do his duty. Not fair, not fair, not fair!

The following week a frustrated Steven came for another regression. "I went to war for all the right reasons…why did I have to die before finishing what I was there to do?" He shook his head as he slid into the recliner I use for regressions. "I'm a trained fighter…to kill the enemy…" He muttered before returning his attention to me and the induction into a trance state.

Diane: What are you aware of?

Steven: I have moccasins on my feet and clothing made of animal skins.

D: Are you male of female?

S: I am a boy – about 15. I am standing outside of my tepee. There are lots of tepees. The women are cooking on open fires. There are small children running around. I am a brave – trained to hunt with the men.

D: Are you carrying anything?

S: Yes, a spear. We are going out on a hunt. The men are gathering. We are excited. Our tribe needs meat. We hunt the buffalo. We are leaving.

D: Move forward in time, just a little. Let's see what happens.

S: We see the buffalo far across the plain. We are creeping up on them. We will surprise them and drive them over the cliff. I am now crawling in the grass with the others. I am excited – adrenaline is rushing.

D: Let me know when you are ready to jump up.

S: We are getting very close to them, behind them; the cliff is on the other side of them. The brave at the front jumps up, we all follow and start yelling at the buffalo, they start running toward the cliff. The stampede is on! We are running after them. Many of the buffalo are turning away from the cliff, a few go over the cliff.

D: So what happens next?

S: We are at the bottom of the cliff. Four buffalo have gone over the cliff and are dead. We are cutting them up to prepare to carry them back to the village. We have poles that we will put the meat on. Everyone is excited – the hunt was successful. The women will be happy – we will not be hungry.

D: So let's move forward in time again to the next important event of that life. What is happening?

S: About a year has passed. We have heard stories of raids by men on horses with a stick that kills – a big bang noise. These men have wiped out whole villages. My people are a peaceful people. But we are making tomahawks and more bows so we can fight if these men come to our village. I want to protect my people. I am sitting outside my tepee making a new tomahawk. The men are worried; stories have come to our village from runners from other villages. We are preparing.

D: Okay – So let's move forward in time to the next significant event in that life. Be there. What are you aware of?

S: I am just waking up in my tepee, it is early morning. I hear the horses in the corral restless, agitated. I'm going to get up and see if maybe there is an animal that is scaring them. I'm getting up but now I hear thundering hooves, loud booming noises! Oh no, it must be the evil men on horses with the sticks that have fire. I grab my tomahawk, head for the tepee opening, and look out. Many men on horses are running through the village – with sticks on fire – they are throwing them at the tepees which are catching on fire. There are braves running about, fighting these men on horses. I must help them – I must save my people!!

D: (pause) Let me know what happens.

S: I open the flap on the tepee and sneak out. A man with white skin on a horse sees me, he is running at me, he points his stick at me, a big noise, I feel a pain in my chest, I fall down – everything is dark.

D: Are you dead?

S: Yes, I am floating out of my body.

D: Look around and tell me what you see.

S: It is horrible – all the tepees are on fire, they are killing everyone – the women and the children. The braves do not have a chance – they are dying one by one – we are brave, but we have no chance against the sticks that kill. They are killing all of my people – we are a peaceful people – why do they kill us?

D: How do you feel?

S: So, so sad. I feel powerless. I see them go into my tepee and kill my sister and mother – they just murder them! I am angry – I want to kill them! But I am dead. I want to rise up and kill them all! They are bad, evil!

Back in the counseling room, in real time, he was in a rage. Fists clenched, his face red with fury, he yelled, "Why do evil people kill innocent people? It is not right. I want to fight evil!"

We processed his anger and discussed his desire to harm those he sees doing evil to others. "Just like school when the jocks go after the band kids, or the seniors attack a freshman…" His voice trailed off.

Steven's favorite subject was history, and now he was aware that human history was full of violence – violence that harmed innocent people.

Week after week Steven came in for past-life regressions. Week after week he saw himself dying a young death as a warrior: in the Civil War, in World War I, in the crusades, basically, in almost every war ever fought between men. He saw himself dying as a police officer in New York City in a raid against drug traffickers, and killed by a grizzly bear in Montana trying to protect his wife. Always brave, always valiant, and always a well-trained killer. He always died young. He was trained to fight for what felt just and righteous in each life. As a small child, he was taught by his people what they believed was "right". He fought for those principles, and life after life he died young…too young, always before he had finished his work.

Life after life he felt rage and anger at injustices he saw and at being killed before he could make his full contribution to his people. Week after week we processed his rage and anger at dying before he could save his people.

After many regressions Steven told me that he had wanted to be a Marine since he was a young boy. Now he realized he was born "to fight, and to die for my country". After all of these untimely deaths, he still wanted to be a Marine. With that understanding, I reminded him that the Marines have very high standards for acceptance into the corps—and uncontrollable violent outbursts on his record might exclude him.

Steven's past life rage was being released. He was becoming less intense, and he had not been triggered into violence in school for about four months. This was huge progress. In my most recent conference, his school principal said, "What did you do to Steven? He has not had a violent outburst for months."

Steven wanted to be regressed one more time to see what happened during his most recent past lifetime. Was there rage still there? Did he die young?

Diane: What are you aware of?

Steven: I have heavy boots on; they lace up high on my legs. I am wearing heavy pants and a flannel shirt. It is fall. I'm in a forest with big trees.

D: Do you have anything in your hands?

S: Yes, a chainsaw. There are some other men nearby.

D: How old are you?

S: 18.

D: Who are the other men?

S: One is my father; one is my older brother, and my uncle. We are loggers, and live in Montana. We are poor.

D: Look into the eyes of the other men and see if you recognize any of their spirits.

S: (pause) My father is my Uncle Ron. My brother is my friend, John. I don't recognize my uncle. The day is over and we are going home to eat dinner. We are packing up the truck with all our equipment.

D: Let me know when you get home.

S: Yes, we are there. It is a log cabin in a forest. We live outside of a small town. We're going inside. My mom is cooking dinner for us.

D: Look into your mom's eyes. Do you recognize her spirit?

S: Yes, she is my sister.

D: So let's see what happens next.

S: We are sitting around the table. They are talking about the war. I tell them I want to enlist. There is nothing here for me and I think I will make a good soldier. I'll probably be drafted anyway.

D: What war is it?

S: The Vietnam War. My family is not excited that I want to go. Many men are dying over there. And my family needs my help here. I am young and strong. I tell them I do not want to log for the rest of my life. The army is an opportunity to have a different life.

D: So let's move forward in time to the next important event in that life. What is happening?

S: I am in boot camp. We are training in various maneuvers. I am in really good shape because I was a logger. Most of these guys are not.

D: Let's move forward in time again to the next important event in that life.

S: My platoon is shipping out to Vietnam. We are boarding the airplane. I am sitting down next to a nurse that is going over there too. We hit it off right away. We will stop in Maine, then over to Vietnam.

D: So what happens next?

S: Her name is Jolene. We are talking constantly. I feel like I have known her forever. We spend the entire flight talking, holding hands.

D: So let's move forward in time again to the next significant event.

S: I'm now in Vietnam. I'm assigned to a six man squad with a new sergeant. We are about to head out on a major operation. I'm worried about this new sergeant.

D: What year is it?

S: 1969.

D: So what happens next? Move forward in time and let's see what happens next.

S: We are landing on the beach. We are running up onto the beach. Oh! Sniper fire from the trees on the right. I'm running to the trees on the left. So are the rest of the men. Some don't make it. I'm hiding in the trees. I don't see anyone. I don't know what to do. I'll just wait.

D: Let me know what happens.

S: I see one of my squad walking by in the trees. I'm going to go to where he is. I am walking toward him. Oh! I've been shot in the back! I'm laying face down. I can't believe how careless I was, bad choice. I'm dying. (pause) Everything is dark.

D: So rise out of your body and see what is happening.

S: I don't see anyone. Many bodies. I see other spirits rising up. I can't believe this has happened. I am so young and I could have served my country if I could have just made a better choice – stayed in the trees longer.

This time when he returned from his trance, he was not angry. He was amazed that one more time he had died in a war as a young man. In fact, he laughed. He had become so used to dying in these past life experiences that he saw that his lives were a seamless fabric that included death and rebirth: over and over again.

He never had another angry outburst in high school. He was well liked and made good choices. After graduation, he enlisted in the Marines and will ship out to Iraq soon. He is a warrior who will fight for justice.

Exploring the roots of anger using past-life regression takes fascinating paths. Because of the destruction anger causes in every lifetime, it is the biggest impediment to our spiritual growth. The negative energy that explodes in angry episodes replaces the positive energy we need to move forward on our path toward spiritual growth and fulfillment.

Righteous Anger?

The first time I met Anna was prior to the last election at a political rally in support of women's rights. This mild mannered, conservatively dressed, heavy set woman was apparently enraged at the possibility of "Roe vs. Wade" being overturned if the wrong party was elected to national office.

Covered with campaign buttons in support of the liberal candidate, carrying a hand made sign in support of women's rights, and red faced from chanting her demands at the podium, Anna was every inch the committed political activist. Apparently someone had told her my profession, because she approached me after the rally.

"Can you help me?" she asked, a smile on her broad, Midwestern face. "I hate those people..." She jerked her head toward the right-to-lifers who remained on the fringes of the crowd. "I don't even know them, but I hate them and everything they stand for: religious superiority, intolerance, and trying to impose their beliefs on the rest of us you know, the ones with the brains." This time she laughed.

We made an appointment for the following week to explore the reasons for her irrational hatred and anger at any and everyone who represents the ultra right wing, fundamentalist, conservative, Tea Party movement. She was particularly passionate about civil rights and gender equality. I went home wondering why she considered these feelings a problem, and looked forward to her appointment to learn more.

Carrying a "green" go cup full of herbal tea into my office, Anna slid comfortably into the side chair in my office. The blue upholstery matched her denim skirt and shirt and brought out the blue in her large, expressive eyes. A natural blonde, she had the high coloring of the Nordic people of her ancestry, and their sturdy, broad shouldered build as well. "I don't want to live another year knowing I will be assaulted by Mormons, Jehovah's, Tea Party people, "good" Christians, Jews for Jesus, and recruiters for the Eastern Star trying to shove their narrow minded conservative views down my throat." Her voice rose with the color in her cheeks as she spat out each word as if it were a pejorative rather than a label.

The force of her invective made me pull back into my chair.

She went on to explain this pattern started when she moved to Utah where her new in-laws put extreme pressure on her to conform to their Evangelical Christian lifestyle and to participate in their church. Her mother-in-law was also putting pressure on Anna to become the perfect Christian wife. She gave Anna books on how to accomplish this complete transformation of herself. Regardless of her mother-in-law's intentions, the results matched Anna's perception of emotional and psychological abuse that stripped her of her self-esteem and personal power. She had no support for her values, opinions, or personality as her husband's family wanted to "save my soul." Anna never "measured up", so her marriage ended in divorce.

Anna then related the most violent encounter she had ever experienced, one that left her shaking for the following three days, and she had felt "beaten to a bloody pulp" even though no one had laid a hand on her. It occurred in her last job when the president of her company called to speak to her about his perception of her "takeover" of her office. She had never met him, and had never even spoken to him over the phone before that day. As he berated her pushiness and power tripping in a loud abusive voice, she felt herself quaking inside, and then the anger came. Like a reflex action, her voice rose to meet his as she stated her defense; she was only doing the work he paid her to do, and her associates appreciated her efforts on the company's behalf. Considering the matter solved, she hung up the phone, quaking inside, and went on with her work. Later that afternoon, the president called again to fire her.

For eight years before I met Anna, she had asked herself why this man had behaved so badly, so meanly, and so brutally to an employee he had never met. She had felt for years that somehow the betrayal of her marriage partner, the emotionally and spiritually abusive conduct of her in-laws, and the verbal violence of her employer were all connected. But how? And why? Anna was aware that her rage, resentment and knee jerk reaction to any evidence of intolerance or imposition stopped her in her spiritual tracks. Until she resolved this detrimental distraction there would be no further progress on her spiritual path.

Diane: What are you aware of?
Anna: I'm walking on a dirt road. There is water on the left and desert-like landscape on the right.
D: What are you wearing?
A: A cloth robe with beads.
D: Are you walking alone or are you with someone?
A: I am alone. There are fires burning to keep the insects away.
D: What season is it?

A: Early fall.

D: How old are you?

A: 34.

D: Let's see what else is important about this scene. Share with me what you see as you look around.

A: The square is above the harbor. There is a harbor with ships in it. It looks like ships from many different places. Many different sails. Different kinds of ships. Maybe a dozen ships in the harbor. They are wooden ships, some have oars.

D: What is it you are doing in this town right now?

A: Just walking through the market.

D: Are you just wandering or are you headed in a particular direction?

A: I am headed to the library.

D: Let's see what this library has for you.

A: There are scrolls and codices, it is dark inside, and the only light comes from the top part of the library where windows bring in natural light. There are candles burning.

D: Are you there to find something?

A: I come here every day to study.

D: What is it you study?

A: Philosophy.

D: This city where you are, where is it located?

A: Alexandria, Egypt. I am interested in philosophy and science.

D: Let's see what happens next. Move forward in time now to the next significant event in that life.

A: It is a dinner, lots of very important people here. The servants seem upset, agitated over something. They are doing their duties but they seem to be concerned about something. Everyone else is oblivious, enjoying themselves as usual.

D: I want you to look around and see if there is anyone at this dinner that is particularly special to you, or that maybe you came with, or maybe is an important person in your life.

A: There is one of the servants. A man.

D: I want you to look into his face, look into his eyes, and see if you recognize him. Is his spirit familiar to you?

A: I don't recognize him.

D: Let's see what this dinner brings, what is the purpose of the dinner?

A: Just wealthy people getting together to enjoy themselves.

D: The servants are agitated. Why?

A: It has something to do with the man. The man servant.

D: Let's see if you can find out why, what is going on.

A: He is teaching them to rebel. He is telling them that the aristocrats have controlled their religious lives to keep them as slaves. He is planning to rebel.

D: What is the religion at that time?

A: They don't have a religion.

D: What people are suppressing the servants?

A: It is the Romans.

D: How do you feel about this possible rebellion?

A: Somehow I have learned about it and am confused about what to do because I believe that the Egyptian people are oppressed and that I know that if they rebel they will be destroyed. I don't feel like I can tell anyone about it.

D: Do you mean the aristocrats? Are you one of the wealthy?

A: Yes.

D: It sounds like you know about what they are planning and that you are fearful for them. So let's see how this unfolds. Move forward in time just a little bit.

A: My father, he is angry with me. He has discovered that I knew about the rebellion and I said nothing. He is beating me.

D: I want you to look into his eyes and see if you recognize his spirit.

A: I do, it is my ex-boss, the head of the company. I recognize his energy even though I never saw him. He wants to beat me to death.

D: How did he find out that you knew?

A: They tortured the servants who rebelled. Most of them were killed, some were tortured.

D: What do you do as your father is beating you?

A: I try to protect myself and get away, but can't. He is a large man.

D: Is he a Roman soldier?

A: Yes. He is so much bigger and stronger than I am.

D: Is your mother anywhere around?

A: My mother is deceased. She died when I was small.

D: How does this altercation with your father come out?

A: He beats me until I am senseless. Then he leaves me there.

D: Are you still alive?

A: Yes.

D: Let's see what happens next.

A: I am afraid to move. But eventually I stand up. My arms are bloody from being beaten. There is blood all over the front of my clothes. I am confused, I don't know what to do or where to go. I am afraid if I stay he will kill me. I run to the library. I am frightened; the streets are not safe at night. I get there safely. I am looking for my teacher.

D: You have a teacher there?

A: Yes, an old man. Someone I think I can trust. I find him in the back of the library.

D: Look into his eyes. See if you recognize his spirit.

A: It's Dave (her ex-husband).

D: So what does this wise teacher do for you?

A: He sends me away. He says that I have been disobedient. And that I am not worthy any longer. He acts as if he has never known me. I feel terribly betrayed.

D: Have you been studying with this man for awhile?

A: For 12 years. He acts as if I am some stranger. He tells me to leave and to never come back.

D: Does he know why you are all bloody?

A: Yes. He knows my father very well.

D: So let's see where you go next.

A: I am on the street, it is very dark. (pause) There is a woman standing in her doorway. She sees me and, weak from the beating, I fall. She comes and helps me into her house.

D: So look into her eyes, and see if you recognize her spirit.

A: Yes, it is Carol (a very close female friend).

D: So what does she do with you?

A: She is cleaning me up. Finding me something clean to wear.

D: How are you feeling from that beating?

A: Weak. I hurt. My whole body aches. It looks like some of the wounds are going to scar badly. But she tells me I can stay for as long as I want. It is just across the square from where my father lives and from the library.

D: So let's see what happens to you. Let's move forward just a little bit in time. What is happening?

A: I am in a courtyard. There are plants in the courtyard and a fountain.

D: Are you there alone or is someone with you?

A: The woman who helped me is with me. It is some kind of sanctuary. She is angry with me, though.

D: Why is she angry with you?

A: I feel like I have to fight back. I feel like I can no longer tolerate the injustices. She is angry because she is afraid I will get myself killed. I have been speaking on the streets against the Romans. Also, I have been teaching people, and because I am a woman I am not allowed to teach.

D: What have you been teaching?

A: The philosophy that I learned in the library; along with what the woman has taught me about kindness and love - and how it is wrong for one group of people to dominate another. She is afraid that if I go out again I will not come back.

D: Is what you are teaching in conflict with what is allowed to be taught at that time?

A: The Romans expect us to be obedient. And I am one of them. I can't *stand* that I am one of them. And I have hurt people too. Because I was raised to be as arrogant and proud as they are. I have been unkind to my slaves. And now I feel like something has to be done.

D: So you are trying to change the way it has been.

A: Yes. The suppression of these people is not okay.

D: So what do you decide to do?

A: I go. I go into the market, walking among the stalls, talking to the people one by one.

D: What do you say to them as you are talking to them?

A: I just tell them that they have a right to decide for themselves what their lives should be. That they do not have to give half their wages to the Romans as taxes. I tell them that they need to band together because if they stick together there are more of them than there are Romans. Some people listen, some think I am crazy. And in a way I am afraid for the people that listen to me. I am more afraid for them than I am for myself. I think of it as a kind of penance for what I have done, for the life I have lived. My father is a very wealthy powerful man.

D: Does he know you are out teaching?

A: Yes. He has disowned me. He pretends he does not know me. I saw him on the street once and he acted as if I wasn't there.

D: So let's see what happens as you are out teaching. Are there any Romans wandering around other than the peasants?

A: There are two Roman soldiers coming toward me. They are coming to arrest me.

D: What do they do when they arrest you?

A: They take me to my father. They grab me by the arms. I know that if I resist them in the market others will get hurt. I am now in my father's home. He is angry. He is in one of his rages. He is hitting me with his fists. He hits me so hard I can't get up. He kicks me. He can't stop; he just keeps kicking me and kicking me. He thinks I have betrayed him, that I have disgraced him, embarrassed him. He kicks me in the head. Everything goes dark. I can't feel anything anymore.

My spirit is leaving my body. I can see him still kicking my body. My body is lying there bloody; there is a terrible wound in my head where he has kicked me. There is lots of blood around my head. He hates me, he really hates me. He has killed me.

I slowly brought Anna back into my consultation room. She was quiet for some time. Then she said she had expected to find some terrible incident involving religious conviction, but was surprised to find a lifetime in which she had studied philosophy, science and math. She stated that it was true that she was more interested in the history of religion than the dogma and the philosophy of spiritual beliefs than any doctrine. Then she said that this past life had shown her why she was so focused on individual rights of self-determination, especially in regard to religion, gender and economic access. She said she was surprised to see her lack of interest in religion in that past life, but attributed that to the Roman culture of the time.

Anna went on to reflect that what seemed to be at the core of her anger issue was the abuse of power. The way the slaves were treated brought intense feelings to the surface for her. She stated that people in power believe they are right and the other is wrong. They impose their belief systems on the others. At the minimum, this causes those in power to push their beliefs onto those that are not in power. At the worst, it causes war, genocide and murder. In that past life the ultimate forcing of the will was when her father killed her, "If you do not agree with me, and go against me, I will kill you."

She likened the Roman efforts to force their culture on the slaves to Christians trying to force their beliefs on peoples all over the world. Anna said that when she hears a Christian say to another person,

"Have you found Jesus yet?" she is angered and considers this spiritual abuse. She commented that little had changed since the Roman Empire. Human beings in power were still oppressing human beings who were not in power. Anna sighed, "Why can't we all realize that we are one, and celebrate our difference, and live in a community called Planet Earth?"

Three weeks later I contacted Anna to see how her anger was doing. She reported that she no longer became angry when see saw acts or heard statements that she disagreed with regarding civil liberties or individual rights. She said that she is still promoting the cause of equality, but that there is no more anger associated with her efforts. She said that all her energy that had been put out in anger is now freed to be creatively used to help the world become a better place. She is still passionate, but not angry!

"Speak when you are angry—and you will make the best speech you will ever regret."

Lawrence J. Peter

Chapter Nine

Psychological Pain: Depression

*"My depression is the most faithful mistress I have known—
no wonder, then, that I return the love."*

Soren Kierkegaard

For purposes of presenting past-life regressions as a treatment option for people in mental pain, I'm drawing a distinction between emotional pain (Chapter Eight) and psychological pain in this chapter. Emotions are feelings, energy that may or may not be acted out in behavior. Painful emotions are anger, rage, fear, sadness, and at times, love. The psychological element enters the picture when the emotion translates into irresistible, irrational behavior or any condition beyond the conscious control of the person. One of the most prominent categories of psychological pain is depression.

Another distinction is the duration of the experience. Emotions respond to environmental triggers, stimuli, and their intensity rises and then subsides, eventually disappearing in a finite amount of time. Psychological pain occurs spontaneously with or without an external event preceding or triggering it. The duration varies depending on how successful treatment is. Psychological pain is chronic and almost always requires treatment to improve the client's quality of life. Emotional pain is transient and requires treatment if the associated feelings translate into actions harmful to the client or others.

Depression: a Physical Solution to a Mental Challenge

Depression kills our motivation to do life. We sit around, sleep, read novels, or watch TV, sometimes over-eating or not eating at all. We have trouble sleeping or we sleep too much. We withdraw from our relationships and activities we used to enjoy. Unlike emotions which are all about energy, depression is obvious in that it drains our energy. Fatigued and unfocused, we feel worthless, useless, and hopeless. At its worst, depression kills us slowly by depriving us of our vitality and willingness to create full, self-actualized lives.

If the depression is a result of a recent trauma, such as loss of a loved one, job, or a marriage; the origins of the condition are obvious…especially if they were preceded by past life events contributing to them. When one of my clients lost her closest female friend in a car wreck, she told me that she felt like she had lost her reason to live. Treating her depression from the point of view of traditional psychotherapy and this life alone did not work. My client did not improve. When she decided to investigate the spiritual connection with her friend using past-life regression and life-between-lives regression she found out that this female friend was her soul mate. This information brought clear understanding to the huge impact this loss had for her. She fully understood her depression over the loss and then moved through the depression and forward with her life.

With regard to depression following a divorce that has been caused by infidelity, past-life regression helps to shed light on whether the relationship between these two people had a pattern of this behavior in past lives.

One of my clients came into my practice because his wife's infidelity had devastated him, resulting in his depression. He was thinking about divorce, but continued to be very much in love with his wife. Past-life regression showed that in a recent past life he had cheated on her. These two spirits had designed their current life together so that this man could learn how it felt to be cheated on. This role reversal of the villain/victim roles is common among spirits who want to learn a lesson from both sides.

The feeling of remorse is a powerful teacher. Once aware of his betrayal in a former life with his wife, his understanding was complete. His sense of justice allowed him to forgive his wife. Their relationship deepened; and now, a few years later, they have a stronger marriage.

My work has shown that we learn more from the villain role than we do from the victim role. Ask any actor which role brings out the best in them; it's always the villain. Villains are more complex, more interesting, and more challenging because of the ways they rationalize their actions.

As human beings, we are aware of the pain suffering causes; we avoid it whenever possible. The speech every father says as he lays the belt to his child's rear end, "This hurts me more than it hurts you." is never understood by the child (victim) until he becomes the parent (villain).

Past-life regression allows us to clarify the current situation through understanding of former life events. By re-experiencing them, we are able to discharge the negativity surrounding them. Thus healed, we are then free to move forward on our spiritual journey in this life.

Chronic Depression

When 55-year-old Nancy came to my office, she had suffered from depression for decades and there was no obvious precipitating situation to cause it. Anti-depressants provided no relief, years of traditional therapy had done nothing to alleviate her symptoms, and she was here because she had run out of alternatives and was considering suicide.

When I suggested past-life regression as a possible treatment, Nancy's immediate response was "no". She was raised Catholic and even though she no longer practiced it, she considered herself a religious person. Even though she had not yet sought help in her faith, she was wary of trying something so "out there".

Shrugging, I opened my hands in a helpless gesture, and told her, "I cannot, in good conscience, turn you away when in my professional opinion you need hospitalization for your own safety."

Her eyes opened wide, and she began to retreat toward the door. "What? Why?" Her fear was evidence in the tremor in her voice.

"Because I am concerned about you." I replied. "And all I have to offer you that differs from what you've tried before is past-life regression…"

Pushing her long grey bangs off of her forehead with a work roughened hand, Nancy's brown eyes rolled toward the ceiling and she heaved a large, heavy sigh. "Okay, we'll do it your way…"

"Please understand, hospitalization is not off of the table…"

She nodded her assent and moved toward the recliner with heaviness in each step.

After an easy induction, I directed Nancy to a past life that would help her understand her current depression.

In her most recent past life, she was the only child of very poor parents living in a Chicago tenement building. Her father was a severe alcoholic.

Diane: What are you aware of?

Nancy: I have pink shoes on and a pink flowered dress.

D: How old are you?

N: I am seven.

D: Please describe your surroundings. Where are you and who is there with you?

N: I am in the living room of our small apartment. The furniture is broken down and dirty. My mommy is sitting in an old rocking chair and daddy is standing over her yelling.

Nancy's face crumbles like a small child. She sniffles.

N: I am afraid.

D: Why are you afraid?

N: They fight lots and sometimes daddy hits mommy. It scares me. I don't try anymore to stop them because daddy used to push me down if I tried to stop them. Daddy is drunk again and mommy is mad at him. She wants him to stop drinking. She says we can't afford for him to drink.

D: Look into both of their eyes. Do you recognize either of their spirits?

N: (pause) Yes. Mom is my sister, Susan, in this life. Dad is my dad in this life. He is dead now.

D: What kind of work do they do?

N: Daddy works at a factory and mommy takes in people's laundry and some sewing. The fight is getting worse. He is swearing at her, she is yelling back. I'm afraid he will hit her.

Nancy's breathing quickens as she makes little mewing sounds.

N: I'm running into my room!

D: What is your room like?

N: Dark and dirty. There is an old small bed in the corner with some blankets on it. My clothes are sort of all over. Mommy doesn't have time to do much in our apartment. I have my favorite stuffed bear on my bed – I'm on my bed with my hands over my ears. I hate the yelling. It happens every night. I'm curled up with my blanket and bear. I'll be okay if I stay in here.

D: Let's move forward in time to the next significant event in that life. What is happening?

N: I am older – about 10. Same apartment. The landlady is talking to mom. Dad is not here – he is at work. It is during the day. The landlady is an old lady. She and mom have become friends. Mom is working on her mending. The landlady gives mom money sometimes when we have no more food because dad drank all the money.

D: What are they talking about?

N: The landlady is trying to talk mom into leaving dad. She is afraid he will hurt my mom bad some day. I can see the landlady really likes my mom.

D: Look closely into the eyes of the landlady. Is her spirit familiar to you?

N: (pause) Yes, she is my grandma in this life. I loved her so much! (Her grandmother is deceased) She is trying to help mom. She gives mom some money because we are out of food.

D: Okay. So let's move forward again in time to the next important event in this life.

N: Mom and dad are in the middle of a huge fight. Dad is very angry. Mom is sitting in her rocking chair. I am scared.

D: How old are you now?

N: Thirteen. I am in my room but this fight is worse than most. I am afraid for mom. Dad is really mad and he is very drunk.

D: Let's see what happens.

N: I am peeking out of my door. My room is dark so they don't see me. It is late. They think I am asleep. Dad wants money to go buy beer. Mom says she doesn't have any. He is standing over her screaming at her. Oh no! He is going to hit her! He hit her so hard that she fell over backward in her chair. Her head hit the heater behind chair. Now he is kicking her as she lies on the floor. She is not moving. I am really scared. I need to hide!

D: Let's see what happens next. ...

N: Dad yells and swears at her. She is not saying anything. I hear the door to the apartment slam shut. I think he might have left. I'll peak out. Yes. He's gone. I am running to check on mom. (pause) She is lying on the floor and will not talk to me or open her eyes. I'm going to get the landlady.

D: Let me know when you get back.

N: (pause) I got her, she is here now trying to help mom. She has mom lying on the floor and is wiping up the blood from mom's head. She is bleeding a lot from a cut in her head. And it looks like he kicked her in the side of the head. I'm so scared. Mom is groaning – so I guess she is alive. The landlady is trying to get mom to sit up, but she won't. She is telling me she is going to call a doctor. We don't have a phone so she is going to her apartment.

D: Let me know what happens.

N: The doctor is here now and is looking at mom. He says she needs to go to the hospital. He is going to take her with the landlady. I'll stay here. The landlady is very upset.

D: Let's move forward in time just a little and see what happens next.

N: I am older now, 15. Mom is sitting in her rocking chair. She never got better. She can't talk much; she just sits in her chair and stares. Dad never came home again. I take care of mom when I'm not in school. The landlady takes care of her during my school. I am taking in laundry now and mending. I stay up late every night getting my homework and the laundry done. I'm tired. Mom just rocks in her chair and stares. The landlady gives us a break on our rent because I can't make enough to cover the rent and food.

D: How are you feeling about mom's state?

N: I am depressed most of the time. I try my best to do everything. I love mom. I want to help her but don't know how. I kiss her and tell her I love her but she just keeps staring out at nothing. I am very sad.

D: Let's move forward in time again to the next significant time in that life.

N: I'm on my way home from school, walking. I'm sixteen. I'm tired. I stay up really late to get everything done. I walk into the apartment. I see mom's rocking chair tipped over and mom is lying in the middle of the floor. Oh! No!

D: What's wrong?

N: She is lying in a pool of blood, her blood. She is dead. She killed herself, cut herself! I am lying next to her in her blood, crying. (long pause)

D: What do you do next?

N: I don't want to do anything – just die with her – I love her so much. I'll go get the landlady. I am dragging myself to her apartment. I tell her what has happened. She is coming back with me. She calls the coroner. He is coming. I am sick. I am throwing up. The coroner arrives. He takes my mom away.

D: Let's move forward in time again and see what becomes of you.

N: I'm 18 now. Same apartment. The landlady let me stay. I dropped out of high school after mom killed herself. I still take in laundry and mending. But I am so depressed. I miss mom so much. I don't feel like doing anything. The only person I am friendly with is the landlady. She understands. She is getting very old, but she is like my mom now. She checks in on me. I spend lots of time lying on mom's blood stain on the living room rug. It makes me feel closer to her. I can feel her spirit when I do that. It is the only time I am comforted. But I don't care about anything. I just want to die. I have nothing to live for anymore.

D: Okay. So let's move forward in time and see what you do with your life. What is happening now?

N: Same apartment. I am now 19. I just can't go on. It is now 1945. Everything is the same. I have no reason to live. I am getting ready to kill myself. I'm going to do it the way mom did but not make such a mess. I don't want the landlady to have to clean up such a mess. I'm going to cut myself in the bath tub. I'm putting on some simple clothes. I write a short note, thanking the landlady, telling her I just can't go on, that I have no reason to live. She will understand. She knows how depressed I have been. I put the note on the kitchen counter. Now I'm getting into the bath tub. I don't feel anything. I cut my wrists with a razor blade. It does not hurt, I can't feel anymore. I am numb to life. (pause) I feel light headed, sort of floating, no more pain. I am rising up out of my body, looking down at my body. I think I am dead.

D: As you look down at your body how are you feeling?

N: I just made a big mistake! I did not try hard enough. I did not value my life! It is wrong what I did. It is wrong not to value the precious gift of life.

     I brought Nancy back from that past life into my consultation room. She was stunned. I was quiet. Finally she said, "Well, I can see that suicide is not the answer. What surprised me the most is that consciousness is seamless. I didn't get one moment of peace – I knew immediately that it was a mistake!"

     I watched her brown eyes open in sudden comprehension as she sat upright and stared at me. "Why would I want to do that again?"

     "This is a good question." I replied, and then paused to wait for another comment from Nancy.

She looked at her hands folded in her lap. Shaking her head slowly back and forth, "As soon as I left my body I realized the depth of my mistake."

"We are attracted to that which we have done in our past lives – the good, the bad and the ugly," I said, then paused again. When Nancy didn't respond, I continued. "You used suicide in your most recent past life as an exit route when things were not going well. It worked then as far as your body was concerned and that is why you are attracted to it now."

Nancy stayed in my office for another hour processing this past life experience. Unlike the isolation of her past life, this life was filled with a large extended family, many friends, and work that she loved. Whereas her former life had been lonely and empty, and a struggle to survive; this life was filled with support and positive activities. She was unaware of this until the past-life regression brought it into stark relief.

Her realizations renewed her hope for the future and the possibility of positively influencing the rest of her life. While this was not an overnight undertaking, she was willing to take it on as a long term project. As she walked out my door I could see that her step was lighter, as was her mood.

Nancy continued weekly counseling and the word "suicide" was never mentioned again. Nancy had clearly learned that not only is life a precious gift, but that each one of us is responsible for the quality of that gift. Our obligation to our spiritual agenda, our responsibility in this incarnation, is to create the most positive reality we can for ourselves on this earth plane – and, according to Nancy, that is a "God given opportunity".

Chapter Ten

Hatred for Others: A Learned Attitude

*"An eye for an eye only ends up making
the whole world blind."*

Mahatma Gandhi

Bigotry and animosity toward another race, religion, ethnicity or political affiliation, is a learned attitude. Depending on the time and place of our birth, our significant others who raise us, influence us, or have any power over us; their attitudes, positive or negative opinions, hatreds and resentments become ours. When there is no basis in fact for the prejudice directed at a specific sub-group, what is the reason for it?

We learn through regression therapy the source of such unreasonable antagonism directed at an individual because of his or her race, ethnicity, or religion. Throughout time, certain groups are known enemies even though the origins of their mutual hatred lay hidden in the past. Blacks vs. whites, Arab vs. Jew, Catholic vs. Protestant, Conservatives vs. Communists, Tea Partiers vs. Progressives; the list is as endless and as varied as the people on our planet.

When experiencing the spirit world, it is apparent that individual spirits are without skin color, gender, religious affiliation, or political persuasion.

- Does the purity of our spiritual existence exist only during the time we spend in the afterlife, or in our life-between-lives?
- Is it possible to live our lives free of hatred for others, even if our society declared them the enemy in the past or present?
- How can we, as individuals, resist the pressure to hate from our fear-based parents, peers, priests and politicians?

Cowboys & Indians...

Ed came to my office from a significant distance to do a past-life regression because he had been enduring an exceptionally difficult boss for seven years. From the moment his boss, Lois, had seen Ed she had disliked him and let everyone else in the office know how *much* she disliked him. He worked in an office where he was the only non-Native American employee. He was a Caucasian male. He also was an excellent technician. Because of the nature of the company, new employees were hired from out-of-state. His immediate boss, and the highest ranking person in the office, had never met him or seen him prior to his first day of work.

Ed told me that he would never forget that first day in the office. He had arrived early, before his boss had arrived for the day. He was at his desk, settling in, when Lois arrived. She walked into the office building, looked at him, and said, "What is a white man doing in this office!!??" She was truly indignant. This statement was made in a loud voice meant for everyone to hear – and hear they did. A hush fell over the office. Ed was shocked at this statement from his new boss. As she looked at him she had a scowl on her face, a look of pure disgust.

For seven years Ed had done an excellent job despite the constant negativity hurled his way. He had been as pleasant as he could be to Lois, hoping that she would judge him by his performance instead of his race. No matter how hard he had tried, nothing made Lois change her mind about him. She made his life miserable. By the time he came to my office he had decided he could take no more. If the situation did not change soon he was going to seek employment elsewhere. He loved his job, but certainly could find another. He decided he would first try past-life regression to see if that would improve his work situation.

Given these circumstances, we entered the regression with the intent of going back to a previous life when Ed and Lois had known one another.

Diane: What are you aware of?
Ed: I'm standing in some bushes – no, I'm hiding in the bushes.
         Behind me is a stream.
D: Are you a male or a female?
E: I'm a boy.
D: What are you wearing on your feet if anything?
E: I have some sort of moccasins on my feet. My pants are made
         out of skins.
D: How old are you?
E: I'm 5 years old. I'm scared – there is a lot of noise coming
         from a ways off.
D: Try to look toward the noise and see what is happening.
E: I'm really scared to look!

D: Well then, what do you hear?

E: Guns, horses, yelling, screaming, and it smells like smoke. I can see flames in the distance through the bushes and tepees on fire. Lots of screaming – women and children.

D: What do you think you will do?

E: Stay here – I'll die if I move. I'm really scared they will find me.

D: Who are "they"?

E: The White Man.

D: Yes, stay where you are – maybe you can move in a while.

E: The noise is stopping – it is getting quiet. But I don't want to leave this place yet.

D: Let me know when you feel it is safe to venture out.

(A few moments later)

E: Okay. It is very quiet – I'm going to sneak toward the tepees.

D: Tell me what you see as you move away from the bushes.

E: I'm crawling – I see all the tepees are burned – smoke coming from everywhere and some flames still. Nothing is moving. I think they killed everyone. I see no movement. I'm standing up and walking toward my tepee. There is no one alive. I see bodies everywhere. Everyone is dead.

D: Where are you now?

E: I'm standing by my tepee. I see my baby sister strapped to her board – she's dead.

D: I know this must be very hard for you. Can you look into your sister's face and see if you recognize her spirit – is she familiar to you?

E: (pause, then sounding amazed) Yes, it's Lois, my boss.

D: So what do you do next?

E: I'm wandering around the camp. My parents are dead. Every-
        one is dead. No one moves. I'm alone. I'm the only one alive.
        I'm scared. What will I do now?

D: Let's see what you do next.

E: I can't do this anymore, I can't stay here, it's too sad – bring
        me out.

I immediately brought Ed back to the counseling room. He felt
sad about what had happened in that past life. It took him awhile to get
the horrible images out of his mind. He looked shocked over the entire
event. Slowly he came all the way back to this life.

We began to process what had happened in that brief scene as a
Native American boy many years ago. Ed said that he had always had
great compassion for the Native Americans and how they had been
treated by white men. Experiencing this first hand in a past life had
greatly impacted Ed. But what about seeing his boss there as his sister
in the papoose carrier? This fact seemed to be of secondary importance
to Ed. What concerned me was the fact that the baby was dead, and did
not see Ed in that past life. I had never had this happen in a past-life
regression, where the other person in the difficult relationship was dead
when my client first recognized them. Would the negative energy leave
this difficult relationship? I didn't say anything to Ed about my concern.
In addition to this concern, I was also concerned because neither Ed nor
Lois had done anything to the other that would cause anger or bad feelings. This was a puzzle for me. Ed seemed glad to have found Lois in a
past life and was hopeful that the relationship would change as he prepared to leave my office. I asked him to call and let me know how things

went when he returned to work that following Monday. He assured me he would.

I did not hear from Ed for three weeks. Then he called. I asked him how things were going with his boss. He said he had not called me because he wanted to see if what had happened would last. He reported that when he came to work the Monday after the regression, he arrived to work before his boss as usual. So he was at his desk working when she came into the office. As she came through the door she said, "Hi, Ed. How was your weekend?" Her tone was happy and pleasant. Usually she would say nothing to him. Ed went on to say they had a pleasant conversation about what each had done over the weekend. He did not tell her about his trip for the regression. Never before had she asked a question about his private life or shared anything about hers. Basically, she had never cared about him or his life prior to now. Ed said he "held his breath for two weeks", waiting to see if she would continue to be nice. He said it just got better and better. She had even called his wife to see if she could go to Weight Watchers with her. Ed and Lois went to lunch several times together. She had become interested in him in an authentic way, dropping all of her former dislike for him.

I was truly amazed and asked Ed what he thought had changed her attitude toward him. He replied, "She no longer sees me as a white man. She sees me as her brother." At this statement, I was filled with awe. Ed was thrilled with the outcome, I was amazed. All I could imagine was that the spirit of the dead baby was still nearby and had seen Ed; and that this had been enough of a connection to shift the negative energy that Lois felt toward Ed. She now saw him as a "kindred spirit".

As you can see, past-life regression has a remarkable ability to go to the heart of the problem, find the negative energy that is being held between two people involved in a difficult relationship and dissolve that negative energy. This dissolving allows both people to get on with their lives in a positive way. The negative energies accompanying anger, hatred, resentment, and jealousy prevent us from experiencing true joy in our lives and hinder our spiritual growth. Ridding ourselves of this negativity is essential to the expansion of life, to the experience of peace, compassion, and hope. It is in our relationships that we struggle the most, yet have the most opportunity to grow.

International, Intimate, Irrational Enemies...

Once upon a time, the people who lived, worked, and wandered throughout the Fertile Crescent lived in harmony with each other. Hunting, fishing, trapping and trading; gathering and cultivating crops; marrying, bearing children, living and dying; settling in one place or wandering over vast areas with the change of the seasons, these early human beings cooperated with each other for their mutual benefit.

Today, that same geography is divided between two factions, religions, and cultures who vow to eliminate each other from the face of the earth. Borders shift; walls with concertina wire encircle communities that were villages belonging to the other side a few years ago; guards wearing M-16's and AK 47's patrol the perimeters; boys throw rocks at other boys across the DMZ; and the leaders of both sides believe in their own righteousness.

What about the people? Do they really care where the other person worships, works, or walks their dog? Most care about the roof providing their shelter, sufficient food on their plate, and living in peace with their families.

Karma: Lessons Learned...

When most of us think of the concept of karma, we think of balancing the scales. Paybacks, even-Steven, what goes out, comes back…in spades. When someone says the word "karma", most people hear "tit for tat." Good deeds then equal a good life now and vice versa. Past-life regressions continue to enlighten the therapists and our clients by pointing out the fallacy of that thinking.

Most believe that karma implies the quality of the current life based on our actions in previous lives: if we are born rich, then we must have done a lot of things right in our past lives. On the other hand, the disadvantaged obviously deserve their fate because of their behavior the last time around. This thinking is a perversion of the concept of karma in more ways than oversimplification. As regressions indicate, in both past-life and life-between-lives, karma concerns lessons we *choose* to try to learn to progress on our spiritual path – not paybacks or punishment for prior bad behavior.

There is balance in karma, for born rich is not always an advantage, any more than being born in poverty is necessarily a disadvantage when looking at the continuum of the human spirit over time and eternity. Each one of us has in multiple lives been both rich and poor. *We* chose the setting and circumstances most likely to help us learn the lesson we are working on then and now. More specifically, if you were a Nazi in a past life, you may choose to be victimized by a Jew in this life. If a murdering colonist in a past life, you may choose to be murdered by a "local" in this life. If a member of the Roman Catholic priesthood during the Inquisition persecuting the infidel a few lives ago, you will want to learn the lesson from the other side this time around. Justice? Perhaps, but that concept is not relevant when we seek to discover our purpose in any incarnation. The key word here is "choice", always. Never are we required to take a specific role in a script. As individual spirits our desire is to learn the principles included in the lessons of kindness, compassion and generosity to every person we meet.

Regression therapy demonstrates the ability to undo learned hatred from our childhood. This kind of dislike or animosity toward a person who is not like us surfaces in regression work regularly. However, no one comes into counseling to work on their issue of discrimination or bigotry because all of us feel justified in our opinions. Rather, the undoing of this hatred is a curious by-product of regression work. My experience is that this kind of learned hatred evaporates when we see ourselves in a past life as that which we currently hate! This is a very powerful reality check. Just a few of the examples I have seen in regression work that show how this kind of learned hatred toward another type of person or a particular group of people is undone are:

- A 65 year old white man who felt justified in feeling superior to both women and black people found himself in a past life hundreds of years ago, before slavery, in Africa as a black woman who was very skilled in the ways of her culture.
- A middle-aged woman who intensely disliked loose women for religious reasons found herself in a past life as a prostitute in the old West.
- A woman who had an intense hatred for the Nazis found herself in a past life as a male Nazi guard at a concentration camp.
- A man who promotes peace and detests violence saw himself in a past life as a Mongolian warrior.
- A woman who hates those that kill animals for food saw herself in a past life as a Native American man hunting deer to survive.
- A devout Christian woman saw herself in a past life as a Roman soldier who participated in the persecution of the early Christians.

- A woman who was committed to peace, meditation and a non-harming life style saw herself in a past life as a man who murdered both of his parents.

All of the people in the regressions mentioned above were stunned to see themselves in a past life in the role of that which they hate in this life. All of them said that their dislike for this type of person was instilled in them during their childhood by either their parents or their culture, or both. None of them came for regression therapy to work on their strong biases. In each case, and many more, the hatred evaporated as these people saw clearly that their spirit has been both genders, most races, all religious denominations, and lived under most political regimes. Each past life body was chosen for an important reason to learn a specific lesson. They also realized that when we see another engaging in an action that will bring them negative karma we should have compassion for them, not hatred. As these examples demonstrate, regression therapy helps each of us realize that hatred and bigotry have no place on this earth. They only promote emotional and physical harm to many. Rather, compassion, kindness and a helping hand should be the appropriate response.

Learn Love...

As Rogers and Hammerstein so effectively stated in their musical, "South Pacific", "They must be carefully taught...to hate those people their relatives hate..." We are not born with bigotry, hatred, and resentment toward another group of people; we are taught how to hate. One of our life lessons appears to be overcoming that narrow minded manipulation.

When we hate, we betray our essence.

When we succumb to someone else's prejudices, we lose our opportunity to learn and grow.

When we stop seeking the source behind others' opinions, we abdicate our responsibility to ourselves, and our own karma...our destiny.

Hatred is based on fear.

Love and fear cannot co-exist.

Choose love!

Chapter Eleven

Addiction, the 21st Century Pandemic

"Every form of addiction is bad, no matter whether the narcotic be alcohol, morphine or idealism."

Carl Jung

Addiction affects each and every one of us.

Addiction in our families, in the workplace, in our neighborhoods, and among our friends touches everyone today.

Chemical substances such as alcohol, marijuana, pain pills, prescription drugs, methamphetamines, cocaine, acid and other mind-altering drugs are the primary sources of misery caused by chemical addiction. Pornography, gambling, sex, computer games, and addictions to the internet are not as obvious, but just as destructive.

According to past-life regression research, these addictions are not by accident; rather they are choices made by the spirit to accept this challenge to learn an important lesson. Addicts never exist in isolation. They affect family, friends, and associates who must deal with the adversity caused by the addict in order to learn their lesson in this lifetime, too, from the other side of the equation.

Every client that I have regressed to a past life specifically to look at the issue of addiction in this life has been working on the problem for a minimum of three consecutive past lives. And they have failed to learn the lesson in those lives – this is a huge statement showing the difficulty of this problem. Addiction is one of the most difficult lessons to overcome.

Overcoming addiction requires the addict being sober enough to make the commitment to maintain his or her sobriety. When we are "high" on our drug of choice, the drug is in control of the addict, and has no interest in relinquishing its power. Much like any parasite that devours the host leading to the death of both, the substance increases its influence until both cease to exist.

No Excuses…

The following two cases are representative of a large group of past-life regressions focused on the issue of addiction. In this lifetime, they have much in common: loving, supportive families, and no precipitating event or trauma that would cause them to choose to escape their reality into the fog of addiction. Nor is there a presenting mental health issue to cause them to "self-medicate", rather both clients just like to get "high"…regardless of the consequences to themselves or their loved ones.

No Problem!

This 14 year old, shaggy haired, gangly young man came to me for counseling from a local adolescent treatment center. Most teenagers don't understand why their parents go "postal" at any evidence of substance abuse.

"Hey, what's the big deal?" he asked. "I like getting high. So, I smoked a little weed, and popped a few pills…"

"And?"

"And, I got caught." His grin indicated no remorse at his actions, only chagrin at his parents' discovery of his use. "That won't happen again!"

Having been in a lock down facility for six months, he was clean and sober…and apparently looking forward to his return home and return to his drug use. All was going well in his life, perhaps too well. He has loving biological parents who are happily married and two sisters, one older and one younger. He had a very healthy childhood – no trauma at all. And yet, he began using a year ago, at age 13.

"I was bored and wanted to try something new," he said with a shrug. "My buddy showed up with some weed, and I was hooked." The grin again.

He hid his use from his parents for a year—a year that included various prescription pills from friends who got them out of various medicine cabinets around town. They took handfuls of pills without knowing what they were or what they were for—hoping to get high.

After working with Chris for six months on relapse prevention, I asked him if he would like to do some past-life regression. "Cool!" He was extremely enthusiastic about the possibility. I explained that I wanted to explore his past lives to see if addiction had been an issue before. He did not care what we explored, he just wanted to "check it out." Teens love regression work. So we set a date.

"Awesome!" Chris said before his experience. Like most teens, he was fascinated by the possibility of an adventure. The therapeutic benefit held little or no interest for him.

Diane: What are you aware of?

Chris: I am in a house with yellow appliances and shag green carpet – it is an old rundown house. Mom is doing the dishes. I'm afraid. Don't know why. Dad is sitting in the corner of the living room wearing shorts, flip flops, and holding a beer. He has darker skin.

D: What happens next?

C: An older man comes charging through the front door with a rifle! Oh! He is pointing it at dad. A second man comes in with a gun. Ouch!

D: What is happening?

C: The first man grabbed me by the hair and dragged me into a corner, pushed me down. Mom freaks out and drops a dish – she is screaming. The man grabs mom and throws her in the corner with me – telling her to shut up. He goes over to dad. Both guys are over Dad. The first one takes out a knife and is putting it to dad's throat. Oh! He slits dad's throat – then the other one shoots him in the head.

D: What do you do next?

C: I jump up, crying and angry, I jump on the guy with the gun. Mom is screaming. He throws me down. Ouch! Both guys run out of the house. Mom is screaming and crying in the corner, covering her eyes. I get up and go over to Dad. There is blood everywhere; he is slumped in his chair, dead. I am mad. Mom comes over, gets on her knees, head on his knee, crying hard.

D: Let's move forward in time now to the next significant event in that life.

C: I am at school in the halls. Some guy is talking trash to me.

D: How old are you?

C: I'm 13. I'm really angry at this guy. He keeps talking trash to me. I attack him, beating him up. Slam him against the locker. Beat his head against the metal. I'm being pulled off of him by some guys.

D: What is happening now?

C: The cops and ambulance are coming. I think I killed him!

D: Let's move forward in time again.

C: I'm in Juvy. I'm an 8th grader and I did kill that kid. They say I'll be here until I'm 18 and then I'll be moved to a prison.

D: Let's move forward in time to the next important event.

C: I'm in the parking lot of the prison – being moved from Juvy to prison. I'm 18.

D: Okay, so now let's move forward in time to the next significant happening.

C: I'm in prison on the bottom bunk. I'm in my mid-20's. The guy in the top bunk is a real problem, everyone hates him. I'm going to kill him the first chance I get.

D: So let's move forward again.

C: I am sleeping on my back. The guy in the top bunk jumps off his bunk and stabs me in the stomach. I get the knife and stab the guy – I kill him. I'm bleeding, holding my guts in – fall down. The guard comes in. Everyone hated that guy – they are happy he is dead. It is a large prison – they take me to the doctor – the hospital.

D: Let's move forward now.

C: I'm about 30. They let me out of prison. I have a scar the shape of a cross on my stomach. I'm living at my girlfriend's house. I don't work. She is a waitress and pays the bills. I drink all the time. I'm very angry and hate my life. I want to be dead. She loves me and wants me to not kill myself. All I want to do is drink and die. My life sucks – and has since they killed my dad. I am afraid I am going to kill someone else.

D: Let's move forward in time.

C: She and I are in a motel room. We took a weekend drive. I am in the bathroom, drunk. My hair is buzzed. She is pretty but I just want to be dead. I take a bunch of pills. I want to die so I don't hurt anyone else.

D: So what happens?

C: I am flying upward through a vortex – right past my spirit guide – I want to go home! Oh no!! I am dropping back down, fast, I see the hospital – I'm back into my body – my girlfriend is squeezing my hand. This sucks – I am back! She wants me here – I want to die.

D: So let's see what happens next.

C: We are back at her house. I'm in the bathroom, drunk, she is at work. I cut my wrists – the right way. I am bleeding to death I hope. I leave my body and am floating upward.

D: What do you see below you as you float up?

C: I am looking down at Seattle, the skyscrapers, the ocean.

D: What year is it?

C: It's 1976. I am floating, it is so peaceful – I am finally away from that horrible life. I was just a drunk and a murderer. I'm rising up fast now to the spirit world. I'm so glad to be released from that life. My guide is here with me. I'm at the place of music – I need to rest. My guide is trying to help me feel okay about my life, but I know I screwed it up. I do not want to go back – he wants me to try again.

D: So what happens next?

C: It is two earth years later and my guide has convinced me to try again. I'm not really wanting to, but will. He thinks I can do it. I just want it to be a short life. He says no. So I'm about to be born.

D: Let me know when you are born.

C: I'm born, screaming, bright lights, doctor cuts the cord. Oh no, I'm here again. I see the doctor; they put me in a plastic crib in the hospital. My mom looks Italian, she has curly hair. Dad is a big Italian with a polo shirt on, dark hair slicked back.

D: Okay. So let's move forward in time to the next important event.

C: I'm seven, playing baseball. I hit the ball hard, it goes flying. I watch it but forget to run. Dad is yelling at me – he is mad. I feel bad. I can't please my dad. He puts me down all the time. We are now in the car driving home in a station wagon. He backhands me. I cover my face and go inward. I'm scared of him – we have a bad relationship. He is a hard ass.

D: What happens next?

C: We are home now. Mom is cooking spaghetti. Mom loves me, she is kind, and I want to be around her.

D: Okay, so let's move forward in time to the next important event.

C: I'm 10 and in summer camp on a lake. This kid throws some chicken in my face – I am depressed about it – he teases me all the time. I go and hide under my bunk. I have a friend there; he tries to cheer me up.

D: What happens next?

C: It is the next day. We are all fishing. That kid is teasing me again – says I can't do it right. I get a bite and mess it up. The line breaks. Same old message as dad gives me: I can't do it right. I feel depressed.

D: Okay. So now let's move forward in time to the next important event.

C: I'm 13. Wearing shorts and flip flops and smoking weed for the first time. There are 8 to 9 boys and girls here. My friend brought me here. It is at night, we are sitting in a circle outside, and it is sort of cold. There is a girl sitting next to me. I like her.

D: Where are you?

C: In the Southwest – Arizona. We are now dancing around – wasted – feels good.

D: So let's move forward in time again.

C: I'm at school. I'm in the bathroom. The same boy gives me a baggie with something in it that looks like a prickly pear. He says, "Eat it now or take it home – it is way better than weed." He leaves. I am eating it.

D: So how does it make you feel?

C: I go back to class. Everything starts moving – I am hearing noises. The room is moving up and down, in and out. Wow! This is cool!

D: So let's move forward in time.

C: This guy becomes my drug buddy. It was peyote. He gives it to me often. I am an only child and am a huge disappointment to my dad because I can't do anything right – so I get high all the time. I stop trying to make him happy. I love being high. Dad works nights so I stay in my room a lot and get high on weed and peyote. My mom is out a lot these days so I am home alone at night. Don't know where she goes, but I'm glad she goes so I can get really high.

D: How often are you using now?

C: I'm doing peyote every two to three days and smoking a bowl of weed two times a day. I'm also sort of dating that same girl. I take her to a movie and give her peyote. She likes it, says it makes the movie better.

D: Why do you use so much?

C: Because I really have no family – my dad puts me down so I stay away from him. I feel rejected by him. Some kids tease me so I feel like I can't do anything right. I feel good when I am high. My friends feel like my family – we have fun together getting high and doing dumb things.

D: So let's move forward in time to the next important event.

C: So I'm on a school bus heading home. It is the last day of school. My buddy gives me a bag of peyote. He tells me there is going to be a desert trip coming up. It is the end of the 10th grade. They are all going to celebrate. The place is two hours away. He tells me to talk my parents into me going.

D: So what happens next?

C: I'm home now and telling mom about the trip. She is okay with it but she says I'll have to talk to my dad. He is home. I tell him. He finally agrees but does not like it. It is a three day deal.

D: Okay. So move forward in time.

C: We are on the trip. It is the first night. My girlfriend is here. We are all sitting around a camp fire getting high. It is hot – we are out in the middle of a desert. We are all talking and laughing at stupid stuff. Go to bed. Get up the next morning. I need to pee. So I head out into the desert. There are huge sand dunes, not flat, just up and down all over. I'm walking and walking. I brought my bag of peyote. I'm eating it along the way. Chilling. I eat three large pieces. Very high. Everything is moving up and down, in and out. I'm just kicking it. Now I'm staggering, very high. I'm lost. Oh well. I'm now crawling on my hands and knees – I lay here for half an hour. I get up, am walking. The hills around me are sliding in and out, up and down. I am aware of my girlfriend's presence somewhere nearby. I'm petting a shrub. I stagger on. There is sort of a step down – oops – it was a cliff – I fall. I leave my body and watch it fall – at least 100 feet down. It crashes on the ground below. I see my body – it has cargo shorts on and a t-shirt. I am dead. I float over and see my girlfriend. She was 30 feet from where I fell. She sees my body over the cliff. She starts crying.

D: What year is it?

C: 1992. I'm 16, or was 16. I am floating upward – now in a vortex that is pulling me up fast. I see my spirit guide. What will he say now?

I brought Chris out of trance. He opened his eyes—wide. His mouth fell open in amazement. There was no need for me to connect the dots for him. He knew the truth of his ongoing addiction issue.

He shared how lucky he was to have such great parents in this life. He commented that both sets of parents in those two past lives were not so good. "You know, if my parents didn't put me in this program when they did I might be dead now."

I asked him how he felt about using now. He replied, "Not such a good idea. Obviously I need to not use anything. I want to make a good, long life for myself. None of this checking out early stuff! I need to do it right this time."

Chris also said he was glad he did not have the problem with anger that he had had in the first life. He was not very interested in alcohol in his present life. He realized it was all about getting high to avoid life – not really wanting to be here on earth. But, since he was here, and had such great parents, he said he would give it his best shot!

Chris has since returned home to his parents and is doing very well. He works hard on maintaining positive relationships with his parents and siblings. He continues to be grateful for another opportunity to create a meaningful life. He wants his parents to be proud of him. He has no interest in using any mind-altering substances. He keeps busy and leans into his gifts in this life: intelligence, creativity, and loving relationships. He is grateful for the opportunity to have learned about his past lives that have brought him to this life and the knowledge that he personally has chosen to work on addiction. And that is his goal – to conquer it this time around.

David...

He came for counseling at age 35 after a twenty year roller coaster of alcohol, drugs, sobriety, employment, only to lose everything again to his addictions. Like Chris, David liked getting high. During his 15th year he began using marijuana, alcohol, methamphetamines, and LSD, as he transitioned from a "straight" appearance to "stoner": long dirty hair and baggy clothes. He skipped school and associated with other drug users.

At 18 he overdosed on LSD and suffered a psychotic break that lasted six months. After that he decided no more acid, but alcohol was legal and enough of it provided escape. After being fired from job after job, he escaped into cocaine. He began suffering severe paranoia. As a result, he switched to marijuana. He never gave up alcohol.

David married, had a child, and was drunk all of the time. His wife supported him and their daughter. After three years of drunkenness, he switched to methamphetamines to get and hold a job. This worked until the meth habit got out of control. His wife threw him out, causing another recovery…for awhile. Then he became a weekend alcoholic, eventually adding pain pills, cocaine and valium.

When he came to see me for help, his routine was predictable: take uppers in the morning, and then begin drinking midday through the evening, finally taking downers to sleep. The next day the cycle repeated itself, yet he was still employed. The irony of his situation did not escape him: the better his life became the more afraid he was of losing it all again due to drugs and alcohol. One day his fear overcame his addictions enough to drive him into counseling.

David's story is not unusual. Many addicts use multiple substances daily depending on the mood they want to create. Most addicts get hooked on being high during their teen years. They have never experienced reality. Creating their mood with substances, the habit, mood creation, becomes an art in itself. Eventually, it catches up to them: an accident, damage to their body, being dumped by a loved one, disease, or poor self esteem finally brings them to their knees. If this happens prior to their substances killing them, then there is hope for recovery.

This is what happened to David. With every drink, every pill, every snort, his disappointment in himself swelled until his fear took over. Fear of losing his new wife, fear of losing his children, fear of losing his life drove him to ask for help.

When David began counseling, he quit using every substance. Outrageously courageous, he brought new meaning to the term "cold turkey". Without the safety of isolation in a rehab center, without the security of a treatment facility, without the 24/7 support of professional drug counselors, David simply quit.

We processed his entire life story and he started meditating. After uncovering personality traits leading to his addictive habits, he wanted to explore past-life regression. This man wanted his life back for good, not just one more attempt at giving up his mood creators.

When David arrived for his first regression, he was anxious. The strain was obvious in his freshly shaven face. His healthy color had returned since giving up the substances, but this morning he was pale again. A few nervous ticks appeared that were not apparent in earlier appointments, but he was aware of them and took a deep breath to reduce his anxiety.

In spite of his concern that he would be unable to be hypnotized because of his history of mind-altering substances, he was able to relax and slip into trance easily.

Diane: What are you aware of?

David: I am in a wagon being pulled by two horses. We are bumping along on a dirt road in a town in the old west. My dad is driving the wagon; mom is sitting next to him. My brother who is seven and my sister who is three are sitting in the back of the wagon with me. We have come to town for supplies and are heading home.

D: What happens next?

Da: We are home. We live in a two story small farm house with trees and a stream that goes by. I'm inside now. There is a white ceramic wood burning stove in the kitchen, a table, and a ladder to the loft. We are all very happy. I am close to my dad.

D: Move forward in time to the next important event.

Da: The whole family is having a picnic down by the creek. Mom has made this huge basket full of good food. I am playing in a tree on a limb that goes out over the creek. I'm scared. My foot slips and I fall into the creek. I can't swim. I am under the water, sinking. I feel a hand grab me. It is my dad. He pulls me out and lays me on the bank. I am choking from swallowing water. He is upset with me. I am all wet.

D: So move forward in time and let's see what happens next.

Da: I am in a small school house. I have gray pants on. I'm 10 years old. My brother is here – there are about eight kids – all in one room. Someone has come to the school to tell my brother and I to get home quick. We leave.

D: Let me know what happens when you get home.

Da: We get home. Oh no! Mom is dead. She died having a baby. The baby died too. Dad is crying. He is heartbroken. I feel sad for Dad. I am not feeling anything else. I have moved forward in time and am at the funeral. We live in Nevada cattle country. The funeral is in our back yard. Everyone is sad, especially Dad.

D: So move forward in time to the next significant event.

Da: There is a gold rush going on. Lots of young men are leaving for California. My brother has his horse all packed up with supplies, plus he is leading a second horse loaded with supplies. I want to go, but I am only seventeen. I know that this is the last time I will see my brother. I am sad.

D: What year is it?

Da: It is 1859.

D: What happens next?

Da: I am now in my 20's. I am a blacksmith in the same town. I make horse shoes. This is Lancaster, Nevada. It is hot. I have my own shop and live over the saloon. I play cards – poker – and drink whiskey. I am in the saloon now playing cards. The whiskey tastes bad! Four of us are playing. I am drunk. I fall out of my chair, laughing. My dad comes to the bar to pick me up because the bartender is complaining. Dad throws me in the back of the wagon and takes me to his house. My sister is there – she pities me. Dad is disgusted with me – I do this all the time. My life style is being a blacksmith and a drunk. I also use the girls at the saloon. I am overweight and my face is puffy from drinking too much.

D: So let's go forward in time to the next important event of that life.

Da: Okay. So I'm in the saloon playing poker and I am drunk. I'm twenty-eight. There is a mean guy yelling at me. He calls me a blubbering fool. I am tipping back in my chair looking calm but I am terrified. I think he might kill me. I see him draw his gun. I see the gun go off. Everything becomes like in slow motion. He is a left-handed gunman. I fall to the dirty floor. I can see a cast iron stove and the dirty boots of the man standing next to me. I leave my body – I'm dead. It is 1871.

D: Look at your body – what do you see?

Da: I see a very unpleasant sight – it is slovenly, unkempt, and dirty. I hurt those people who cared for me. I see that life style is bad; it creates pain and suffering for those around me.

D: You have died young. I want you to now move forward in time into the life that you live right after that life. One – two - three – forward in time into your next life. Let me know when you are there and what is going on.

Da: It is another farm house similar to the last life – but smaller. We are very poor. I am about three and am outside of the house playing in the dirt. It is hot and dry. I am waiting for Dad to come back on his tractor.

D: Where is your mom?

Da: She is in the house cooking with my little sister. I see Dad coming! It is a very old run down tractor. He looks tired. I run over to him. He grabs me and picks me up. I am happy. We go into the house. Mom is there with my little sister. I am very close to my mom. We all sit down and eat dinner – it is a very happy family.

D: Let's move forward in time now – to the next important event.

Da: I am in the fields helping dad. I am 10. Dad is drunk and barely able to stand up. He has a flask that he is sipping out of. He looks worn out – like life is getting the best of him. I look around and all I can see is corn fields – flat for as far as I can see. It is the end of the day and we are heading in. We get to the house, Mom has dinner ready. Dad is staggering. She is angry. The family is no longer happy. It is all about Dad's drinking. He is not getting much done in the fields anymore. I am doing much of the work. We are dirt poor. This is Kansas, near Wichita.

D: So let's move forward in time again.

Da: I am sixteen. Dad is drunk all the time in the saloon in town. I go get him when he is really drunk. I am in front of the saloon now. I have my horse. I do not want to go in. He gets very angry at me and sometimes hits me. He scares me when he is drunk – and now that is all of the time. It is dusk. Mom asked me to come get him. This is a familiar scene. I hate it. I hate him. I go into the saloon. He angrily tells me to leave. I tell him he needs to come home. He pushes me down. I get up and go out. He finally comes out. I feel so sorry for Mom.

D: Move forward in time to the next important event.

Da: I'm in town getting supplies. We have a rundown old car now. I am heading home. I want to spend time with my friends, but can't. Mom and my sister need me to work the fields. Dad can't get much done cause he is drunk all of the time. He is in the fields today. I'll see what he got done. I have met a girl in town that I want to date but have too little time. I get home – he is drunk and passed out in the field. I just leave him there.

D: Okay – so move forward in time.

Da: It is my wedding day. I'm twenty. It is the girl I wanted to date. We are so happy. It is a big wedding in a big old barn. Mom is helping serve the food – and Dad is over at a table drunk. He always embarrasses me. I can't take my eyes off of him – I am afraid he will do something or say something embarrassing. Mom looks good, and my sister is flirting with some boys. I go over to Dad and take him outside to have a cigarette. He sits down and passes out in the chair. I'm glad he is out of the barn passed out – now I can relax and enjoy myself.

D: Do you drink?

Da: No, I have never had a drink or smoked cigarettes. I do not want to be like my dad. My wife and I rent a place in town, but I still go work the corn fields for Mom. Dad does about nothing. My wife works at a shop in town. The town has grown a lot since I was little. We have a little place, but we are very happy.

D: Move forward again – what happens next?

Da: I am in the field and it is the end of the day. I am looking for Dad. I see the tractor. He has fallen off of it and is on the ground. I am leaning over him. He is dead, there is a flask lying next to him.

D: What do you do?

Da: I am getting the car – I'll take him to the morgue.

D: How does his death affect you?

Da: I am glad he is dead. Maybe Mom can be happy now.

D: Let's move forward again.

Da: I have my own shop in town. I fix small things like clocks. My wife and I are very happy. We bought a small yellow house. We have a better car. We have two children; a very happy family. I have stayed away from alcohol. I make good money and support my mom. She is still in the same house but I sold the fields to a neighboring farmer who now works our old fields. She is happy – plays with the grandkids. My sister married a man in town and has moved to Wichita. They are doing well.

D: So let's go to the next important event in that life.

Da: Mom is sick and in the hospital in Wichita. My sister visits her every day. Mom has some sickness that is lingering on.

My kids are grown and my shop is doing well. I'm in my forties. The phone rings, I'm in my shop. It is my sister – Mom died. I feel empty – heart-broken. I am walking home. Our home is near the shop. I am leaning up against a building. I want a drink.

D: Have you ever had a thought like that before?

Da: No! I don't even know where it came from. Why now? I start walking again. I feel so sad.

D: So let's move forward in time again.

Da: I am old now – about sixty. I am sitting in my chair at home. It is in the evening. My wife is in the kitchen. I am sad all of the time. I'm not doing well. I still love my wife. Next to my chair is a table with a bottle of rum on it. I am in the habit of drinking rum in a shot glass – just sipping it of course. I want to show myself that I can control it – that I am not like my dad. I am all about hard work and the Lord. I will control the alcohol. It will never control me like it controlled my dad. I am not working anymore. I am bored and do not know what to do with my time.

D: How long has this rum habit been going on?

Da: Since mom died. I seemed to just lose my interest in life. My reason to live sort of left me. I spent most of my life making sure she was okay. My dad was such a loser. I also wanted to prove to myself that I could control alcohol and not be like my dad.

D: How much are you drinking in the evenings?

Da: Too much. I am falling asleep in my chair from it. I am losing a lot of time with my wife. I just don't seem to care anymore. I'm just not interested in doing any of the things I used to love to do.

D: Is your health still good?

Da: Yes, there is nothing wrong with me.

D: Any chance the way you feel about life is due to the rum?

Da: Never thought about that possibility. I just don't know what to do with my time.

D: So let's move forward in time to the next significant event.

Da: I am in the hospital. I am tired. My wife has fallen asleep in the chair in the corner of the room. I do not want to go. My son comes in with his wife and four kids. My wife wakes up. We all are talking about days gone by. They all seem to know I am not going to last much longer. They don't stay long, I am very tired. My wife gives me a kiss and goes back to the chair. I am very sleepy. I fall asleep and do not wake up.

When David came back from his past-life regression he realized that addiction has been a struggle for him for a long time. He also thought that his most recent past life watching his dad drink and then becoming a "controlled" alcoholic as an older adult set him up for his current life. He knew he had not conquered the addiction in the last life. He reflected on the fact that he had been an addict in this life for twenty-two years so far. "Enough!" He made a heart-felt commitment to never use again – anything mind altering. He was learning to like himself, and this was new for him.

Time has passed and David is doing well with his resolve – he has not used any drugs or alcohol. He feels that he is finally being a good role model for his children and his marriage is doing very well. He feels he has gotten *himself* back.

Healing What Hurts....

The purpose of all therapy is to heal what hurts. Whether the method is hands on, as in massage or pressure points; sensory through scents, music, chanting, visual biofeedback, or motor skills; or purely cognitive through talking, reading, listening; the goal is to ease the suffering, eliminate the pain, and excise the fear that prevents the client from living the rest of their life in fulfillment. At this point in time addiction is one of the most common and destructive problems affecting all of us. If regression therapy can help entrenched addicts recover, if it can cure an addict who is in deep denial, then this process, whatever it may be, should be used in rehabilitation centers world wide. Is it important to believe in reincarnation or past lives? Or is it important that *your* loved one heals from this debilitating condition?

Part Three

Life-Between-Lives Regression

A Time to Gather Information & Knowledge

"The only real misfortune, the only real tragedy, comes when we suffer without learning the lesson."

Emmet Fox

Want happens to *you* after the death of your physical body?

Cultures, civilizations, religions, cults, societies, communities and individuals seek the answer to that question. Scientists tell us that the material body eventually disintegrates into dust. Ultimately, we are recyclable. The physical "we", like wood, water, or wool goes back to the earth to benefit the world we leave behind.

What about the personality, the energy, the essence of each of us?

What happens to you; what happens to me?

What happens to "love"?

Many answers are "best guesses" based on the perspectives of the person or institution responding to the question. Some deny the existence of a "hereafter"; others declare a resurrection experience; or a "judgment day" that determines the fate of the individual for eternity; and still others believe in a Heaven or a Hell, often separated by a "Limbo" of vagueness.

Death is the "fear" word of our existence.

Based in fear, representing loss, decay, and finality, the "d" word means endings, abandonment, vulnerability and invisibility. We cease to exist. We have left the "building". Completely, permanently….and forever.

To cope with these paralyzing fears, human beings created belief systems to answer the original questions:

- Where are we when we die?
- Who are we when we die?
- Do we still exist when we die?
- Why?

Life-between-lives regressions answer those questions and many more.

As children we learn the belief system of our parents and extended family. Those beliefs come from ancestries, ethnic identity, or the significant people who influence us during our lives. As children we know only the information we receive from our families or caretakers. As we mature and our exposure to other belief systems occurs, our individuality kicks in. We are curious. We ask questions. We receive satisfactory answers —or answers that provoke other questions.

Often we simply accept the information as accurate and true.

This is because we trust the source of that information: our parents, our religious leaders, our politicians, our boss, our lover, or our peers; we are afraid to look any further for the truth.

Having worked with thousands of people in my practice, I have seen that one of four things occurs:

1) We live out our lives continuing to believe our parents.
2) The answer that satisfied us as children, adolescents, or young adults seems to miss the point: "What happens next?"
3) We begin to doubt the integrity of the source of the information.
4) A near-death experience shatters our belief system.

Arguably, near-death experiences are the closest human beings come to knowing what happens after death. People who are reported as clinically dead for a brief time relate their common experiences: their essence left their body, then pulled toward an intense white light, then joined and comforted by a "wise being". This "being" discusses the life they had just left.

This conversation with the "wise being" often gives a choice for the spirit to either continue upward toward the bright light or to return to their body here on earth. Those who return report that the experience of dying is most pleasant, and that they felt released from their earthly problems. Some of these people "died" during surgeries or accidents, while others were attempting suicide. Interestingly enough, whether intentional or unintentional, those who have had near-death experiences report going to a place of unconditional love and peace accompanied by a loving, supportive "being". They say that this place is more inviting than the often stressful and depressing earth plane.

The Beginning...

My role during a life-between-lives regression is to be a facilitator or a technician, not a medium, seer, or clairvoyant. Based on my life experience, I have certain beliefs about the afterlife. As a therapist, it is not my job to persuade you to accept my beliefs; rather, I hope to help you access your own truth through this experience and to report, as objectively as possible, what has happened in my office.

All of us have beliefs about what happens when we die, some are dictated by our family's religious tradition, some through meditation, some through research and investigation, and others through cultural rituals. Regardless of our individual conceptions of what happens next, evidence indicates that the experience is much the same for all of us. That is not to say centuries of literature, tradition, and rituals are wrong or misguided. Rather, that life-between-lives regression reveals an option that makes sense emotionally, psychologically, and spiritually.

My client Carol, a non-practicing Catholic, was depressed to the verge of suicide when she came into my office seeking help. Her spirit guide knew the experience she needed to correct her course in this lifetime - and that is exactly what she received. She had come for a past-life regression and instead her guide took her directly to the spirit world. Her guide showed her that there is a "heaven" and what it is like. Also, her guide refreshed her memory as to what she had chosen to work on here on earth. This experience converted her *belief* in an afterlife into *knowledge* of the afterlife. What an empowering experience for anyone!

"Where did you learn how to do that?" The formerly depressed Carol returned to the room with a broad smile expressing a renewed excitement for re-engaging in her life. She literally skipped from the room in eager anticipation to accomplish her chosen purpose here on earth.

The process of regression is not a trick or a gift that is mine alone to share. Rather it is the way it works: the client's spirit guide directs my guide to the maximum benefit for the client. I simply facilitate the process. Because "show me" is at times a human limitation requiring demonstrable experience prior to acceptance or belief, clients who need to access the spirit world during a regression usually do so for their own benefit…taking the concept from belief to knowledge of their guiding principles for the rest of their time here on the planet.

The spirit world is a place to gather knowledge and information to light our way on earth. Most who come into counseling are groping in the dark as they desperately try to figure out why their life, their relationships, and their emotions are the way they are. They have tried every traditional and new age therapy available to solve the problems, heal the pain, and end their suffering. Some work for awhile…some have no effect at all…and my office is often the last stop in their journey to heal.

Through access to the spirit world during life-between-lives regression, we find a place where there is hope, and where the answers exist for our spiritual growth.

While in the spirit world we can:

- Learn which lessons we chose to work on in this life
- Learn who is helping us learn these lessons
- Learn who we are helping to learn their lessons
- Meet our spirit guide and hear their advice
- Learn who is in our soul group
- Learn who is our soul mate
- Learn where to find meaning and purpose in our life
- Find out if we are on "path", or how to get back on "path"

- See and communicate with loved ones who have passed on
- Meet with our Council of Elders and receive their advice
- Go to the spiritual library and access our "life book"
- Find out why we chose the life we are currently living
- And much more – your imagination is the only limit

Through the experience of a life-between-lives regression, we can transform our life into a place of clear understanding, direction, and purpose now. We can self-actualize according to our spirit's agenda – not that of our culture. In addition to all of this, we have the experience of a place that wraps us in unconditional love. A place filled with compassion and kindness for all spirits, regardless of the quality of their choices. During a life-between-lives experience, we feel nurtured and supported in a manner never experienced here on earth. We return with a sense of renewed energy to carry on with our current life's work.

A life-between-lives regression usually lasts between three to five hours, but is often perceived as very brief by the person having this experience. I have facilitated almost two thousand life-between-lives regressions for many unique people from all over the Northwestern United States. It is as if time stops and the spirit world begins…as we ask questions and receive answers that are not obtainable any other way…we are empowered and energized to continue life here on earth with purpose and meaning.

Each regression is both alike and unique. It never ceases to amaze me how alike all clients see the spirit world, but also how uniquely different each person's experience is, and how it is always according to their needs at that time in their life. Those courageous enough to undertake this experience gain information and knowledge that propel them forward in their life on earth with conviction in their every step.

Chapter Twelve

Spirit Guides and Soul Mates

"When my grandmother was alive,
she told me that every time God created a soul in heaven,
he creates another to be its special mate."

Anonymous

Michael Newton, Ph.D., in his book *"Journey of Souls" (Llewellyn Publications,* Woodbury, MN, 1994) takes the reader beyond the boundaries of human senses into the world of spirits. A product of over ten years of research, Dr. Newton's book details the experiences of his willing participants when they explore life beyond the earth plane. In his ground breaking work on the spirit world and the creation of life-between-lives regression, he brilliantly maps the spirit world. Dr. Newton has made it possible for therapists who have followed his work to guide those seeking the truth into this place of unconditional love.

Dr. Newton has documented the progression of spirits through the spirit world from the moment of physical death to the moment of rebirth. Whereas we all see the spirit world remarkably alike, our experience there is uniquely different according to our individual needs.

Spirit Guides – Always Loving

What makes each experience of the spirit world unique? Our spirit guide does. Who is this guide? This is a spirit that is always with us, both here on earth and when we are in the spirit world. This guide has been with us for many lives. This spirit not only guides us but is our teacher, coach, and friend. Our guide knows us better than we could ever know ourselves.

When here on earth, our guide works very hard to keep us on the path that we created prior to incarnating. Our guide tries to keep us safe and out of harm's way by alerting us to danger as best he can. Our guide helps us see the sign posts and triggers that we created to keep us on path. He or she tries to help us make positive choices so that we will progress spiritually according to our plan.

When in the spirit world, our guide helps us to learn and grow. They love and encourage us whether we succeed or fail in what we have set out to accomplish on earth. In the presence of this spirit, we experience infinite acceptance and love, even when they tell or show us something that we really do not want to hear or see. It is our guide's sole purpose to assist our spiritual progress through time eternal. The speed with which we learn is not important. Our education is not a program that must be completed on a certain schedule. The earth plane is a fast track to learning and provides us with adversity so we can practice having responses that promote our learning. We have free will. Although we incarnate with a plan that we created with the help of our spirit guide, when in human form we are tempted off path. Our guide tries to keep us on path, but often our human agenda overrides their efforts. Frequently free will moves to the forefront on earth. This may derail us for awhile, or for the remainder of our time on earth. Regardless, our guide is still here for us, always helping.

Upon our physical death, as our spirit leaves our body, we feel a sense of relief as we shed any remaining physical or emotional residue from the life we have just lived. Some spirits exit the body and return to the spirit world in a nanosecond. Others feel moments of sadness and longing as they leave their loved ones behind, many of whom may be at their bedside during their passage. Some who die in massacres, genocide, or war, feel heavy and burdened by the physical residue of that life and death. They struggle to rise. Some need to say goodbye to a loved one before leaving, and some need to say goodbye to a beloved pet. Eventually, along the way to the spirit world, the soul lightens during the movement home to that all-loving realm.

As our spirit is released from our physical body, and we have said our goodbyes, we then experience our spirit moving upward and away from our body. We can look down and see our home, and then our town or countryside moving farther away, then the planet curved, and then round in the distance. We feel a pulling sensation upward and toward a bright light. Some enter an energy vortex or tunnel shaped cone that pulls them upward rapidly.

Some spirit guides will meet our returning spirit just after this ascent begins, and will take us by the "hand", and lead us to the spirit world. Some guides will meet the homecoming spirit half-way there, others when our spirit has arrived in the spirit world.

No matter what takes place while we are on earth, when we die and our spirit is released from our physical body, we move upward toward the spirit world and are usually met by our spirit guide. Our guide welcomes us back home and communicates to us telepathically how we did in the life we just left. There is never any judgment associated with this conversation. This exchange focuses on the learning of lessons that we chose to work on during the life we just left. Our guide communicates the progress we made in learning our lessons. Our guide inquires how we feel about our performance in this most recent life. These interchanges are always positive and supportive.

Spirit guides appear in different ways and with interesting names. Some appear as male, some as female and some as gender neutral. Some look like Gandalf, sporting a white robe, pointed conical hat, and white beard. Some have female features and wear long flowing gowns. Some appear young, some old. Some appear in a globe shape with few features at all. No matter how our guide appears to us, we always recognize them immediately. Spirit guides have names that we would not hear on earth. Examples I have heard are Bli, Jru, Nembus, and Urel.

Sometimes, rather than our spirit guide, we are met by our soul mate. This may happen because the soul mates chose not to be together in that past life. This choice always makes the life more difficult because our soul mate is our primary source of comfort and support. If this was the plan made by these two very close spirits, it is a huge relief to the homecoming spirit to be greeted by their soul mate. Sometimes the soul mates depart the life together, and this was their plan prior to incarnation. When this is the case, they rise up to the spirit world together. When they arrive they are relieved to be home and their spirits can communicate about what was learned.

Jean, Lessons in "alone" ness

At 48 years old, Jean's life had been marked by adversity since birth. Her life was filled with physically and emotionally abusive parents, estranged siblings, and two marriages to abusive, angry and alcoholic men that produced two adult children who were involved in their own lives. Jean had come for counseling off and on during her journey. We had worked on several issues, but she expressed no interest in regression therapy. I had not seen her in three years when she called requesting an appointment - for a regression.

"I'm afraid of dying," Jean said after sharing her recent terminal cancer diagnosis with me on the phone. She continued to tell me she was happy with her current simple life and a job she liked, so it was not all bad. "I'm almost grateful that soon I'll leave this world behind me...if I had any idea what comes next."

We scheduled a regression for the next week. When she arrived, the intervening years had not been kind to her, as her sallow complexion, stooped shoulders, and ragged appearance indicated. Her dull grey brown hair that she had kept stylishly cut when we first met was now drooping onto her shoulders. I kept my shock at the change in her appearance to myself as I watched her force a smile as she slipped into the chair beside mine.

"I guess I want to know why love has not been present in my life..." her voice dropped to a whisper in an apparent attempt to refrain from tears.

"Then, let's find out..." I answered before beginning the relaxation induction.

Jean's lined face smoothed as she went into trance. The process took years off the history written on her face. A slight smile played on her thin lips as she returned to a past life long ago in Venice, Italy.

In that life she was happily married to a loving man. She was happy although that life had its own share of adversity. At the end, sick with fever, she lay dying in her bed, her husband by her side. As her spirit left her body and she looked back over her life, the important lesson was about love and companionship. She had both in that life. Her spirit then left her bed and rose quickly to the spirit world. She felt the relief at being released from the trials of life on earth.

Diane: What are you aware of now?

Jean: I am moving rapidly toward the light.

D: Let me know when you can see off into the distance.

J: I see a bright light off to the left. I am moving toward it. It is moving toward me.

D: Let me know when you are close to the light.

J: We are together now. (stronger voice, smiling)

D: What do you mean?

J: My soul mate is here, he has come to meet me. He is so bright. Our energies are entwined together. I feel so safe, so loved, and so warm. (softly spoken)

D: I will leave you two alone to be together for a few minutes. (several minutes pass) What is happening now?

J: He is telling me that he is not in my current life. He was my husband in that past life in Venice. He is telling me that we agreed not to incarnate together this time because I needed to work on being on my own. I have become too dependent upon him in my past lives for security and support. We usually choose to incarnate as mates. We have spent many lives together married.

Jean stopped and exhaled a ruffled sigh that caught in her throat before continuing.

> *I need to work on my fear of being alone.* That is what I am working on in my current life – to make it on my own without his love and support. I am telling him how hard it has been for me. He is telling me that I have done a great job, and it is almost over. *I miss him so much.* It feels so good to be

with him again, home. I want to stay here. I do not want to
return to my life.

D: You will return to your current life after visiting the spirit
world for awhile today…and then…

J: Oh, that's right, I am not dead yet!

Jean went forward to experience much of the spirit world after
this wonderful reunion with her soul mate. When I finally brought her
back to my consultation room, she just sat there for awhile, speechless.

"I now see why I have not felt love in this life. That kind of love
does not come from children. It is so comforting to know where I am
going when this life finally comes to an end. I know he will be there
waiting for me." She said after a few minutes. Color had returned to her
face, her smile was broad and genuine, and she stood up abruptly and
stretched her arms up and toward the ceiling.

Her fear of death had vanished.

I regressed Jean many times after that first regression. She went
back to several past lives with her soul mate there to support and comfort
her. Together, they had many difficult lives with much adversity, but as
long as she was with him she was happy and felt safe. Her experience in her
current life had been the opposite. She had been plagued with fear and
anxiety and had never felt safe for one moment. Many of my clients have
this generalized anxiety shadowing them on a daily basis. Medications provide temporary relief for the stress and may lose their effectiveness over
time. Traditional talk therapy may get to the core issue in this lifetime, but
takes many sessions and sometimes does little to alleviate the pain.

Jean's visit to the spirit world answered her question, explained
her loneliness, and assured her of her successful responses to her current
challenges. She arrived at a peaceful place in this life.

Prior to the regression, when she received her terminal diagnosis, her fear overwhelmed her and death seemed worse than current loneliness. Now she was no longer afraid of death, but indeed welcomed it. Just a few months later she passed on, joyfully, to reunite with her soul mate.

After being met by our spirit guide or our soul mate and doing a life review, the next stop in the spirit world is our soul group. Sometimes our spirit guide feels it is necessary for us to pause in isolation after a particularly difficult life. Isolation gives the incoming spirit an opportunity to rest and be nurtured by spirits whose specialty is to care for those homecoming spirits who are tired from their earth bound life.

One such client, a man whose most recent past life ended as an eight year old boy in a gas chamber in Auschwitz, had managed to survive for several years in the concentration camp. Prior to his death he was used for multiple experimental surgeries in the death camp. When he returned to the spirit world, he was met by his spirit guide and they reviewed that horrific life he had chosen before incarnating.

He was not only exhausted, but needed help to remove the emotional and physical residue from the horrors he had seen and personally experienced in that life. His spirit guide provided that assistance and support. He was taken to spend time in the area of isolation and healing.

After his healing, he was welcomed into his soul group with congratulations and celebration for his earthly experience and the spiritual progress he had accomplished. Victims of horrific cruelty have chosen those experiences to learn compassion. The Nazis who volunteered to play the persecutor role during this period in history also chose those roles. Perhaps the lesson for all of us is forgiveness and compassion for the cruel choices others make. As we have compassion for the victims, we also need to have compassion for the villains, for they suffered too.

While in the spirit world this spirit went on to be shown the preparation class he attended with millions of other spirits prior to that incarnation to train for the Holocaust and to be prepared for the damage to the energy of all of the souls, victims and villains. He was told that this event was planned in hopes of teaching humankind an important lesson. Will we ever learn? Violence continues to march on...

One persistent question we all wonder about is why we would subject ourselves to the horrors on earth when we have the option of learning in the spirit world. The only information I can contribute to this discussion is that our learning curve is steeper and faster on earth than in the spirit world. Many of us clearly select this tougher route. I feel we make this choice because we are so held in unconditional love in the spirit world, with our cheering squad telling us that we can do it and they will be there for us, that we are convinced we can succeed in learning. We incarnate having created a difficult script and then the veil of forgetfulness falls and adversity begins.

OAO: One and Only, Soul Mates – Twin Flames

Fact, Fiction, or Fantasy?

The Western myth has us believe we have one soul mate, and that person is probably out there somewhere waiting to join us and live happily ever after. This is the consensus regarding the concept of soul mates that is held by the overwhelming majority of people that have entered my practice over the years. In fact, many blame their problems on not being partnered with their soul mate, and believe that they should have held out for that special person.

That is not only not true, but it is irrelevant. You wrote the script. After many years of doing regression therapy, I have learned that most of us here on earth now did not plan to marry our soul mate in this lifetime. For various reasons, most of us have chosen steep learning curves in which we are not going to partner up with that one and only special spirit. However, even though we have decided not to have this person as our marriage partner, most commonly this spirit has incarnated close to us. We did plan to have our soul mate's love and support in our lives – just not as our intimate partner. This is what I have seen in the vast majority of clients – in fact, more than 90% of those who have come for regression therapy. And it was their plan to have it that way.

Yes, it is true that we have one soul mate. We were created together – they know us and read us well. In a very real way we are "twin flames". We feel a strong affinity toward this spirit. We will form a close relationship with them, usually one that will last the entire time both spirits are incarnated on earth. Sometimes these two will be in different generations. I have seen soul mates incarnate as grandparent and grandchild, so the overlapping of their lives may be only 10 to 20 years. But during that time they are very close, and often that grandparent is one of the primary caretakers of the child. I have also seen soul mates incarnate as parent and child. When I see this they usually remain close in proximity to each other throughout their years together on earth and are of significant support.

Another common way soul mates choose to incarnate is as siblings, most commonly as same-sex siblings, but not necessarily. I have also seen soul mates incarnate as best same-sex friends. On occasion, I have seen them as close opposite sex friends. This is a risky plan as these two will be sexually attracted to each other even if the possibility of marriage is not open to them. Another combination is as first cousins, same or opposite sex. Also, I have seen an aunt or uncle as the soul mate of a niece or nephew. The important point is that these two have chosen to be in each other's life in a supportive role; there, not only for those difficult times, but also to enjoy the good times together. Having our soul mate present in our life somewhere makes it an easier ride. Easiest is of course as our intimate partner, but close by is also wonderful. Those who choose not to have their soul mate anywhere in their life have chosen the most difficult ride, and this is an unusual choice.

When I say that choosing to incarnate with our soul mate as an intimate partner is the easiest life, I need to clarify this. When soul mates have chosen to be together as intimate partners in this life, they have done so because the lessons they have chosen to learn are often very difficult and each feels they need their soul mate in that role to give them the greatest level of support possible. I regressed an older woman who had been married to her soul mate for 45 years. This couple had two sons. One son was killed in a plane crash in his 30's. Regression therapy showed that this was a planned "accident" in that it was in the script for their life together. Their son "volunteered" to play that role. This son was one of their soul group members. Recovering and continuing with their lives was almost an insurmountable task after this loss, but together they managed. The lesson they chose to learn was about love and loss – and how these two always come together. So when a soul mated pair chooses to incarnate as a married pair beginning in early adulthood, they usually write a script for themselves that is full of adversity.

I have noticed another pattern for soul mates that have chosen to incarnate as intimate partners; they both marry one or more times prior to partnering up with each other. The marriages prior to their one together have been very difficult. But these marriages were also planned.

The soul mates decided to learn important lessons through other relationships before finally ending up with each other. When they do come together they create a happy union – with great relief to both.

Even though soul mates have chosen not to incarnate in their current life as intimate partners, when I regress someone to their soul group and they see their soul mate who may currently be their best friend, the reunion in the spirit world is as profound as the reunion of current intimate partners. It is important to remember that it is the spiritual connection of these two spirits that is paramount, not the type of earthly closeness that defines their love.

There are three reasons why a soul mate would not be in a person's current life. The first reason is that the two planned that they would not incarnate together this time, as was the situation with Jean. The second is that the soul mate was in the person's life but has already passed on. The third is that the soul mates have not met yet, but plan to be together at a later date.

During a life-between-lives regression, we will see our soul mate in our soul group. This is a golden opportunity for these two, regardless of their current relationship on earth. I frequently ask my client to ask their soul mate to take them back to their favorite past life together. If these two have planned to come together later in the client's current life, then he will get a direct energetic hit of what his soul mate feels like and is more likely to recognize her when they meet. If the soul mate has already passed on from the current life, there will first be a very emotional reunion for the two in the spirit world. Then, to have the soul mate show the client his or her favorite past life demonstrates that they have been together many times and death has parted them before. This experience will hopefully make the parting in this life easier to handle for the one left behind.

I had one client who found out through a life-between-lives regression that she was dating her soul mate. He was struggling with making a marriage commitment to her due to other issues. When this woman was in her soul group, I asked her to see if he would take them back to his favorite past life with her. He did. This regression had a positive energetic effect on him and untied a Karmic Knot. Within three months he was pushing for marriage. She graciously accepted, not telling him of the regression! That was two years ago, and they are now happily married.

The most difficult path on earth, as I have mentioned, is to have chosen not to have your soul mate in your life. As we saw with Jean, we have the constant feeling that something is missing – a pervasive feeling of loneliness.

Beneficial Betrayal…

A 52 year old successful business man, Bob, had everything going for him until he discovered his wife's affair. He knew he had to let go, move on, and get a divorce…but was distracted because of his general level of unhappiness surrounding the rest of his life, even though his children were loving, and he loved his profession. Although he had never been alone in his life, he had felt alone throughout his life. After processing his current situation and his childhood he decided to see if regression therapy could shed further light on his life.

A little anxious at the beginning of his first regression, Bob took longer than usual to relax into a trance state. Bob went back to a past life as a Buddhist monk high in the Himalayan Mountains. It was a life of much solitude, but he had close relationships with his teacher and a few other monks. This was a peaceful life that was very fulfilling to him.

In his current life he had already been attracted to meditation and found this practice grounding. Upon his death as a monk he rapidly rose to the spirit world.

When his spirit guide took him to his soul group he was surprised to find that none of his soul group members were close to him in his current life. He had met most of them over the years. Two had been close male friends in past years but he had little contact with them now. Two were casual acquaintances. Others were here and there in his life, but he had not seen these relationships as significant. Further, all had been male figures in this life.

There was one member of his soul group he did not recognize from his current life at all. She was showing herself to him as a beautiful Native American woman. He was very attracted to this spirit, and he was sure she was his soul mate. But, he was confused.

Diane: You don't recognize her? It seems like she is giving you some sort of clue with the clothing she is wearing. Can you ask her what her dress means?

Bob: Yes. But she's now doing a native dance for me and singing. I will ask her. She says that her dress is to remind me of a life we shared together.

D: Can you ask her if she will take you back now to that life, and show you so you can remember?

B: She says she will.

D: Let me know what you become aware of as you return to that life.

B: I am in a place with many trees and creeks. I'm alone.

D: What are you wearing?

B: Long pants and boots. Dark colors with fringe. Sort of a jacket with the same fringe. They are made out of animal hides.

D: Are you a man or a woman?

B: I am a man about twenty-eight. I am a trapper. I have some traps in my hand that I'm about to set. I'm near a stream. I am setting them.

D: What else do you see around the area you are in?

B: Nothing, just lots of huge pine trees. It's a dense forest, so I can't see much through it.

D: Okay. So let's see what you do when you finish setting your traps.

B: I'm done. I'm now walking back the way I came, through the trees. I can see something off through the trees. Oh, it is an Indian village. Many tepees. I'm walking toward a particular tepee. I go into it. She is there, she is my wife. I am glad to see her – we embrace.

D: What else is in the tepee?

B: Lots of buffalo hides. Skins. She is beading a dress.

D: Do you have any children? How long have you been together?

B: No children. We have been together several years. I came to this area to trap. The natives are very friendly. Some of the white people are not. They befriended me and I make sure the white men treat this tribe well.

D: How big is the tribe?

B: Fifty, sixty maybe. We have lots of horses. The white men come here to trade. They try to take advantage of the Indians. I make sure they don't.

D: Let's move forward in time to the next significant event in that life. What is happening?

B: There are three white men here to trade. One is not nice and he's insulting some of the Indian men and putting their goods down. I'm talking to them, to let them know they are either respectful or they need to go.

D: What sort of men are they?

B: Mountain men, trappers like myself. Rough men. Not at all friendly. The one worries me.

D: Is your wife there with you?

B: Yes, they're leering at her. They're angering me. I ask them to leave. The one wants to fight me. My Indian friends draw their bows and tomahawks. We outnumber them. They back off, and move toward their horses. I watch them ride off. I have a bad feeling about these men.

D: What do you feel you need to do?

B: Nothing I can do. These kinds of men are around. Hopefully they will not return.

D: How is your relationship going?

B: We are so happy. We are so much in love. Her people are good to me. I like living with them.

D: Let's move forward in time again to the next significant event in that life.

B: She and I are riding our horses away from the village. It is mid-day, a beautiful day in the fall. She is wearing that same beautiful dress. We are just riding slowly along, enjoying the beauty around us.

D: What happens next?

B: I hear a gun-shot, a bullet just misses me. It came from behind us. Our horses start running. We are running now out into the plains. Very fast. She's a good rider. We are side by side. I look back. It is the mean men – three of them. They are chasing us – they must want to kill me! They are a ways behind us; we are faster. Another gun shot. It hits her, she falls off her horse. I stop. Get off. Run to her. I hold her. She looks up at me with love in her eyes, and takes her last breath. I'm so sad, sick. I jump up and onto my horse. The men are close. I'm out-running them. (pause) They give up.

D: What do you do next?

B: I'm older now. I didn't go back to the village. I moved into the plains area and live alone. I miss her. I feel lonely without her.

D: Okay, now I want you to return to your soul group in the spirit world.

B: Yes, I'm here now. So is she. We are embracing – sharing our energy – it feels so good to be with my soul mate.

D: Can she tell you why she is not sharing your current life with you?

B: She is saying that we planned it this way because I am working on lessons that are best worked on without her. Life is much easier with her even if there are difficulties. I'm alone now to deal with adversity on my own. It is hard for me – that is my lesson. I have chosen not to have any of my soul group members close to me this time – I have been too dependent on their support – I want to learn the hard way this time. And it sure is hard.

D: So right now take a few special moments to be with your soul mate before we move on. Let me know when you are ready to move on in the spirit world.

B: Yes, I will.

Bob's favorite part of the regression was the time spent with his soul mate. He now understood why he felt so alone. He now knew that he and his soul mate had agreed not to incarnate together this time. So he had chosen this path. He was going it alone not only without her, but also without any of his soul group members in close relationship to him.

This plan is highly unusual. Most spirits choose to have a strong support system here on earth. Bob is an example of a soul that has chosen a tough learning curve by minimizing his support system. The life as the Buddhist monk also showed him a part of his spiritual past that he could use now to help him through his current difficult times. His spirit guide had chosen his past life experience well. Bob made a renewed commitment to his meditation practice that day. He realized that he would need it to get him through. He left with renewed energy to continue the life that he had set up before incarnating. He was determined to learn the lessons he had chosen in the way he had chosen to learn them!

Someday Her Prince Will Come...

At 15 years old, her parents going through an ugly divorce, Kendra was sent to me for support while her parents ended their marriage. After processing her childhood and the important relationships in her life, she became interested in regression therapy. At that time I was only doing past-life regression. Kendra re-experienced many past lives.

She learned a great deal about the path her spirit had been on for hundreds of years. She also learned much about the primary relationships in her current life as she kept running into these spirits in her past lives. Kendra also became very clear about the lessons she was working on in this life because they kept reappearing in her past lives.

What was particularly interesting to her as an adolescent was that the same man appeared as her husband in many of her past lives. Sometimes she would be the man and he the woman. Then they would reverse roles. These unions were always caring and loving. She came to believe that he was probably her soul mate. She also knew that she had not met him yet, if indeed it was for her to meet him. She had a very good feeling for his energy after so many lives with him.

Just about the time Kendra was leaving for college I began to do life-between-lives regression therapy. She let me know she wanted to be one of my first clients to do this new therapy model. She was very excited. Kendra became almost beside herself when she realized that she would be able to see her soul group and her soul mate. The day arrived for her first life-between-lives regression. She decided that the past life she went to this day would not be important – so we decided to not direct that choice, but to let her spirit guide decide. Kendra's main goal was to see her soul group and her soul mate. She was 18 years old when this regression took place in 2004.

As usual Kendra went into trance easily. Although I directed her to go back to a past life, her spirit guide decided to have her go directly to the spirit world. She was a seasoned traveler! When a client goes directly from the induction to the spirit world the trip there is but a moment. She simply arrived into the presence of her spirit guide. Kendra's guide was a woman in an elegant flowing gown. The two spirits embraced. Kendra instantly recognized her and said she had been her guide "forever". When I asked Kendra her spirit guide's name she lovingly said, "La Madre." After this touching reunion, La Madre took Kendra straight to her soul group. It soon became clear that she is an example of a spirit who has provided herself with a close and strong support system in her current life. Many of her soul group members are in her immediate family.

Diane: So as you look around in your soul group, who is there?

Kendra: Wow, my mom is here, my sister, my sister's best friend, Sue, and even Granny and Gramps. Oh! I see HIM! He is showing himself as he was as my husband in the Norwegian life! He is so handsome! And his energy is so warm, so loving, so caring. We are like magnets to each other.

D: So have you met him yet in your current life?

K: No.

D: Can you ask him what the plan is for this life?

K: Sure. He says the plan is to meet each other when I am twenty-three. He says we have much to accomplish in this life. But he is afraid I will not follow the plan for this life.

D: Why is he afraid you will not follow the plan the two of you have laid out?

K: He says because I didn't in one of our past lives – he says sometimes I get stuck in being too attached to what my humanness wants to do and do not follow my heart. He says that this life is very important for both of us – that we need to be together to accomplish the goals we have set up.

D: Can you have him show you the life where you did not follow your heart and the triggers that were set up before you incarnated?

K: I'm asking him to show me that life so I will not mess up again. He says he will.

D: Let me know when you have arrived back to that life.

K: I am there. I'm a man about twenty. I'm in college. I'm very serious about college. I study a lot and don't do much for fun.

D: Where are you right now?

K: I'm in a pub with a few male college friends. I'm quieter than my friends, who are sort of rowdy. They've had a few beers. I'm just looking around the pub. There are horses and buggies going by on the cobblestone street out front. It is a big town.

D: What town is it?

K: Copenhagen, Denmark.

D: See if you can see the year flashing before your third eye.

K: Yes, it is 1833.

D: So let's see what happens next.

K: I am still looking around at the people in the pub. My eyes have fallen on a girl who is there. I do not recognize her, but she is beautiful. Her eyes meet mine. I am shy, I look away. I can feel her heading over to our table. She knows one of my friends.

D: So what happens next?

K: My friend introduces us and she sits down. She is carefree and silly – the opposite of me. She is not doing anything right now, no school. She is telling me that her father is a merchant who owns a large shipping company.

D: Look into her eyes and see if you recognize her spirit.

K: She is not in my present life. But she is the spirit that I have been partnered with many times – she is my soul mate.

D: So how do you feel about her now as you sit there with her?

K: I am very attracted to her! But she is my opposite – carefree and okay with doing nothing. She has no ambition. We are so different. The way she is scares me. Also, my family is not rich. Her family would never approve of our dating. She is out of my reach.

D: So let's see what happens. Move forward in time to the next significant event in that life.

K: It's a year later. We are dating but her family does not know it. Her father is paying me to tutor her. There is a big expedition that is leaving for Africa to do some archeology digs, looking for something. I am studying archeology and should be going but do not want to. I'm just not adventurous. I like being home. She has told me I am too serious. She thinks I should go on the expedition – be adventurous. I think she is too frivolous; she wants to do everything - have kids and travel all over. She and I argue over our differences.

D: So let's move forward in time again and see what happens next.

K: We are at the dock. She is leaving on a huge ship going to England. She wants me to follow on the next ship. I told her I don't want to go but I'll think about it. I am not adventurous, just want to stay here. Besides, she and I are so different. I'm not going to follow her all over. It's just not proper. What would people think of me chasing a woman all over? I am sad as I see the ship heading out to sea. I don't think I will ever see her again.

D: Okay, so let's move forward in time and see what happens next.

K: I didn't follow. It has been two years. She met someone else and is getting married. I am shy, driven, serious, and focused. She and I would never get along.

D: Now I want you to return to the spirit world and your soul group. Let me know when you have arrived back there.

K: I am here with him. He says he showed me that life because he is afraid I will do the same in this life. He says we had planned to be together in that life but I missed the triggers we set up. He says I was so worried about what people would think if I did something outside of the cultural expectations that I did not do what we had planned. He says that I was committed to being proper and did not follow my heart.

D: Is your spirit guide still there?

K: Yes she is.

D: Can we get some help on this from her? Can you ask her how this past life that your soul mate has shown you relates to your current life?

K: Yes. I am asking her. She says that the lesson of that life was supposed to be that adventure is good and important. La Madre says I was supposed to go to Africa and become an archeologist. I also was supposed to take a second ship and go after her to England. I was supposed to learn in that life to follow my heart. She says I tend to be serious and driven. I miss triggers because I am caught by stability on the physical plane – not adventure.

D: How is this important for you to know regarding your present life?

K: La Madre says that it is possible that I will not keep to the plan this life if I do not want to be adventurous. She says that my soul mate and I will be meeting in an adventurous sort of way – specifically, that we will meet in a sort of Peace Corps type of experience! No, that is definitely not me. I want to be successful – never would have thought that the Peace Corps would be part of a successful life!

D: What else does La Madre have to tell you about your life this time?

K: She says that when I have an opportunity to take it. Follow my heart. It does not matter what society thinks. I need not go by the rules. Love it, that is important. She tells me I am not to create obstacles that stop me from my life plan. She says lighten up! Don't be so serious! Balance serious with relaxed. She says I am pushing myself too hard. I am afraid I will not meet my soul mate in the future, that I will mess it up!

D: Ask your guide if you are afraid you will mess up again because you did in the life your soul mate just showed you.

K: She says yes, that is why I am afraid in this life now that I will mess it up and we will not meet, because I have before. La Madre says she will help. She says remember Mendoza, Argentina. That it is important. She says I will meet him and we will travel for at least three years. She says do not plan the future – that it will plan itself. She says I have an important role in the future – that things will be very different – but that I am not to worry about that. Do not be like you were in that past life! Be adventurous. She says she wants to help me do as I have planned. It is important for many that the plan is kept. Don't study it, just do it. That past life was a turning point – she says I wanted to go but could not bring myself to go. Do not repeat that, she says. Just follow my heart.

D: How is your soul mate feeling as your spirit guide is sharing all of this information with you?

K: He is really happy that she is telling me all of this because he too is afraid I will mess it up again! He wants to spend this life with me as planned.

D: Does your spirit guide have a final message for you before we move on to another soul group member?

K: Yes. She says in the future just do it, don't cling to the known, she says all is one, all are one in the world, everywhere is my home, don't get attached to any one place, just do what is in front of me.

D: Before you move on to the next member of your group, take a few minutes to connect deeply with your soul mate so that there is no chance of your missing his essence when you meet him.

Kendra finished her trip through the spirit world and returned from her trance amazed at all she had learned. She was very grateful for all of the information she was given about her future, as she felt she could have easily had a rerun and missed spending her life again with her soul mate. She left my office that day in deep contemplation.

Kendra's story brings up an important reality about the plans we make prior to incarnating on earth: it is possible to get off course by missing triggers that were set in place in the life preparation class in the spirit world that is held after we select our next life. In this preparation class we set up very specific triggers that cause us, hopefully, to take certain directions in our life on earth that are in accord with the life script we created. Some triggers cause us to fall in love, and some cause us to do what we might not otherwise choose to do in our life on earth. Sometimes we miss the triggers, get off course, and do not lead our life the way we had planned. Kendra had done that in a past life and she was experiencing anxiety in her current life, but she did not know where it was coming from. Her life-between-lives regression pointed out clearly that both she and her soul mate were afraid of a rerun of the past life where she did not see the guide posts that were set up so that they would spend their lives together.

As we have seen, our soul mate plays a very important role in our lives here on earth. They provide loving support when adversity presents itself in our life. Their presence and caring makes the difficulties we face somewhat easier. When we write a script that does not have that very special spirit there to help us get through, life can become an even greater challenge. Both our spirit guides and our soul mates provide the support that enables us to persevere on our chosen path regardless of the steep grade we have chosen here on earth.

Chapter Thirteen

Gathering: The Soul Group

"Happiness is having a large, loving, caring, close-knit family in another city."

George Burns

After our de-briefing with our spirit guide, we rejoin our soul group. Our guide takes a back seat – behind us – while our group greets us. Emotional and warm reunions are experienced with every member of our group whether they are currently on earth or not. This spirit group was created together and has traversed many roads together on planet earth. This is our "family", our closest spirits. Within this group all of these spirits have played every role to everyone: grandparent, parent, child, spouse, cousin, best friend, aunt, uncle, etc.

Also, within this group, these spirits are soul mated. So if there are eight spirits there are four soul mate pairs. When we return to our soul group from a past life, usually the first spirit to greet us is our soul mate. It is also important to remember that when we incarnate on earth we only bring approximately 40 to 60 percent of our spiritual energy with us; the remainder stays in the spirit world. So at all times our spirit is present in the spirit world. When we do a life-between-lives regression we are able to encounter any spirit in the spirit world regardless of whether they are incarnate on earth or not. This makes it possible for us to have a conversation with the spirit of anyone we know or have known on earth in the spirit world.

Our soul group is one of the most special places to be in the spirit world. It is always an honor for me to witness the reunion of these spirits that are so important to one another. This place is also lots of fun for me as the facilitator of the life-between-lives regressions. All kinds of experiences are possible in and from the soul group.

Most soul groups seem to have six to ten members. The number of the soul group members that are recognized as being in one's current life will depend on the client's age. A teen will know very few whereas an older adult will recognize most as being in their current life. Most teens and young adults will recognize between two to four members. This is true because they have not yet met key people in their current life. Adults 50 or older will usually recognize all of those in their soul group. However, sometimes there will be one or two members that are not and have not been in their current life. These spirits are familiar, but cannot be assigned to a particular person on earth. Furthermore, not uncommonly, a client will recognize a soul group member that was in his or her current life but has already passed on – for example a grandparent or a friend or child that died prematurely. These reunions are particularly heartfelt and full of opportunities for the person being regressed.

If, for example, we see a grandparent who has passed on already, there is first the initial emotional reunion of these two spirits. This usually entails reminiscing about loving memories between the two. If this soul group member has been gone awhile, I have the client ask that spirit if he or she has incarnated again. If the response is yes, then I encourage the person to ask who he or she is now. It is not at all uncommon for this beloved person who has passed on to have been reborn as someone who is close to the client. For most, this is a wonderful realization. She will often remark to me that a "likeness" can be "seen", energetically speaking, in the deceased person to the incarnate one.

This is a powerful moment. Reunions between loving spirits are always powerful for the participants and those privileged enough to share the event.

Sisters in Spirit...

Karen, 32 years old and still single, lost her older sister in an auto accident a dozen years ago. Karen never got over the grief of losing this dear friend and one year older sibling. She felt something was missing in her emotional make-up after losing her sister.

"I'm a hole in the donut..." She said, then immediately looked down at her hands twisting a Kleenex in her lap. "I am living without a life - my life."

After experiencing her most recent past life Karen rose quickly to the spirit world. She conversed with her spirit guide about that life just experienced, and then her guide took her to her soul group. Upon reaching the group, Karen's eyes filled with tears, her voice shook with emotion and her body curled into itself as if in pain.

Diane: Why so much emotion now?

Karen: It is my sister, she is here. We are hugging and blending our energy. It feels so good to see her. I have missed her so much.

D: I will be quiet for a few moments while the two of you share this time together. (pause) Does your sister have a message for you?

K: She is telling me that the accident was planned. We planned it before being born so that I could learn the lesson of love and loss. She made this sacrifice for me! She is also telling me that I need to learn acceptance and get on with my life. She knows that I have been stuck since she left. But it is sooo good to be here with her!

D: So it was not an accident but an opportunity for you to learn the lesson that you chose – and she signed up to help you learn that lesson. How beautiful. With her spirit there before you, ask her if she has incarnated again. Is she currently on earth?

K: She says she is.

D: Ask her who she is now.

K: Wow!! She says she is my nephew, Steven. Susan's son. (another sister)

D: How do you feel about this?

K: I see it now. I am surprised I did not see this before. Steven is just like Sharon was as a child. I am sooo happy that I have her back with me! (Karen lives in the same town with Susan's family.) We are hugging again. I am feeling her spiritual energy – imprinting it so I can always recall it when I go back to earth.

After finishing the entire life-between-lives session, I brought Karen back to the consultation room. She was still bubbly and happy about finding her sister and finding out that she was now her nephew. This was the highlight of her regression. In following up with Karen a year later it was clear that she was following her sister's advice and getting on with her life. The depression was gone and she had a renewed interest in life. She told me that she now felt the way she had prior to the accident. And she reported, she had become a very active aunt to her nephew, Steven.

Rachel + 1's Regression

Rachel, in her early thirties and very pregnant with her first child, came to me for therapy around the child's father and her live-in partner, Ron. She had had two prior miscarriages, so this was considered a high-risk pregnancy, and therefore was told to leave her job until the baby arrived. Ron was not happy about the loss of her income, particularly the reason for it, his baby.

Her regression work was focused on learning about her spiritual connection to Ron and to determine how she could help him deal with his stress about their reduced financial circumstances. In the life-between-lives regression, Rachel had just finished a wonderful past life with Ron and was now in the spirit world in her soul group. As the facilitator of this regression, I became acutely aware of the baby's spirit being in the room with Rachel and me.

I don't regress too many pregnant women – so this was an unusual experience. While regressing clients, I go into a mild trance – it is unavoidable in this work and actually helpful in connecting the spiritual energies between me, my guide, the client, and his or her guide. I have received many messages from my client's guide as to where to go with the regression. This was no exception. The spiritual energy in the consultation room was palpable.

Diane: So as you look around at these spirits, who do you recognize as being in your current life?

Rachel: Well, Ron is here. He was my husband in the life I just left. We are hugging – it feels so good! We are spinning, blending our energies. He is my soul mate! I can see that. We are so happy here. He feels no stress here.

D: Can you talk to him about the current situation and the stress he feels?

R: Yes, I am telling him it will all be okay – that he can relax. He says he knows from here in the spirit world that it will be okay, but that his body, his humanness, does not believe that. He says one of his problems is that he worries too much. He will try to get his worry under control. He says he knows he has been irritable, but asks me to be patient – he is working on one of his lessons – acceptance of what is. He says my not working was planned to help him work on acceptance. We love each other so much. (pause) I can see that everything will be okay!

D: Who else is there in your group?

R: Oh! My grandma is here! (Rachel was very close to her grandmother as a child. Her grandmother died when Rachel was 12 years old.)

D: Does she have a message for you?

R: Yes, she says she misses me. To rest and prepare for the birth. And that all my loved ones here are sending energy to me now during the pregnancy. She says she loves me. It is so wonderful to be here with her!

D: Ask grandma if she has incarnated yet.

R: She says no, she has not yet, but will soon. It has been 20 years.

D: Ask her what her plan to incarnate is – sounds like she has
        one.

R: Oh!! She says she is my baby! She will take this body. A girl
        baby. She is excited about this upcoming life and sharing it
        with me again. Oh! I am so happy about this – we are spin-
        ning again, celebrating this life to come! Ron is happy too.
        We three do many lives together.

After Rachel had finished the rest of her life-between-lives
regression, I brought her back to the consultation room. She was ecsta-
tic to know that her baby was her grandma. Then she talked awhile
about how close the two had been before grandma had passed on. Now
Rachel would have her back in her life. She left a happy person.

Two weeks later when Rachel came for her next appointment
she reported that Ron had been much more relaxed. She said he was
trying hard to not stress out about the bills. They would get paid!
They were also taking more time for the relationship and focusing on
having more loving moments, as the baby was due soon. A Karmic
Knot had been untied during the regression. And the pregnancy was
going very well according to the doctor. Four months later Rachel
brought her new baby to my office for a session. A beautiful baby girl
and the bond between the two was clear. The relationship with Ron
was going well.

Sadness Eased in the Soul Group...

Bruce, mid-sixties, lost his wife to cancer five years before coming into my practice. He came for counseling because he had been
depressed since her death. He told me that he felt his "life ended when
she left," that he could find no reason to carry on. He was not suicidal,

just constantly sad. No one could make him feel happy, not his children or his close friends. He had an excellent support system, but it just did not matter to him. He did not want to be here on earth without her. After we spent time processing his life story and looking for ways he could re-engage in life, he asked if I would do some regression work with him so that he could perhaps get more knowledge and understanding about his sadness.

Bruce came in for his life-between-lives regression feeling some hope that he might find an answer to the reason for his prolonged sadness. Until his wife's death, life had been good to him and he thought he should not be sad. Because the issue was the loss of his wife, we decided to have him first go back to a past life he had spent with her before going into the spirit world.

Bruce found himself on a midwestern farm married to the same wife that had passed on. They were very happy together and had three children. But there were plenty of difficulties in this past life that centered on crop failures and monetary problems. They made it through all of this together. Bruce became very sick when he was 62 years old. With his beloved wife and children by his bedside he died peacefully. As he rose above his body he felt the extreme grief and sadness of his wife. She was sobbing uncontrollably. His spirit went to her to try to comfort her. Before, when she was upset he would kiss her behind her ear. His spirit moved to do that now in hopes of letting her know that she would be okay without him. As he did, her sobbing stopped; she was indeed aware of his spiritual presence in the room. She was comforted, but still felt the loss of her beloved. Bruce then said goodbye to his children and began to rise up to the spirit world.

Rising up was not easy for him because he was leaving her behind. For awhile he felt the heavy human emotional residue hanging onto his spirit. The further away he was, the less he felt this heaviness.

After being met by his spirit guide, who said he had done well in that past life, Bruce was taken to his soul group. Here, he was immediately greeted by his wife, Kara, from his former and current life. The reunion of these two was heartfelt and emotional. Bruce was clearly glad to see her, not only as part of his soul group, but as his soul mate.

Diane: Who is there in your group?

Bruce: Kara is here – we are embracing – I am so happy to see her. She is my soul mate.

D: I'll leave you two alone for a few moments. (pause) Does she have a message for you?

B: Yes. She is telling me that we planned her earlier departure from our life together this time so I could learn the lesson that she learned in that past life I just left where I died first and left her.

D: What is the lesson that the two of you are working on together?

B: It's about love – that love and loss are one, that they come together. When you love someone on earth you will also experience loss. But you don't lose them, because we really don't die. Our spirit is eternal. We have lived many lives together and are also here in the spirit world together all of the time. We test our learning as humans on the earth. This is where we learn our lessons. She says we will be together here again. But she wants me to enjoy the rest of my life on earth and not be sad because she's not there now. She says she's always with me and I'm to be comforted by that.

D: Does she want to show you another past life that you shared together?

B: No, she says that I just saw her favorite past life with us together. She says that what she loved about that life is that we had so much time together – working on the farm. She says adversity is just how we learn our lessons on earth. It is always part of life on earth. It's how we handle adversity that is important, she says. So I see that I'm not handling the adversity of losing her well at all. She tells me to not be hard on myself but to return and work on helping others be happy – that will bring me happiness, she says.

D: Is there anything else for you and Kara to do or say before you move on to your other soul group members?

B: She is showing me how our spirits can spin together, mixing our energy. It feels so good. We are spinning faster and faster. Our energy is mixing so that I feel one with her. Wow!

D: Let me know when this blending of your energies is finished. (pause)

B: Okay, I am ready to greet the others.

After the regression, Bruce was quiet. Finally he said, "I can still feel her energy in and on me. I feel like I am wearing her!" The experience of seeing her in the spirit world was profound for Bruce. Knowing where she was, that she was happy, and that he would be joining her one day enabled him to be with his loss more easily. He realized he had not lost her. She was waiting for him. Further, it was important for him to learn the lesson he was working on. This knowledge would release him to find happiness on earth at this stage of his life. He also learned that we do live life after life and that dying is just a movement to the between stage. He left my office a renewed man, planning to find happiness here, now. She had given him the hope and the direction to do so.

This Life, a Clarifying Moment...

James, 19, lost his father in a plane crash five years earlier, and his grief had turned into a deep depression that lasted until his mother brought him in for counseling. She feared he might be suicidal, as he had lost all interest in life.

A recent high school graduate (barely), James did nothing but play video games. When I asked him what he was planning to do with his life, he said "Nothing. What's the point?"

Rather than deliver a lecture on the preciousness of life, or waste both of our time indulging in self-esteem cheerleading, I cut right to the chase.

"Would it help to talk to your father?"

His shaggy head popped up and his dark blue eyes narrowed in resentment, "My father's dead."

"I'm aware of that," I said gently. "His body is no longer present in your life, but his spirit..."

"Shut up!" James said, his hands making fists on the side of the chair.

"...is eternal." I finished my sentence, and sat quietly while James reacted to this information. He shook his head back and forth, back and forth, back and forth in denial of this possibility I had so recently suggested.

"Really?" His voice cracked and his question came out in a whisper.

I nodded and we scheduled a regression.

When James arrived for the regression he was apprehensive, and cracked his knuckles in an effort to spend some of his anxiety. I suggested since Dad was the primary issue, we take him back to a past life that he shared with his father. I moved him into a trance state with that suggestion. He went back easily to one of those lives with the same father-son role. This life was during the Roman Empire. It was a difficult, but good life; the two were very close. Upon James' death he went quickly to the spirit world. After meeting his spirit guide and processing the life he had just left, his guide took him to his soul group.

Diane:	Who is there in your soul group?
James:	I see my dad!
D:	Move toward him and let's have you talk to him.
J:	We are hugging – it feels so good to be with him again. He looks just like I remember him before he died.
D:	Do you have a question for him?
J:	Yes, I am asking him why he had to leave me so early.
D:	What does he say?
J:	He is telling me that he was not happy on earth. He didn't know how to deal with life. He says that after his boss killed himself he just lost interest in life – did not know how to move on.
D:	Ask him if the plane crash was a planned departure.
J:	He says yes. He says he had dreams all of his life that he would die in a plane crash. Now he realizes that these dreams were true – that the plan he made for his life before

incarnating was that he would die in a plane crash. I am asking him that if he had those dreams why did he keep flying. He says he actually began flying more so that he could leave his life sooner – he had lost hope.

D: Does he have advice for you at this point in your life?

J: He says, "Don't do as I did, do as I say. Pay attention to your plan for your life – follow your dream – be strong – be James – my son. Live life – don't do as I did. Be who you are: be strong, forgive, live, laugh, smile, love. Be you – you have it all – live happily. Do not lose hope like I did."

D: How do you feel about that message?

J: It makes me feel like I want to make my dad proud of me. He wants me to get on with my life.

D: Ask him if he has anything more for you to hear.

J: He says he is always with me. He will help me move on in my life. If I am still I will know he is there.

D: How does that make you feel?

J: Really good – that I will have his help.

James finished greeting all of his soul group members. It turned out that many of his soul group members were close to him in this life. They all offered their support. James had clearly set up a strong support system so that he could weather the loss of his dad. He also met his soul mate who told him that they would meet later and be together in this life as partners. This pleased him and gave him hope and purpose to live and to move forward with his life.

When I brought him back to my consultation room when the regression was over he was clearly amazed by the whole event. He was grateful and clearly had renewed energy to begin to make some choices for his life. We spent some time talking about what he was interested in and how he would begin to construct his life. James accepted his responsibility for his life.

A Clarifying Summary of the Post-Death Process...

We have seen a variety of experiences that people during a regression have immediately after physical death. We have seen how they leave the body, say good-by, and rise up to the spirit world. We have seen how they are met by their spirit guide when they arrive and sometimes before they arrive. We have seen how the spirit guide communicates to the incoming spirit about the past life they just left. We have also seen how the guide usually takes them to their soul group first, but not always. Sometimes either a traumatic life or death will see them going into isolation for a time. In other situations, the spirit guide will take them to their Council of Elders before taking them to their soul group. Sooner or later, however, they are always reunited with their soul group.

Once in the soul group, we have seen the various possibilities that exist there for homecoming souls to experience: reunion with the soul family and soul mate, experiencing past lives from that group, learning about the lessons they are working on, getting information about why they planned their current life the way they did, whether a soul group member who has died has reincarnated into their life again, and seeing the spirits of those who have passed on in their life. These are just a few of the many experiences the spirit can have in the soul group. This information and knowledge helps us make sense of our current life. Knowledge that helps us move on in our life in a way that is more likely to be positive and create happiness for ourselves and those around us. This information gives us direction and hope that we can, in this very moment, create peace and harmony for ourselves and for those we are here to help.

We are now going to move forward in our experience of the spirit world. What kind of knowledge can be learned from the other areas in that place beyond this physical plane? The most common stop after spirits leave the soul group is to be taken by their spirit guide to their Council of Elders. This is a group of wise elders who help us in the progression of our spiritual knowledge. They help us process our most recent past life and construct our upcoming life so that maximum learning can take place.

Chapter Fourteen
Council of Elders

"The world is proof that God is a committee."
Bob Stokes

Your Personal Steering Committee

An exception to going directly to your soul group after passing over from a life on earth is in the case of suicide, or voluntarily ending your physical life on the earth plane. If this is the situation, your spirit guide will take you directly to your Council of Elders, bypassing the reunion with your soul group temporarily.

In his mid-fifties, underweight, his sparse hair stretched across a bald pate in a bad comb-over, unfashionably unshaven, and clearly in need of a dentist, Ben was referred to me for clinical depression and suicidal ideation.

"Doc, I've had it up to here." He dragged his gnarled hand across his Adam's apple in a familiar gesture of slashing his throat. His attempt at stretching his lips into a weak smile was designed to hide his missing teeth. "And you can't talk me out of going home to my .357 and my bottle of Jack that I've saved for this momentous occasion."

I'm not sure what shocked me more, his awarding me a Ph.D. or M.D. that I hadn't earned, or his use of the word "momentous". That will teach me to make assumptions about a man from his appearance, I thought with chagrin.

To my surprise, there was no resistance to my suggestion of past-life regression. "Do what you want," said Ben, slipping into the recliner and jerking the handle to flatten it out. "Won't matter any-way."

During the past life segment of his regression, he went back to his most recent past life. There he successfully committed suicide after having had enough of the adversities of that life. As he died and his spirit left his body, he immediately realized he had made a bad choice. He quickly went to the spirit world and was greeted by his spirit guide. His guide's first message to him was, "You are back early. I'll take you to your Council of Elders. They want to speak to you." Normally this stop is after the reunion with one's soul group. But it was clear that the gravity of his actions required that he first see his counsel. This is what transpired at his Council of Elders meeting:

Diane: Where are you now?

Ben: In a great domed building with large pillars. We are going down a hallway. Now we are going into a large room – the ceiling is a high dome.

D: Who is in there with you?

B: My spirit guide is behind me to the left. There are five very wise-looking male spirits here. I am awed by them. I feel humbled.

D: What are these wise spirits wearing?

B: Robes, red robes with hoods.

D: Does one seem like he will act as moderator?

B: Yes, the one in the middle.

D: What message does he have for you?

B: He says I did not value my life. That a human life is a precious gift, an opportunity to learn and grow spiritually. I did not value that opportunity. He is not judging me, just making a statement. And it is true. I did not value my life.

D: What does he feel you need to do?

B: He says he wants me to study here for awhile before returning to earth. To study how to better deal with difficulty when it arises on earth. He asks my guide to give me special help in my studies. He says the council will give me much support in choosing my next life and those that will go with me and help support me. I can feel their love. They want to help me succeed in my next life. They do not want me to repeat what I have just done. My guide says it is time to go now to my soul group.

Ben continued his regression through the spirit world. He studied there for two years, earth time, before he incarnated into his current life. He received much help in choosing his next body in the life selection room and attended his life preparation class with many reminders of what he was to do when times became difficult. Prior to incarnating he had another meeting with his Council of Elders who gave him much encouragement for his upcoming life. At the end of that meeting they told him, "Value this new opportunity on earth, this time grow and progress spiritually with this new precious gift." He then went to the exit portal and rapidly fell into his mother's womb.

As Ben came back into my consultation room he was astonished. The message was clear: he was not to kill himself again! That regression was several years ago. Ben is managing the difficulties in his life much better. He seeks out healthy people and healthy solutions when problems arise. He has direction and purpose in his life now.

I have had several clients who have killed themselves in their most recent past life. All have incarnated about two earth years after their past life suicide. This two year time frame is also true if one dies naturally as a child or young adult. However, those who live long, full lives reincarnate after an average of about 20 earth years. There is no indication that those who take their own lives are punished in any way – unless you feel that returning to earth with only a two year break is harsh! Returning is also voluntary. We return because we are given so much support and love in the spirit world that we feel we can take on new challenges and handle them. Then we are born, and the veil of forgetfulness falls. We forget that we are spirits learning through the human body, and that those here with us are here to help us learn the lessons that we have chosen.

Suicide is always spiritually unplanned, never part of our life design.

Council of Elders

Our Council of Elders is a panel of wise spirits who help us plan our future lives on earth. On earth, adversity is a given. The elders are aware of the challenges we face here and are interested in how we responded. They understand our trials here, and are never judgmental about our behavior. They help us see how we might have handled a situation or relationship in a more constructive way. Knowing the lessons we have chosen to work on, they clearly see our progress. They comment on what they see and provide recommendations for us to manage our present life better on earth. They also help us set up our next life so that we can continue our spiritual progression through time.

When our spirit guide brings us before the Council of Elders, the council focuses on helping us. Our spirit has just arrived from a past life and has always struggled there in many ways. When our spirit comes before the council, we are anxious to learn. We are open to help and ready to listen to the wise elders. While in the spirit world, it is easy for our spirit to listen and understand recommendations and advice on how we can improve while on earth. That does not mean we succeed when we get back to another incarnation, because our humanity gets in our way. We are tempted on the earth plane by many unproductive choices. In the spirit world, as pure spiritual beings, we are open to hear the opinions of the council and to follow what our council recommends. These wise ones help us plan our lives for the greatest opportunity to learn and progress spiritually.

This opportunity is an amazing gift. The council always has many comments on how we are doing in this current life and ways for us to improve. Not only will the council comment on the past life we just left in the regression, but they will make suggestions for our current life as well. The Council of Elders is one of the greatest opportunities in the life-between-lives regression process. We can ask questions we feel are important about our current life. The council is always respectful and does not judge. These questions can be about relationships, our work, or behaviors with which we are struggling. Also, the council will answer questions about our progress to date, where we have struggled, and to varying degrees, what lies ahead. Our spirit guide is present during this meeting, but usually does not participate.

Problems with Paul

Gwen is a woman in her late forties. As a registered nurse, she helps many people in her life. She was happily married with three adult children and was struggling with one of her sons who was in his mid 20's who loved to have a good time. He was having trouble getting serious about his adult life. Gwen was at a loss with how to deal with him.

During her life-between-lives regression, Gwen found out that her son is a member of her soul group. This was a surprise to her. In the soul group his message to her was to please keep trying to help him. His spirit told Gwen that he did want to get on with his spiritual agenda in this life, but that all of the temptations of the physical world were distracting him. This conversation with her son's spirit was fresh on her mind when Gwen entered her Council of Elders' chamber.

Diane: What do you see as you arrive in the hall?

Gwen: The council room is huge! But I can see right through it! How strange. As I am walking in I am close to a column. I am going to try to touch it!

D: Do you?

G: Yes, it feels like soft velvet, but it is not solid. I am now standing in front of my council. It's a humbling experience. They look so wise, I feel so small.

D: Please describe the set up in the room.

G: The council is seated behind a large curved table. I am standing in front of them. My guide is standing on my right somewhat behind me.

D: How many elders are there?

G: Four. Not a big group. There is one in the middle who has on a dark purple robe with a hat like my guide's – conical shaped

– purple, too. He looks very wise. These people help me plan my lives. The one in the middle says I am doing a good job in my present life. He is pleased that I am helping people who are sick. He says that I am doing what I came to do – I have contracts with some of these people to help them.

D: Does he have suggestions on where you could learn more?

G: I'll ask. (pause) Yes, he says that judgment is one of the things I am helping people to let go of. But he says I need to work on letting go of my judgment of my son and the way he is handling his life issues. He says this is where I am stuck. I am falling short by not letting go of my judgment of my son. He says that fear is driving me in that relationship. I need to let go of my fear about where my son's actions may be taking him. He is also saying that learning and teaching is all that is – I need to be a role model only.

D: Does your elder have any suggestions as to how you might let go of your judgment of your son?

G: I'll ask him. (pause) He says that my son is doing well. He says this is the path he has chosen to help learn his lessons, through the situations that he creates. He will come to know. He says that my love for my son gets in my way; my fear causes me to judge him. He is saying that I love him so much that I do not want him to suffer. I want to help him leap over the garbage and difficulties of the physical world. He says I can't do that, it is not possible; this is his learning, not mine. The elder is saying that we all must go through what we have planned to go through so that we learn our lessons. He says don't judge, rather share with him.

D: Does he have any other ideas how you might be different with your son?

G: Yes, he says if I accept his stuff it will allow him to see the situations more objectively. I need to be present, loving, and stay in my knowing that everything is as it is supposed to be. It is as it is, it is meant to be this way. He also says that my son has set up a strong support system and will make it this time. He also says that it is not for me to decide what is potentially harmful. Don't judge his playing. That is for his spirit to sort out. He needs to listen to his spirit, not me. It is not my responsibility to show him the way, the path – right now he is resistant. They say I need to just let him be.

D: Can you ask your elder how all of this is affecting your progress?

G: He says that I judge myself for not having the ability to not comment on his playing. I judge my judgment. My son wants to do his spiritual agenda but is stuck in his human agenda of playing. My fear is he will not get it. He is determined to have fun here on this plane – this frustrates me. My lesson is to learn not to judge him and to let go. He says my contract with my son is to help him overcome his resistance so that he can progress spiritually by my simply being loving and kind. I am to love him and to accept him as he is, so he can figure it out himself. He has not chosen to embrace his life yet, his spiritual work. He is the most challenging of the spirits I am working with.

D: Can you ask your elder for help in how to let go?

G: Yes, he says I get hooked by my fear of failing him in my contract to help him wake up and do his spiritual agenda here. Only he can help himself – I just need to be present. He says

I have watched this many times before and it is for me to watch it again and practice loving presence. He says I need to push forward in my work – tend to my goals. My son needs to be peripheral in my life now. I am expending too much energy in his direction. My work is important – my energy needs to be there – he will be fine. When he needs a helping hand, give it lovingly. The elder says I still have a lot to do in this life. My work is out in the world. I am siphoning off too much energy toward him needlessly.

D: How do you feel about your elders' suggestions?

G: I am feeling relieved. I want to put my energy into my work and let my son deal with his issues.

The council understands our trials here on earth. After all, they helped us set up these difficulties so that we can learn the lessons that we have chosen to work on. The council will give us helpful suggestions on any issue we choose to ask them about during the life-between-lives session. They are patient and non-judgmental in the reflections that they offer us.

The difference between your spirit guide and your Council of Elders is a question of degree and development along the spiritual path. Your spirit guide is your supporter, sounding board, and friend along your journey. Your Council of Elders offers advice, observations, opinions, and guidance specific to your challenges, issues, and concerns. The latter group makes suggestions about the lessons you will learn, the choices you make prior to incarnating, and advises you about the percentage of spiritual energy they recommend incarnating with to successfully accomplish your life plan. They are generous with the knowledge and information that they share with us during our journey through the spirit world.

Chapter Fifteen
Spiritual Library

"I go into my library and all history unrolls before me."
Alexander Smith

As we progress through the spirit world during the life-between-lives regression, the most common stop after the Council of Elders is the spiritual library. This place of endless bookshelves contains the "life book" for each of our spirits. In Michael Newton, Ph.D.'s book, "Destiny of Souls" (Llewellyn Publications, St. Paul, MN, 2000), his clients refer to their record as their "life book". The spirit's life book holds all past lives since the creation of their soul, and is often referred to as the "Akashic Record".

Akashic means "sky", "space", or "ether". This term describes knowledge encoded in a non-physical plane of existence. The Akashic Records are similar to a cosmic or collective consciousness. These records have recorded all human experience and history throughout time. They are a "universal computer" containing all that has happened in human history. These records can be accessed while in a trance state. Some of us are able to access them while in a meditative state.

Every heartbeat, thought, action, word, and deed throughout time has been recorded in your personal, spiritual Akashic Record. Every spirit has a life book as each energetic element makes an impression on the pages of your Akashic Record. Because each event is an expression of energy, it is the energy that creates the impression on the page. That impression expands to a vision accessible to the soul and their spirit guide when they explore a particular past life present on the pages of the Akashic Record or life book.

During the life-between-lives regression your spirit guide will take you to the spiritual library to look at your life book if he feels it is important for you to see a portion of a particular past life. You will sit at a table that seems to extend endlessly into the distance in both directions. An archivist will recognize your spirit, retrieve your book from the library shelves and bring it to you and your spirit guide. This is one of the most powerful ways to teach us how to better handle certain situations and adversity here on earth. Seeing how we acted in a previous life, and the results of our actions, enables us to learn better ways to handle the same adversity in our current life.

New insights begin when your guide opens your book to a specific past life. What you learn there will benefit you in this life or the next. As you look at the page, you will see a still photo of a particular day in that past life. Often in black and white, the picture then morphs into color and motion as your spirit is pulled through the page into that life. Instantly you relive that life. You assume your role in that life and re-experience the events, choices, and consequences you made at that time. The purpose of this visit to a past life is to enlighten your spirit with regard to the results of your choices in that past life. Your guide's intention is to provide you with information for your use in this life.

The presentation is always without judgment, rather the events roll out as a film with your spirit assuming the lead role in the past life drama. You can see what lessons you chose to learn and what Karmic Knots you hoped to untie. You can see the path you chose, when you exercised free will that changed that path, and the events and outcomes created by your choices. Your guide may want you to see how a partic-ular relationship in your current life became entangled in negative energy in a past life, how you have worked on a particular issue already in a past life, or how a particular event in a past life has affected your current life. The purpose of this visit to a specific past life is to enlighten your spirit by showing you the results of your choices in that prior life.

After you re-experience that part of your past life, you will return to the spiritual library. In my practice, I have my client ask their guide for advice on how to handle the specific similar issue in their cur-rent life. The client benefits from the therapist's guidance when directed to ask certain questions in order to gain specific knowledge. Then the client's guide responds by relating the previous life's experience to the current life's issues. Once the client acknowledges the connection, their spirit guide offers advice to achieve a better result now. This is possibly the most powerful teaching tool in the spirit world.

If the Akashic Record contains the entire life of the spirit, the question arises if there is future information available during the visit. Newton asserts in his research that the future pages in the spirit's life book are available, but only in short, vivid glimpses. Future incarnations are the results of choices made by the spirit with the help of their guide under the supervision of the Council of Elders. The power always resides in the spirit, whether he or she complies with the script they wrote, or chooses to exercise free will to jump script and go in a differ-ent direction, and experience the consequences of those choices.

Regardless of the spirit's decisions and life choices, there will always be evidence of the energy resulting from those choices in the spirit's life book, or Akashic Record.

Once the visit to the spiritual library ends, the next step is to take that knowledge to your Council of Elders for your second visit. Your Council assesses your current awareness and aids you in planning your next incarnation. At this meeting, your Council helps you select the lessons to learn and the spirits to accompany you on that journey. After you leave, your Council creates four or five separate bodies with an accompanying script for your selection when you arrive at the life selection room. There you will view the selections your Council of Elders presents for you to choose from for your next life. Because you are there in a life-between-lives regression, you will see the other options you had been offered before choosing your current body and script. After seeing the alternative choices, my clients understand the purpose of their choice in this lifetime.

While in the spiritual library during a life-between-lives regression, following the specific past life chosen for review by the client's guide, the spirit focuses on this life to ascertain how near or how far they are from their chosen path. This awareness brings clarity to my clients. Based on this information, they know whether or not they are living their pre-selected script. Some may choose to change the direction of their life, while others benefit from the validation of their current choices. In both cases, when they return to the present, they have direction for a more meaningful future.

Regardless of the choices the spirit makes during any incarnation, their acceptance into the spirit world is guaranteed. During any visit to the spiritual library, the learning/teaching cycle continues as the spirit interacts with other spirits in the hope of increasing their level of spiritual attainment.

Chapter Sixteen

Unique Spirit World Experiences

"If death meant just leaving the stage long enough to change costume and come back as a new character... would you slow down? Or speed up?"

Chuck Palahniuk

As the facilitator of life-between-lives regressions, I am privileged to be witness to many surprising and remarkable happenings in the spirit world. In the spirit world, *the sky is the limit.* My client receives whatever experience or information that their spirit guide hopes will benefit him or her in accomplishing their agenda for this current life and increase their level of spiritual awareness. The goal is always to help resolve issues, meet challenges, and learn all we can to live a loving, compassionate life here on earth.

During most life-between-lives regressions, the spirit guide shows us our soul group, our wise Council of Elders, our life book in the spiritual library, why we chose our body with its script in the life selection room, the contracts made between various spirits for this life-time and the lessons we chose to work on. All of this knowledge and information enlightens the client as to whether he or she is on track or whether a course correction is needed to fulfill the client's purpose in this incarnation.

Through over one thousand spirit world regressions that I have facilitated, this has been the standard fare. When each regression seems to be winding down, I will ask my client to ask their spirit guide if there is a special activity or experience for them today.

The following is a sampling of the types of experiences that various spirit guides have chosen that enhanced the experience of the life-between-lives session:

- Meditating in a beautiful meadow or a thick grove of old growth trees
- Receiving special training in a healing skill
- Visiting a particular spirit of someone currently incarnate to gather important information to help them
- Joining a prayer group that is lending support to a person who is struggling on earth
- Joining a preparation class for a spirit you have contracted to help in their next incarnation
- Joining a large preparation class if you have volunteered to participate in a mass human disaster coming up in your next lifetime
- Experiencing being in the presence of the Creator
- Visiting earth in spirit form
- Visiting another world of incarnation
- Engaging in a special activity with your soul group

The range of possibilities at this point in the life-between-lives regression is probably infinite. Knowing the client's agenda for the session I will ask her spirit guide for a particular experience, or ask the guide if there is a place or activity her guide wants her to experience today. The response to my question can range anywhere from, "That is all for today", to "Yes, I want—." Then the client is off to experience an encounter that is of particular significance to her spirit.

The spirit guide's intentions are always clear. What follows are several unique gifts from spirit guides who knew these experiences would serve the client well along their path.

Jane, a Mother's Grief...

When Jane knocked on the door to my offices, the sound of her knuckles on the wooden door barely registered on me. The soft tap, tap, tap was hesitant and muffled by the thick woolen mittens she wore against the cold outside. Once inside the warmth of my interview room, this 45 year old woman sank into the upholstered chair as if trying to disappear into the fabric. Grasping her elbows, she was hunched over, clearly in pain. Knowing her history, I knew her pain was from the loss of her 19 year old son over a year ago in a pedestrian automobile accident.

Shivering in spite of the oppressive heat from the wall radiator, Jane pulled off her mittens to reveal broken finger nails partially covered with slashes of violent red polish in random spots on her chapped and reddened fingers. Her hair was badly in need of a wash, and I noticed food stains on the front of her woolen t-shirt. This was clearly not the professional woman who took excellent care of herself prior to her son's untimely death.

"My son," her voice shook with emotion. "He was walking home from a meeting after dark and was hit by a car that jumped the curb and k-k-killed him."

I nodded, waiting for her to continue her story.

"I quit my job a year ago," her pale grey eyes scanned the walls of my room before focusing on me. "I'm not interested in anything. Anything at all."

She wanted to explore a life-between-lives regression to understand why her son had been taken from her and what she was supposed to do with her life now. She felt all alone on the planet, even though she knew she was supposed to be doing something, but what? She needed some closure around her son's death and some direction for her life.

Jane went into trance easily. After finishing a difficult past life she went to the spirit world and was greeted by her spirit guide. She and her guide processed that past life. They were just finishing that conversation when we begin here.

Diane: What is your guide's final message about how you could have better handled that past life?

Jane: He says that I should not complain so much about situations; rather I need to take action.

D: Can you ask your guide about your son? Perhaps he could bring his spirit there to you? So you could see him and talk to him.

J: Okay, I will.

D: Is your son there?

J: Yes. We are embracing. It is so wonderful to see him, he is glowing.

D: Ask him if his passing was something the two of you planned.

J: He says it was.

D: Can you ask him why the two of you planned that, what is the contract?

J: He says he had some things he needed to learn, but he didn't need to spend a lot of time here. He has other things to move on to.

D: Can you ask him what lesson you signed up to learn from his early passing?

J: He says, "That love doesn't die. It is the only thing that is real." (she is crying) He says he always knew that I loved him. (crying harder)

D: What else do the two of you have to share in this special moment?

J: He says not to worry; I am going to be seeing him again.

D: Good. Ask him if he has any advice for your life right now; for the direction you are going?

J: He says I need to stop procrastinating and start writing.

D: Ask him if this is where you are going to find purpose and meaning in your life.

J: He says it is the vehicle for my life's work. It is where I am to fight the fight. It is a political fight for more economic freedom. The battleground is the economics. It is the same old story.

D: Is it about economic suppression? Or crisis?

J: It is about economic suppression. About oligarchy. The crisis being created by the oligarchy.

D: Is this the crisis being created right now?

J: Yes.

D: Is there anything else he can share with you about what is coming up so your book can be more directed toward what exactly the problem is going to be.

J: He says I need to keep a sense of humor about it. People won't listen if I am too passionate about it. He says I should not scare them. It is about showing them a different way.

D: Are these writings to be directed toward the common people or the leaders that are being oppressive?

J: The middle class. Showing the middle class a new way. He says direct it toward the women of the middle class.

D: What would this new way look like?

J: He says more cooperative, more caring, more human. He says the children need to be the center of it.

D: How so?

J: He says if we learn to care for the children, we will be caring for everyone.

D: What else does he have to suggest?

J: That is all.

D: So what else do the two of you need to do today before you move on in the spirit world?

J: I just need to know that I was there for him when he needed me. (crying) He says I was. I helped him learn what he came here to learn.

D: So is it time for you to say your good-byes?

J: Yes.

D: Let me know when you are finished. And know that at any time you can access his spirit, feel his energy.

J: He is ready to go.

Jane went on to finish her trip through the spirit world. When I brought her back to my consultation room she was grateful to have seen her son and know that he was doing well. She found it interesting that the guidance for her life at this time came from him. She realized that he had given her direction for now. She had been putting off writing a book for some time. She also did not feel alone anymore and she saw in her soul group that several of her close female friends were in that group and that they had made a specific plan for the future that was about to unfold. She was told by one of her soul group members, that she did not recognize, that she would meet two group members soon that would take her into the plan this soul group had for this life. She learned that her soul group comes here to earth to be activists – to help inform people of new ways of being – they are always met with resistance – but play an important role in the formation of new ideas and ways. Jane was excited that she had not only learned that there was a plan for her life, but that it would be unfolding soon. Being with her son was joyous and comforting for her.

Laura, Experienced Meditation Practitioner...

Many of my clients are spiritual seekers who participate in regression therapy on a regular basis to receive direction and guidance from the spirit world. Laura, a civil servant in her mid-fifties, spends as much time as possible out of doors, both professionally and personally.

Her tan face and smile lines fanning from her deep brown eyes reflect the serenity of her soul. Her naturally sandy grey hair was gathered up into a long French braid bisecting her shoulder blades. Long legs in faded blue jeans, with a tear above her knee that was a result of her latest hike in the nearby national forest rather than a fashion statement, broad shoulders beneath a long graceful neck, indicated the presence of a strong, serious woman. That image held until she threw back her head in a braying throaty laugh more familiar in a smoky tavern than in a therapist's office.

Always curious, and at times impatient, Laura felt there was something missing in her meditation practice and she needed reassurance and guidance as to the time she devoted to meditation. Confident that her guide was there waiting to respond, Laura eased into the trance state under my direction.

During this regression, her guide wanted her to participate in an event in the spirit world that was taking place at that moment.

Diane: What does your guide have in mind for you today?

Laura: He says he is taking me to a gathering.

D: Let me know what happens along the way.

L: We have arrived at a huge amphitheater. I don't know what is happening but there are millions of spirits gathered here.

D: Please ask your guide what is happening.

L: He says it is a huge group gathered together in meditation to pray for a person on earth who is about to make a bad choice that could affect the entire planet.

D: What do you do next?

L: He and I are joining the prayer group. Moving to the front of the group. There is a spirit leading the meditation.

D: Do you recognize the spirit who is leading this group?

L: Yes, it is the spirit of Jesus. He is guiding the group in prayer. My guide says that humans have been given free will. But that when one is about to make a bad choice, much support is given. He says the amount of support depends on the magnitude of the potential bad choice. This choice now could destroy the planet.

D: Ask him what happens when an individual is about to make a smaller bad choice, one that might just cause harm in their own life.

L: He says any bad choice we make affects many people, not just us. He says our actions on earth always have a 'ripple' effect. But he says that our spirit guide will work hard to guide us to a better choice. Also, the balance of our spiritual energy that we left in the spirit world will try to influence the person to follow their life plan. In addition, those spirits with whom we have contracts will also attempt to guide us in the right direction. He says we get lots of help.

D: So what are you doing now?

L: We are praying for a person in high power. His choice is important.

D: Can your guide tell you who this person is?

L: No – he says that is not important. He wanted me to participate because I am here – and they need everyone to help. He also wanted me to see how free will and guidance work together to create what happens on the planet.

D: Can you say more about the spirit who is leading this group?

L: Yes. He is very wise. Highly evolved. Compassionate.

D: Does he still incarnate?

L: My guide says no, not unless times on earth are dire. He comes as a spiritual leader to earth now and then – to guide humanity. He is needed here to teach and lead spirits in the work of the spirit world. Like this meeting. My guide says he is not the only highly evolved spirit here. There are many others who teach and guide here. My guide says we need to be quiet now and pray.

D: Okay. Let me know when you are ready to leave this meeting.

L: (minutes pass by) We are leaving now.

After Laura had finished her life-between-lives session, she commented that the experience of being in the prayer group had affirmed her belief in the power of meditation and prayer. Thoughtful and reflective, she shared her thoughts with me. "It's not all about me "—A rueful laugh. "It's about all who are struggling with decisions, choices. Rather than worry about my issues, I will double my efforts to pray for people who are struggling."

Laura's experience in the mass meditation group was unusual, but the desire of a spirit while in the spirit world to go to a place of solitude to meditate is not. During this phase of the life-between-lives, I will always ask the client if there is something in the spirit world that they enjoy doing. It is not uncommon to have them reply that they would like to spend some quiet time meditating to rejuvenate and increase their energy.

John's Initiation to Meditation...

When John stumbled into my office, he was in the throes of early adolescence. Gangly, long-boned, a shadow of fuzz on his upper lip, evidence of adolescent eruptions colored his smooth full cheeks, as he fell into the easy chair next to mine. Leaning forward, he jerked his athletic socks from the heels of his untied designer sneakers. Having raised three sons of my own, I'm familiar with that stage between childhood and physical maturity—the awkwardness, the self-consciousness, the discomfort in their skin.

I waited until he settled into the chair, exhaled, and then looked at me and smiled. "Okay, bring it on…"

John had never heard the word "meditate" before his first trip into the spirit world. When asked what he would enjoy doing after he had gained much knowledge from his Council of Elders and experienced a past life from his trip to the spiritual library, John replied that he wanted some time to rest in meditation.

Diane: Is there something you would like to do now that you enjoy doing when you are in the spirit world?

John: Yes. I would like to spend some time meditating to restore my energy.

D: Do you have a particular place that you go when you meditate?

J: Yes, I go to a very special place in a dense forest.

D: Will your guide go there with you?

J: Yes, he will go with me, but I will meditate alone while he waits for me.

D: Do you want to go there now?

J: Yes. We will go now.

D: Describe to me what you are aware of along the way.

J: We are moving fast, we are here now.

D: Describe this place please.

J: We are walking side by side through a beautiful meadow covered with wild flowers. On the right side is a dense forest. We are walking along the edge of the forest. There is a spot where I like to go into the forest up ahead.

D: Are you talking to your guide or walking in silence.

J: We are walking in silence. He knows I need to rest.

D: What happens next?

J: I see the place where I enter the forest. My guide has sat down on a rock to wait for me. I am moving to the right to enter between two particularly large trees. There is a small path there.

D: Please describe to me what the forest looks like.

J: Yes – it is a huge old growth redwood tree forest. The trees are many feet thick; some seem to be grown together. When I look up it seems like they come together. The sunlight filters through the trees. I am coming to my grove. It is like a cathedral – round – the trees have grown in a circle about 20 feet across. I sit in the middle so I can feel their energy circling me. (pause)

D: What does this energy feel like as you sit in the middle?

J: It is hard to put into words – like a hug – I feel their energy as if I were part of them. They give me energy. That is why I love this place – they fill me up with energy – I feel nurtured by them – one with them. (pause)

D: What are you doing now?

J: Meditating – getting filled up with energy.

D: I will be quiet for awhile. Let me know when you are finished.

J: (many minutes pass) I am finished.

D: How do you feel now?

J: Wonderful. Nourished. Filled with golden energy. I am ready
          to go back to my guide.

Those who want to take some quiet time to meditate in the spirit world describe the places they choose as much like natural places on earth. Of the descriptions coming from the spirit world, these are also the most vivid, colorful and detailed. The places where spirits go for solitude are natural settings without running water.

Norma, Further Enlightening an Exceptional Soul...

Norma's peaceful spirit preceded her formidable presence into my office. Small in stature, grey hair cropped short, Norma favored comfortable loose clothing from natural fabrics. Earth tones accented grays and beiges; she wore colorless clothing and surrounded her vibrant energy with tones rather than colors. She sensed her healing energy and highly evolved spirit needed the balance provided by sensory neutral surroundings.

Norma came for life-between-lives regressions in order to rejuvenate her tired spirit. Often meditation over there restores the gifts and energy we need here on earth to fulfill our life's purpose. At times, in addition to resting, the spirit will experience an infusion of wisdom. I refer to this as "swimming in the purple plasma." This experience is never the result of a request from the regressed person, rather it is always offered by their spirit guide. Those who have experienced this opportunity report that it is beyond inspirational. They learn about the truth and purpose of life.

The respect Norma's spirit guide has for her was demonstrated in this life-between-lives regression. After her meeting with her council, he showed her a round disk with a picture on it. As she was describing it to me she was drawn into the purple plasma.

Diane: What is happening now?

Norma: My guide is showing me a medallion, a disk. It is about six inches across.

D: Does it have anything drawn on it?

N: I am going to have to move closer. (pause) Yes, it is a drawing of a pyramid. A mountain. And at the bottom of the mountain is a dense forest. As I look up the mountain the trees become fewer and fewer. The air clearer and the view clearer and there are colors.

D: What colors?

N: At the bottom of the mountain the sky has clouds. Then as one moves up the mountain the sky becomes a light blue and then a darker blue. The view as you move up is clearer and clearer, and what becomes clearer is the truth and the purpose. At the top of the mountain, it is pointed, sort of like Everest; there is a perfectly round deep purple ball. And it is… wow, okay, so I am being asked to move into that ball. I am floating into it. Inside the ball, which is now much bigger, is a purple liquid, kind of like plasma, and I am floating in it. This purple plasma is warm and I am part of it. But it is also millions of spirits. It is like the place where all is created. This plasma, this fluidity, the feeling is pure love, pure. It is not that spirits are created here, but this is where creative ideas emerge from, come from. This is where that creative idea of how to show people how to come into the spirit world came from. The idea of how to open the veil just a little bit to help raise the level of consciousness – this is where that idea came from! This plasma, this fluidity, pure love! It is the source of all creativity. This is the guiding force from which all ideas emanate. This space is huge. Millions of spirits creating ideas to further the truth. (pause)

D: What is happening now?

N: I am resting in this plasma. I am having my energy rejuvenated here by all of this love. I feel embraced by the love of millions of spirits who hold me. I will rest awhile here.

D: I will be quiet. Let me know when you are finished resting. (pause)

N: I am pulling out of the purple ball. I see the mountain and the trees; they represent the heavy veil that separates us from the truth, from the knowledge of the world beyond the seen world of humanity. My guide is here with me – he says it is time to move on.

This experience that Norma's guide offered her was truly a gift. It was a gift that helped her to understand the truth of our existence, both as spirits and as humans. She was awed by it. When I brought her back after the remainder of her tour through the spirit world, she felt she had been given a special view into the makings of that place beyond the physical plane here on earth. She felt blessed and left to share her new awareness with others.

Another experience that a few receive in the spirit world has an impact similar to that of the purple plasma. Whereas the purple plasma is a place of creative thought, the next case gives an example of the experience of being in the presence of the Creator. This too is one of awe – precipitating speechlessness and deep reverence. Like the purple plasma experience, this too is one that the guide just offers to the spirit – unasked, as a gift. Those that have had this experience in the life-between-lives regression see it as normal; kind of matter of fact; "well of course there is a Creator!" The experience comes as no surprise to them. This experience is actually rare.

I often ask my clients when they are in the Council of Elders' chamber if they are aware of a being, force, energy in the room that has a higher wisdom than the elders. Most will respond "yes". When I ask where it is they tell me that it is up above the council members, high up in the large dome above them. They report that it looks just like a very bright white energy. This is the closest most clients get to the experience of knowing that the Creator is near.

Karen's Confirmation of the One...

My client Karen, a happily married woman with children and a job she enjoyed, came to me to address several fears she worried would become phobias without treatment. After taking her history, unless she was functioning in total denial because of a forgotten childhood trauma, I was at a loss to pinpoint the source of her apparently irrational fears. After traditional talk therapy, Karen wanted to go through the hypnotic therapeutic process to discover the origins of her paralyzing anxiety.

Past-life regression revealed adversities during the past that could be carried into this incarnation, but awareness of the resolution of those issues did not dissolve the negative energy surrounding her fears.

Her spirit guide took her to the spirit world in her life-between-lives regression and gave her this experience.

Diane: What is happening?

Karen: (pause) I am with The One.

D: What is The One?

K: You know, the Creator, The One.

D: Please describe The One.

K: The One is a being. This being is a collection of different prisms of light, of energy. It is all colors collected into one – a blinding light. Pure. If you are an advanced spirit you can see all of the colors distinctly, you can differentiate each color. If you are a lower stage spirit, you can just see white. I am a mid-stage spirit so I see sort of a tie dye effect when I look at The One. The One is huge, beyond boundaries, no boundaries. The One is here and everywhere.

D: Why has your guide brought you to The One?

K: To have the experience of feeling the pure love that emanates from this divine being. To feel the awe of being in The One's presence. To help me understand that fear is a creation of my human mind. Fear is not real, only love is real.

These encounters with the creator are usually sudden and do not last very long. They definitely are a gift offered by the spirit guide. Karen mentioned the different levels of spirits.

Michael Newton, Ph.D., in his book *Journey of Souls*, goes into great depth regarding the different levels of spirits. We continue to incarnate on the earth plane to increase our level of actual spiritual attainment. When we are in the spirit world we know the truth. When we incarnate the veil of forgetfulness falls and we have no idea why we are here.

We begin our new life with the family we have chosen; and the script we have written begins to unfold. We experience a complex mixture of adversities and happiness. When adversity presents itself, this is our opportunity to grow spiritually. How we deal with adversity is the key to growth. If we meet it with anger, depression, addiction, or violence then we do not grow. If we bring kindness, compassion, and a helping hand to it, we will increase our level of spiritual growth. When our life is over and we rise up to the spirit world, we once again realize why we incarnated and what lessons we wanted to learn. With the help of our spirit guide, we see the degree to which we learned those lessons. This process goes on, life after life. The degree to which we learn our chosen lessons during our life on earth is the degree to which we advance in our spiritual attainment.

During the life-between-lives regression, the homecoming spirit sees that all of the spirits they encounter, including their guide and council members, have a specific color emanating from the core of their spirit. These colors denote the actual level of attainment that each spirit has reached. There is no judgment placed on these levels, rather it seems that this system makes it clear in the spirit world who we can learn from and who we can teach. The various colors have seven basic levels: starting with the beginning spirits and moving to the most advanced spirits: Level I - white, Level II - reddish pink/light orange, Level III – yellow, Level IV - green/brownish tones, Level V - light blue, Level VI - dark blue/lavender, Level VII – purple. Moving from one color upward to the next is a significant achievement and usually takes many lives. During some lives we make no progress, while in others we achieve a quantum leap forward. When we do progress in our learning, our spirit guide makes us aware of this attainment immediately upon entering the spirit world.

Donna Awakens to the Healer Within...

Donna had been referred to me by her best friend because she was worried about her deep depression. Donna's life had been chaotic, with marriages to two raging alcoholics and an unusual amount of adversity punctuated her life from childhood. When she began counseling two years prior to the following regression she was overweight, struggling with addictions, and clearly unhealthy in appearance and demeanor. She was struggling simply to survive the ghosts from her life up to this point.

When a client is in that much pain, they rarely see beyond their own misery to their place in the overall picture of their life. We celebrated every positive step in her life, we accepted her setbacks without judgment, we shared every inch of the therapeutic process seeking a breakthrough, an aha! moment, an epiphany to explain her pain.

When Donna's spirit guide knew she was ready, he revealed to her that her purpose in this life was to advance in her work as a healer. This came as a surprise to her, as she knew nothing about healing. Her guide showed her several past lives where she had been a healer. He also showed her the progress she had made over time. As this knowledge unfolded for Donna, she began learning a few healing practices. As time passed she became recognized as a healer. Her reputation grew as an effective healer, as her clinical depression faded with each day she applied her gift to benefit others. After two years of hard work and acquiring skills and gifts, Donna became established as a gifted healer in her community. Highly motivated and with a good support system, Donna actualized the plan she had created prior to incarnating for this life.

On her next visit to the spirit world, Donna's spirit guide greeted her with excitement. Apparently, her guide had something special for today's visit. Donna had been aware of her level of attainment since her first life-between-lives regression: she was a yellow spirit. This is a mid-level spirit.

Her spirit guide ushered her into an initiation ceremony that would move her into the next level: a light blue color – level five. This was a huge step forward in her spiritual attainment. Her guide indicated this was the result of her commitment to her life's plan and the hard work she had done since then. He led her to a pool with other spirits.

Diane: What is happening now?

Donna: My guide is leading me to a pool filled with yellow liquid. I get in. I have on a yellow gown that is floating in the liquid. It's a round pool and other spirits are in here too. We are all yellow spirits. There are about eight of us.

D: How deep is the liquid?

Do: It is waist deep. We all have our arms on the side walls of the pool and our fingers are touching. We are cleansing our spirit in preparation to go somewhere. There is an energy force near. A deep purple light comes and surrounds us. Each of us is asking to be freed from a particular block that we have: lack of trust, hesitation, frustration, fear, or feeling unlovable. Each of us has set up a particular dilemma in our life that has been difficult. There are high level healers here to help us let go of our particular problem.

D: How are you helped to let go of this dilemma?

Do: There is an arc above the pool. Each spirit sends upward their strengths. These strengths are captured by the arc which then sends down to each spirit what they feel they are lacking. This cleanses our spiritual energy. Wow!

D: What happened?

Do: The liquid in the pool just turned red and is humming! We in the pool are all healers. We have all requested this cleansing. The arc amplifies the strengths coming to it and sends them back down multifold.

D: What happens next?

Do: There is a gate. We are moving through the gate. As I move through the gate my understanding increases. We are going down a walkway toward a central place were many are gathered. We will be prayed over by all of the spirits in the amphitheater. There are hundreds of souls praying for us.

D: What does the amphitheater look like?

Do: There are seven columns, each a different color. They are the seven different colors of spiritual progress. We are walking down into the center. Oh!

D: What is happening?

Do: I am being lifted up – I am floating above all of the praying spirits. I am floating with my arms held out. It feels so very un-alone. The others that were in the pool with me are also floating up here with me. We are transparent, it feels like we are being touched by all those who are praying – it must be that we are being embraced by their energy! Wow – what an incredible feeling!!

D: How are you feeling with all of this?

Do: I feel full, complete, like nothing is missing – all is easy and perfect now.

D: What happens next?

Do: We are being brought down to a white round platform in the middle of the amphitheater. We are standing in the middle of it. Wow! Now the praying spirits are rising up in a single file and moving over us – we have been announced as the advancing group. All of these hundreds of spirits are rising up; I feel their energy move through me as they send their prayers of advancement to me. They pass over me and the others in a single line. These floating, praying spirits form a lavender circle of energy as they pass over each of us.

D: Does this ceremony have a name?

Do: Yes. It is an anointing, a rite of passage, as we in this group move up to a new color: light blue.

This experience in the spirit world profoundly affirmed Donna's commitment to her healing path. The evidence of her hard work and extraordinary effort to accomplish the commitments she had chosen prior to this incarnation renewed her faith in herself and the afterlife. Donna's current life is a testament to her spiritual progress once she re-connected with her life's plan.

Chapter Seventeen
Life Selection Room

"Each man is an architect of his own fate."
Albert Einstein

When our guide takes us to the life selection room we are shown the possible body selections we were offered for our next life. We are shown about four different possibilities, each with a specific body and life story attached. By now, our council has suggested lessons we might want to address in our upcoming life. We have also chosen the spirits who will help us learn these lessons: from one or the other side of the equation, a helper or a hinderer.

Each potential life focuses on those lessons and with those particular spirits, but each has a different story line. One of those bodies is the one we have already chosen for our current life. These choices are shown to us in a room that resembles an IMAX theater: a huge screen on which we see many short vignettes of each potential life. You can either watch the scenes or choose to participate in them, to see how it would feel to live them. Since we have already chosen our current body we gravitate to that body choice.

It is interesting to view why we did not choose one of the other bodies. As we watch the scenes we are in charge of the controller. When we come to the life we are actually living now we can view scenes from birth to our current age. Generally, we cannot view into the future. We are shown how the lessons we will be working on will be learned, and with whom.

Almost all of the time we see how and why our current life has unfolded as it has. On rare occasions a person will see that he or she has missed an important cue that was set up to indicate a particular path. Each of us sets up specific cues and triggers that will cause us to go this way or that way. For example, if we are to fall in love with a particular person, that trigger is set up before we incarnate. This is true with all significant choices in our life. These triggers and cues are set up to keep us on track with the life story that we have chosen. These triggers will also include where we will live, and what career we will choose. Generally speaking, we stay on path.

There are exceptions. If a person has chosen addiction, for example, there will be specific cues to guide him on a path that will lead him to become clean and sober in this life. The goal is to learn that lesson. However, as we have seen in the chapter on addiction in Part Two, there are what I call "failed experiments". If a cue is missed that would have helped us muster the courage to stop using a particular substance, we are most likely to die of a disease caused by that substance, kill ourselves in some sort of accident, or die of an unintentional overdose. These are not planned events. They fall in the category of suicide.

The earlier we cause ourselves to end our lives, the sooner we will return here to try again. That is what our spirit will choose to do as we are all wanting to increase our level of spiritual awareness, whether we are aware of it or not. Everyone's purpose is to learn the lessons that we have selected. So, when we are watching the IMAX screen, we will become aware of missed cues and triggers if we are beyond the age at which we should have seen them. We will notice on the screen that the storyline does not match what we are living. In addition, we will clearly see what the trigger was.

What happens when we miss a guide post we had set up? Our guide, our Council of Elders, and the part of our spiritual energy that we left in the spirit world create a new plan. They invite volunteer spirits to play the various roles here on earth for us – as we missed the set of spirits that we had set up prior to incarnating.

This re-write of the script is similar to what happens in the case of suicide or the failed experiment. This unplanned event causes all of the contracts that the departing spirit made with other spirits to come to an end prematurely. This leaves those left on earth with a hole in their plan. Interestingly enough, many loved ones of those who commit suicide feel adrift when this person leaves. This is not so when one dies if it was a planned departure, part of the original script. This does not mean that loved ones of those who die according to plan don't grieve and feel lost for a time. Suicide is very different – it leaves a big hole in the life plan of many. This hole is filled by those spirits who support us in the spirit world. They diligently come up with a new plan, whether this plan is to cover our missing a trigger, a suicide, or a failed experiment.

Free Will or Fate?

Regression therapy's revelations about the spirit world and life-between-lives activities may lead you to believe that our existence is a pre-planned path with a lock step approach to our progress toward spiritual enlightenment. However, that is not the case. We apply our free will in the selection of our life plan. Some might consider those events as "fate", our destiny.

There are so many lessons to learn, and so many to teach that the number of possible combinations stretches into infinity. Our spirit chooses our plan, which is only one expression of our free will. The others occur during the incarnation when we have an endless series of choices. Each decision, each action may or may not be consistent with our script.

What happens during the incarnation when we exercise our free will and make choices not in keeping with the plan? The spirit world, including the Council of Elders, your spirit guide and the percentage of your spiritual energy remaining there, meet to assess the damage. Regardless of the magnitude, your team writes a new plan. Small deviations may go unnoticed by you; however extreme changes require a new script. The human being intuitively feels they are not leading the life they were meant to live.

It is one thing when the individual alters their own script through other options, it's quite another when a significant player in your drama makes an alternate selection. Does their deviation from *your* plan destroy your script? Yes, until another one is written in the spirit world.

Regardless of your religious beliefs, the presence or absence of a spiritual practice, or total absence of any assumptions beyond the here and now; we are humans and as such we always have choice. That is what separates us from the other species, and that is what separates us from each other - the choices we make, and the results of those choices.

"Sally Go Round the Roses…"

Occasionally I will have a client tell me that they do not feel like they are leading the life they had planned to lead. Even though a new plan is created for us if a trigger is missed, our spirit is aware of the change. Our human body is not. However, we just feel like something went wrong.

What happens when we get off track? What happens when we miss the sign posts that we have set up for this life? How can we find out that we are off track? During a life-between-lives regression the easiest way to find out if we are indeed off track is in the life selection room.

Sally, a 58 year old woman, had done many regressions to past lives and into the spirit world. Her life had been very difficult. She knew who her soul mate was and had a very difficult relationship with him later in life. She had met him late in high school, he had tried to date her, but she had rebuffed him. After marrying another man, raising a family, and going through a very difficult divorce, she met this man again. They began dating and from the beginning, the relationship was filled with turmoil.

During prior regressions, she had relived many past lives where she and Dan had been very happy together. She had learned that he was her soul mate. Sally could not understand why they were doing so horribly in this current life. He always seemed angry with her for one reason or another. No matter what she tried his seemingly irrational anger at her remained. She had ended that relationship two years before she entered counseling with me. After resolving many issues and relationships in her life, one day she told me that she just did not feel like this was the life she planned. She felt that something had gone horribly wrong.

I suggested that we do a regression that would take her to the life selection room. So far, none of her regressions had taken her to this stop. We discussed how this would show her clearly what she had planned prior to incarnating.

Sally's regression began with her returning to her most recent past life. After her death she rose to the spirit world where she was met by her spirit guide. Her guide took her to a room with two chairs. Dan was already seated in one of them. As usual, she and her soul mate had a joyous reunion. Then Sally sat down in the second chair facing Dan. Her spirit guide backed out of the scene. This entire meeting was orchestrated by her guide as he was well aware of Sally's goal for this regression. Sally reported to me that Dan was happy and loving, and had a message for her.

Diane: So what is Dan telling you?

Sally: He is saying that our plan was to meet in high school, marry, and raise a family!

D: Ask Dan if he will take you to the life selection room and show you the plan that you had made.

S: He says that he will take me there. (This is very unusual as our spirit guide usually takes us there).

D: Let me know when you have arrived.

S: (pause) We are there. We sit down next to each other in a huge room that looks like a movie theater. Dan is taking the controls and is showing me a scene when we were both in high school.

D: Tell me what is in this scene.

S: Well, I am standing in front of a fast food place in the town where we both go to high school. I am 17. I am with two of my girl friends, we are giggling, looking at boys, and are going to get something to eat. We go into the place and go to the counter to order.

D: Do you see Dan anywhere in this place?

S: No. I am in the scene now. We three go to the counter and order some food. Now we are turning and moving toward a table. Oh, yes, there he is. He is sitting with a guy friend of his at one of the tables.

D: Ask Dan why he is showing you this scene.

S: He says that the trigger we set up for me to fall in love with him was for me to see the French fries and coke that he ordered. I didn't see them.

D: Ask Dan how this affected the relationship.

S: He says that because I missed the cue we set up that I did not fall in love with him. If I had seen it, I would have accepted his next attempt to ask me out. He had already asked me out several times and I had said "no". I am seeing on the screen that after this day at the fast food restaurant that he asked me out again – which he did – and I say "yes". I see us dating and falling in love! Oh, I feel so bad! I messed it all up! I see now why he made such a big deal out of me not dating him in high school when we met later in life. On earth, his body is very angry at me. But here in the spirit world Dan is forgiving me – telling me it is okay – we will get together in our next life.

Sally's regression shows us that cues can be missed, taking us down a completely different path. French fries and a coke! The moral of this story is to pay attention to details – you never know how important they may be. Another client's trigger to fall in love with her man was when he leaned over a honey bucket in a certain way. When she saw this in the life selection room she told me that she remembered that very moment and that she had fallen deeply in love. Those two married. But

Sally's story did not end so happily. The various spirits in the spirit world, plus her guide, had created a new path for her – and many lessons were learned from that new path. She was not happy about this turn of events, however.

In our journey through the spirit world, we have the opportunity to be shown a wide variety of experiences and to learn much about our spirit's intentions here on earth. We can see who we have chosen to incarnate with and which lessons we want to learn. We can also see how we have chosen to have our lives unfold and where the greater meaning lies. We can find direction in our current life, and see how past lives have brought us to where we are in our current life. We get direct knowledge of who we have chosen to bring adversity into our lives so that we can learn. This knowledge can soften our negative feelings for those bearers of difficulty as we learn that we have chosen these adversities – they are simply meeting the contracts that we made with them.

Follow Your Plan...

Your spiritual growth depends upon following your plan. Following your plan enables you, as well as the other spirits with whom you have contracts, to successfully learn the lessons.

If we choose to learn and to teach with love and compassion as the core of our process, the rewards of achievement and completion are evident in our spiritual progress. If we make other choices, choices motivated by fear, selfishness, greed, envy, arrogance, or any other less than honorable reasons, there is no punishment as part of the consequences. However, our spiritual advancement may be slower and require more lives. Once incarnate the temptations faced by the human body can cause free will to trump our spiritual plan. Free will exists in our choices while between lives and while incarnate on earth and affects our destiny.

Part Four

Reflections on Regression Therapy

"If you want to change the world, first try to improve and bring about change in yourself."

Dalai Lama

Past-life regression enables us to return to the origin of all problems, issues, or difficult relationships. By returning to the beginning of the karmic energy, by re-experiencing the trauma, the energy is released. This process shows us how the problem originated, enables us to understand the dynamics of the issue, and to see with a new perspective our role then and the effect it has on our role today. By untying the Karmic Knot during the past-life regression, we heal with the release of the negativity surrounding the problem and are now able to move forward in today's life with clarity, renewed energy and commitment.

Life-between-lives regression takes us into the afterlife. There we gather information and knowledge about our purpose and mission in this incarnation. Our spirit guide takes us on a tour of the spirit world, encountering spirits whose intent is to provide us with loving support in our current life and to improve our coping skills when faced with adversity on earth. A place of unconditional love where your spirit is nurtured and rejuvenated by your spirit guide and the other members of your soul group, the afterlife is filled with love and acceptance, a true paradise.

By combining these two therapy modalities we heal a problem we chose to work on and then move into the spirit world to experience the loving reflections of our spirit guide, our Council of Elders, and our soul group. This experience is life-changing and gives us the understanding and tools necessary to move forward on a path that has purpose and meaning – rather than living in confusion. Through regression therapy, we begin to understand the master plan of life and the fundamental truth of our existence on earth: as teachers, as students, and as progressing souls. Regression therapy provides access to our personal plan for this life, and the realization that our spirit wrote our script prior to incarnating. This understanding enables us to take responsibility for the difficult spin in our lives and to look for a lesson that is held within them. This allows us to let go of blame and move forward in our spiritual progress.

Learning that we wrote the script for our life is difficult to accept. Many have asked why they would write horrible events into their lives. Aren't we here to experience love and joy? Yes we are, but also we learn through working with adversity. We come to earth to learn lessons we have chosen and also to help others learn the lessons they have chosen. This interaction between spirits in human bodies enables all of us to learn and to teach, back and forth, through time eternal.

One of the most difficult teachings is to learn that we have, in many lives, been the villain as well as the victim. Many struggle with the reality that we need to learn most lessons from both sides of the equation. "We all have both Christ and Hitler in us," is a familiar statement.

However, experiencing it in our own past lives is humbling. As soon as we understand and accept without judgment this dynamic in our learning process we become more forgiving and compassionate toward all others in our lives.

Experiencing past lives as both genders furthers our understanding of the opposite gender in our current life. Many of us have little understanding of how it would be to step in the shoes of the opposite sex. This is also true with different ages and physical conditions. When adults in their prime of life experience old age, sickness, and death in regression therapy, they have a much greater understanding for the struggles of declining body and health. Compassion brings the helping hand to the forefront.

Another benefit of regression therapy occurs when we unexpectedly run into our own prejudices regarding different races, religions, political persuasion or cultures. When we see ourselves in past lives as that which we have been taught to hate in our childhood, we realize that we have throughout time been all races, practiced all religions, and lived under all political regimes. We come to understand that all people on earth seek security and happiness; all of us have the same human right to live in peace and harmony.

Most of us fear death, others' death, as well as our own. When we experience dying life after life, living just one more storyline, we come to understand our purpose here on earth. We realize it is about our own personal spiritual growth. We and we alone are responsible for all of our choices, and we will either learn it then, or now, or we will get another chance to learn that lesson in some future lifetime. When this understanding of life reaches us deep within our soul, we begin to try to make the best possible choice in every moment. Being human, we will fail some percentage of the time, but the hope is that we will get better and better at the game of life and increase our level of spiritual attainment. This accomplishment benefits others in our circle as well.

As this interaction, person to person and spirit to spirit, goes on through eternity here on earth we come to know that true joy is found in our ability to bring happiness to others in whatever way the moment presents. Regression therapy is a gift because it brings this understanding to us quickly, enabling all those in our circle of influence to benefit from our knowledge.

Part Five

THE GREAT REBIRTH

Progressions Reveal
The Enlightened Times To Come

*"To bring healing, it is a spiritual imperative to elevate
the energy of the planet before it is too late.
Our obligation is to know what our Karmic Knots are,
and be willing to untie them. It is a virtual imperative
for the life force of the planet."*

Spirit Guide, 2010

What Does the Future Hold?

Many people around the planet have come to believe that difficult times have begun to unfold. There are many prophecies and theories that talk about what is in front of us. Even global warming is now on the list of potential problems facing humankind. Storms and earthquakes are becoming greater in magnitude, as we saw in hurricane Katrina and earthquakes in Haiti and Chile. Scientists are concerned about the melting ice caps as well as monitoring new volcanic activity in various areas.

Currently, there is a huge amount of information available on the up-coming year, 2012. In addition to the prophecies around this date, also on December 21, 2012 the planets will be in alignment. This alignment only occurs every 640,000 years. Also on that day there will be a full solar eclipse. This is not pseudo-science or astrology; this is astronomy, astrophysics—science.

Added to the planetary changes are political and economic crises all around the globe. Many countries suffer under huge burdens of debt. Politically, worldwide peace seems an impossible dream as nuclear proliferation continues, and ancient enemies continue to threaten each other. There is a tension in the air that intensifies with the news of each natural or manmade disaster. Daily living has become daily stressing, as the pace of our lives ratchets up with the speed of the information assaulting us over the radio, internet, and television.

When I began to do life-between-lives regression therapy in early 2004 this opened a window for me and those I was journeying with into the spirit world. In the course of our travels in the spirit world, we held dialogues with individuals' spirit guides. At first, our queries pertained to the specific needs of the person who was being regressed. On occasion, people's experiences would lead to questions that were more general, that applied to the condition of larger communities, of humanity, and the entire world. During regressions, clients began to spontaneously experience glimpses of where we are headed in the future, and how to prepare for what the future may bring. As the frequency of these occurrences increased, we started asking more questions and becoming fascinated with the answers. I call these glimpses of future times from within the spirit world *"progressions"*.

In 2004, a woman I was working with posed a question prior to a life-between-lives regression. She was struggling with her religious beliefs and was widely read on the subject. She saw many similarities across the various faiths and many differences as well.

"Where can I find the truth?" she asked her guide.

"Seek spiritual teaching and truth from the spirit world," was the answer.

I found this answer profound indeed.

Her guide then proceeded to answer many more of her questions regarding the truth.

"What is the underlying problem on our planet?" she asked.

"When technology outstrips spirituality on the planet, technology will be used for destruction," he added. "Even though technology has benefited humankind, for some time now, technology has surpassed the level of spirituality on earth, so now humankind is on a path of destruction."

"What can we do about it?" she asked.

"This balance in the wrong direction must be corrected so that technology will be used only to benefit humankind," the guide responded. "There is already a plan in place."

He continued by saying the plan would increase the level of spiritual awareness of the human race so that we would no longer want to use technology to harm or destroy groups of people or the earth. When this plan is in place, all humans on earth would practice compassion and loving kindness toward all, regardless of differences in appearances or beliefs.

"What is the plan that the spirit world has devised to make this correction?" She asked.

His response was that at this time it was not for her to know. He did say that the plan would unfold for all to experience and it would create a new reality on earth. He called this "The Great Rebirth".

Enlightened Times to Come...

Since that regression I have been privileged to be present during many uninvited progressions into the future that have shown, in vivid detail, this future filled with peace and love. All of these progressions with different clients show the same reality; there is no conflicting information.

Many times I have asked myself, "Why me? Why is this information coming into my office? And, most importantly, what am I supposed to do with it?" This question lingered in the background of my work for years.

My practice was bringing in more and more clients who wanted to do regressions. During many hours weekly, I facilitated regressions in my office. I was learning a great deal about how to help clients go back in time to their past lives to find the origin of their problems in this life. I saw client after client resolve issues that were devastating their current life. In 2007 I felt an inner calling to write a book about the healing benefits of regression therapy. I felt it was important that all people know that there was a faster way to work on issues than sitting in a therapist's office for years. This is in no way a criticism of traditional psychotherapy, which has a very important role in healing work. But more people needed to hear about this method of spiritual exploration that would teach and help them in so many ways. Hence this book began in 2007.

I thought that writing a book was the answer to the question I had been asking myself for years: why am I hearing all of this information from the spirit world? Not so. During a life-between-lives session in 2008, a client I had regressed many times into the spirit world stopped mid-sentence. She said, "My guide has a message for you." This rarely happens, but when it does I know it is important. So I responded, "What is his message?" She said, "He wants you to finish your book." I then asked her to ask him what was the message he wanted me to give people. His response surprised me. He said, "I want you to tell the people about the enlightened time that is coming. You need to share what the spirit world has shown you through your clients. They need to hear this truth. They need to not be fearful of the future." I must admit that I had no intention of including any of the progressions and the information gleaned during them in this book. Who would believe it?

So, it is a direct request from the spirit world that has guided me to share these amazing progressions that open a window into the future. This view of what is to come is beyond beautiful; it is beyond what any of us could have dreamed possible. It has helped me to know that at this point in time, we are literally birthing a new reality for humanity and the planet. Yes, the birthing process will be preceded by pain and challenge. When completed, before us will be a miracle. A miracle that holds within it all the love and joy of being that exemplifies hope for the future. So, this is the process that we are currently engaged in; none other than creating a new reality devoid of violence, hate, and depression. Rather, we are moving into a reality that speaks of balance, peace, love and harmony among all.

So regarding 2012 and the prophecies that abound; the message from the spirit world is that there will be an end to violence, not a violent end. It is not clear that there is an exact date when this shift will take place. Getting dates out of the guides in the spirit world is sketchy at best. Apparently there is "*now*" time only in the spirit world, but planning is part of their program. What is undeniable from all of the information received is that we are walking into a rebirth, a new beginning of community and harmony. The path between here and there may challenge us and probably will not be easy. When we arrive it will be a new beginning for all.

"Whatever the present moment contains, accept it as if you had chosen it."

Eckhart Tolle

Chapter Eighteen

Flashes Forward

"...it takes great skill to taste the future and not allow your knowledge to spoil your actions or the present."
Alberto Villoldo

So how has this information come through during regressions?

All of the progressions into the future have taken place during life-between-lives regressions where we gather information. The clients who have been shown these glimpses into the future have asked for information about their lives that prompted their spirit guide to move them forward in time.

One woman was contemplating moving to a new area and asked her guide's advice. Instead of answering her question, he showed her where she would be living in the future. Another client, while in the spirit world, asked her guide to see a past life with a particular person.

Instead, her guide showed her a future time with this person. Another client did not want to stay here on the earth much longer; she felt that her work here was done and she wanted to return home to the spirit world. Her guide's answer to this feeling was to show her the role she would have in upcoming years and how important it was for her to remain on earth. A male client was anxious about the state of the world in general, and was considering a radical job change. His guide showed him the "job" he would have in the future. Even though many clients seek information about their future, whether they receive it depends on their spirit guide. The amount of information and the source of the information given during progressions I facilitate is totally dependent upon the spirit guide's discretion.

Regardless of the source, or the client, there is no conflicting information regarding the future on this planet. I have asked many spirit guides to show my client what will be going on for them in the future; these requests are denied almost 100% of the time. Since the progressions are dependent upon the client's spirit guide, please do not assume you can choose to do this work and foretell your own destiny; 99.9% of the time it will not happen. All of the progressions that have happened in life-between-lives sessions have been the choice of the spirit guide and not requested by myself or the client.

Seeing into the future can be unsettling. All of those who have had this opportunity have in one way or another altered their life plan. All of these people are courageous, forward thinking, and highly spiritual. And yet it has still been a struggle knowing what is to come. That being said, I want to share some of these progressions. As the facilitator of regression therapy, I am not seeing directly the vivid detail that my client sees. They only report a percentage of the details to me. Because of this, I asked several clients if they would write their progressions to share them with you.

The first progression occurred during a life-between-lives session in 2004 with a woman in her 50's who was contemplating a move several states away. She asked her guide if this was a good choice. Her guide never answered her question; rather he chose to show her how she would be living in the future. She has been kind enough to share what she saw. The following six paragraphs were written by DSJ in 2004.

"When I asked my guide what he thought of my moving to another state where my only grandchild lived, he did not respond. Instead, it was like he pushed a button on a VCR and the movie began. I was not only in the movie, but I was immediately pulled into the screen, as if I was living it now. The first thing that I was aware of was the feeling of complete contentedness within me. I was sitting in a large vegetable garden with others. I was wearing a handmade dress with a thing tied around my waist that carried my gardening tools. My socks were hand knitted and my shoes were moccasins that were made out of hide. We were cultivating each plant with such loving care. There were purple peppers; tall rows of plants that I believe were potatoes, row after row of corn, and much, much more. There was a light or energy force coming up from the ground bidden by the workers. This energy flowed through the plant and did a kind of turnaround in their hands and returned to the earth.

There was a small child who was four years old running through the garden. His mother was working on some low growing plants and she was asking him to come feel the plant's joy. He was so full of happiness himself it would have been redundant. So he would pass one or another of the workers. He would hug and kiss them on the leg or back or the top of their heads. We were all enjoying and encouraging his game. One of the men who was hoeing, when the child ran up and hugged his legs, pretended to have a blister on his hand so he would be kissed there too. Then on his chin, another kiss, then under his straw hat on top of his head. Then we all started complaining of injuries so we could be healed with this loving child's kiss. I remember a complete absence of rush in this scene.

There was a horse drawn cart being loaded while we worked in the garden. Two men and a woman were preparing to visit a nearby community with our wares and trade for planked lumber and some tools. We are part of a network of small farms that each have and need items the others produce. It is all a barter system. The only means of transportation was your feet, horseback, or horse drawn wagon. We also use boats on the river to go farther distances.

Two other men were working on housing for some kind of pump that would be used to irrigate our fields and bring water to the main house. There was no electricity. The main house is not the largest building on the settlement but certainly the most important. We all take our meals there. Cooking and sewing, and other intricate work of many kinds, happened in this building or on its large three sided porch. Hand crank washing machines are on the left side for our clothes to be kept clean. Forms and racks for making candles are likewise there. Presses and churns are kept in tall closets between the windows.

The largest building that I can see is a barn that sits across the open space in front of the house and the first garden is between these two buildings. A second garden is across the road toward the pond. A third growing place is farther out from our main living space. It is reached down a road we use to travel to other communities. In and around the barn are barnyards. There are chickens. One young man is gathering eggs from the coop. He lovingly gathers each egg – like it is a special offering of love from the chicken. Another young man is milking a cow. As he milks her I can see his thoughts. He has his head against her belly while he sits on his stool. He blesses her gift of milk now, and later the meat she will nourish us with, and the shoes her hide will provide for us. He lovingly milks her and their two energy fields blend and flow together and up and through the earth. There are also goats running around.

As I look around I see mountains and pine trees. On the side of the hills are dwellings where many of us live. These are small cabins. Each family has their own. The young bachelors share one as do the unmarried young women. The trees emanate a glow about them as does the earth itself. On this land hay or some sort of tall, beautiful golden grass grows. The people in our group gather here in prayer for the peace of the planet. We form a circle with our hands brushing the tops of the grass and a resonating hum comes up from the ground. We raise our arms up over our heads and pray. A light shines from each of us and connects to each other, and back into the ground. We are one with each other and the earth."

This woman was awed by the love and joy that all the members of this community shared. She also commented on the visible energy that emanated from all living things including the earth. She did not understand this, but knew that somehow the level of consciousness of all had increased. Also, she spoke in awe that there were no negative emotions in this community. She also said that this was the early stages of the development of this group of people who had gathered together to form a community to sustain its members.

Four years after this first progression, she had completed much hard personal work, and the fruits of this work were obvious in her life. In the spring of 2008 she was shown a second progression to the same community. This time she was older. The best guess is about 12 years had passed between the first stage of the community to the second stage. An important point to note is that between these two progressions my client had realized and developed her skills as a healer here on earth. In this second progression her spirit guide shows her the role she plays in the future of this loving community. The following six paragraphs were written by DSJ in 2008.

"I'm not sure why I was shown this future scene except as a furthering of my healing work. The buildings and grounds looked very much the same. The community was further along in the process of surviving. The main building was different in several ways. The heating and cooking was more compartmentalized. Several wood cook stoves were along the left wall as you entered with large counter tops and tables for work areas. These were set there obviously because of the door and windows that surrounded them. This made cooking in the summer less hot. On the opposite wall was a large wood burning stove by a door that lead out to the side porch and made for easy access to a wood shed.

The biggest difference, however, was a new door on the back of this main room. It had glass windows running down both sides of the door and on top of its frame. The glass was colored opaque in the seven spiritual colors. As you entered this room you found a small bench and peg hooks to your left and the rest of the very small room was empty. The floor was dirt. It was almost completely made of glass – colored glass mostly. Even the ceiling was glass. There were strange marking in the dirt floor. Although it was hard stamped dirt, somehow we had made circles in the dirt, with some lines darker than the others. There were framed vents that opened or closed on either side of the door's windowed frame. These were to let in heat in the winter.

I was one of three healers that used this room. Each morning the three of us stood on different sides of one of our community members and, raising our hands from a prayer position, extended them upward and over our heads and then down their body with our hands out from them about eight inches. We were aligning their energy field, chakras, and meridians all at once. We did this to cleanse each member. This is what the room was called, "the Cleansing Room". The purpose was to help the body stay strong – a kind of proactive health plan as well as centering the spirit for the day's journey. What was interesting is that there was no illness in our community. There were occasional accidents. When these happened the three of us would be summoned to work on the injured member.

We worked our land with an eye on surviving the future. But we lived in the joy and measure of the daily moment. Also, the weather had changed. There was no more snow in the winter. It was warmer and rained in the winter months. The growing season was longer and there was a greater variety of plants that would work in this new climate.

At one point I saw myself sitting at a long table in the community room sewing. People were cooking our small evening meal – our large meals were breakfast and lunch. Ten or so of us were sewing an assortment of clothing items. One of our crew was lamenting on how easy life had been when she was young. We all sat patiently until one of the older women got up and went to the complaining woman and admired the beautiful work she was doing on a shirt and offered to buy it from her. She asked how many kisses would it cost: 20? 30? It was certainly worth 50 but would she barter down to a smaller amount? The young woman was initially caught off guard and then began to laugh as we all did. Our life was hard work but so good. We all rose and smothered the complaining woman with kisses. She then started to work on a special little cloth square for her friend who helped her see.

I believe this progression was shown to me for two reasons. First, and most obviously, to confront the idea of the perfect future. Each thing we have and do must be brought up from ground level. We don't go to the store to buy thread – we must make it. And before we learned how it had to be bartered for from other communities. Secondly and more personally, it addressed my healing nature. I am part of a large group that takes what we are seriously. I am not in charge of everyone's physical or, as in the case of the young woman, mental health. This young woman's comment was a sign of living in the past and if pursued would have caused her unhappiness. Because of my place in our unit, when she started talking I wanted to help her, cleanse her. It wasn't up to me. It was handled by another and I was shown that we are all a part of our community health."

These two progressions give a window into the future showing us the strength of cooperation, love, and healing energy. All involved seemed to understand that a peaceful kindness and living in the beauty of the moment make for a joyous community.

This is the experience of a young woman who asked her spirit guide to show her a past life with a current friend of hers. Rather than going backward in time, her spirit guide chose to send her forward in time to see where this friendship was headed. This progression took place in early 2007. The following six paragraphs were written by RJB.

"I see myself as part of a community that is built just outside of what used to be a town. Most of the town was destroyed. Because there is no electricity, gas, or modern amenities, life is very different from what it is now. There is no communication across countries, and no airplanes. To prosper everyone must work every day, but it is not a hard life. The community is in the mountains, but the climate has changed so that it is warm for most of the year. From where I stand I am looking up at an old chair lift from a former ski resort. But there is no longer snow here. The weather is really perfect. We are able to raise sheep for meat, wool for thread, and collect duck eggs. We grow crops too, though irrigating them is a challenge. We have planted citrus orchards of oranges and grapefruit. Most of our time is spent planting, growing, and nurturing nature's bounty. The surplus of drinking water, food, and shelter is all made possible because the community works together to support each other and take care of each other. The only transportation is walking. But there is nowhere to go. This community is completely self-sustaining. Occasionally a wonderer will walk into the community. These people are seeking to join a community and are welcomed and integrated. We know that only together can we survive. Because of this reality, we view ourselves as one unit, one community – as one.

Everyone works together, cooks together, and eats together. There is a large outdoor kitchen that can be used most of the year. We build small stone houses for the wintertime. During the summer, which is much longer than it was in the past, it is so warm that everyone sets up large colorful tents to live in. We often find reasons to celebrate by preparing large, special meals. During these summer nights, we play music and dance and sing together under the warmth of the stars until the sun rises.

Everything we have is recycled from what was left in the old city. Much like the transformation that we as people have undergone, the things that we use are also relics, transformed into something new. Parking lots are dug up and turned into fields and orchards. Old hardware is taken apart and reassembled into new, more useful tools. Even the clothes that we wear are made of parts of old clothes that were found in the stores of the old town and have been deconstructed and re-sewn. Nothing we use is the same as what it was. Everything has been transformed. This re-creation of clothes, land, and utensils occupies the greater part of our day. People are constantly taking old things apart to make something new. Though it is necessary for our survival to build these tools, this whole process is in large part viewed as a game or even meditative practice.

Humankind's contemporary knowledge has not been lost. There is still a level of understanding of science, etc. An old textbook may be consulted for a new project that is undertaken, but, unlike the current times, technology is always subject to humanity, never the reverse. Technology is only used for the benefit of people and the earth. Children go to school and learn to read and write, but there is a deeper level of learning happening. In fact, teaching and learning is something that everyone takes part in everyday. We learn how to treat each other, relate to each other, and understand ourselves. And build a better community.

The most significant transformation is the way that the people themselves have changed. First of all, since we are so interdependent, there is no crime or hostility. There is never anger. But the transformation runs deeper than a simple need to survive. Kindness and compassion fill every interaction. Stillness fills every heart and mind. This change is hard to describe, but it is as though, rather than constantly seeing problems and emotions as conditions that happen to them, everyone focuses all of their attention inward. Before people were always looking outward for what they did not have, but there was nothing to find. It took this change to get humans to realize that they were looking for themselves. Just like the tools and clothes that we build, we take ourselves apart and try to build something better. The anxious fumbling for answers that once plagued humanity has gone. A calmness and harmony has settled over the people. People know that they must look inward to find answers. Salvation lies within. Light comes from within and we can share it together in community.

Everyone takes responsibility for his or her own emotions. It may sound small, but this constant self-reflection has dramatic effects on the culture of the community. All social hierarchy, rules, and taboos have dissolved. There are still leaders, followers, and a kind of social structure, but everyone is truly seen as peers. No one is judged for his or her differences, but rather celebrated. It is a community and world where everyone is constantly striving to live each other up. It is a world where every person can be filled up with love. The life that we here in this community have built together is a beautiful one."

This young woman's spirit guide referred to these communities as "bubbles of light", many of which he says spring up across the land in the future.

The next progression describes another of these enlightened communities that is created by those who currently live in a small rural town near a river. In early 2008 this woman, who is in her 40's, came to regression therapy as she was feeling that she was at a crossroads in her life's journey. During a life-between-lives session she asked her spirit guide what direction she should take at this time. Instead of a verbal response to her question her guide moved her into a community of the future – showing her what was in front of her and why. This community is very new and, at first, disorganized. The following seven paragraphs were written by SWT in 2008.

"The people of our town are grateful to have their friends and neighbors to form a community based on helping each other. There is sadness initially due to not being able to contact anyone outside of this area because all communications have been cut off. There is no power or gas. There is no transportation except for horses and wagons. Canoes and other row boats can be used on the river. The central government and the economy are no longer functioning. Money has no value and there are no goods to buy. Those who placed value on their 401Ks will need to let go. As this group of people pulls together, there is a calm that falls over them as they realize that simplicity is going to be the order of the day. There is no stress and the only thing to worry about is food and shelter.

The first order of business in this new community is taking inventory of what is available: animals; staples like salt and flour; methods for hunting deer and elk like guns and bows and arrows; and building materials as some people choose to move more toward the town rather than live in the country surrounding our town. Those who are in the country are forming their own communities and pulling together their resources. Some, however, want to be in a larger group than the country communities that are forming.

We know about these other communities because young men on horseback have already started to come in with messages from outlying communities. These messages are most often about what sort of goods they need and what they offer in exchange. A system of bartering is already in the making. These young men are becoming an integral part of the larger network of communities. They are organizing so that there is some system to their efforts. The various communities feed and shelter these men when they layover between the legs of their journey up and down the valley along the river.

The river is also becoming an important path to transport needed goods from one community to another. We can only use row boats and canoes as there is no form of power. Another interesting avenue of transportation is the railroad track. Even though there are no trains, the people of our community have been very creative in "cannibalizing" parts from useless machinery to create rail cars. They chopped up trains and manually move them using a lever, pulley, and cog system as they raided parts from what is not usable anymore. They are demonstrating amazing ingenuity. There is lots of creativity that raises the confidence of the community as a whole. They are even transporting cows and chickens in and out of our community. Whereas there is no communication with any outlying area, we do have communication between the local communities in the valley. The level of cooperation and caring toward all people regardless of their ability to work hard and contribute is remarkable. It is all about the group as a whole, not the individual. No one is left behind – each is included. Peace and harmony punctuate all work and activities.

While one group is working on transportation, another is organizing a system of gardens and local animals. We have cows, chickens, goats, and even some llamas. There is a growing realization of how many people were prepared for some sort of adversity. This is a comforting reality for our new community. Many had food supplies put up. Skills in canning, growing, candle making, sewing, carpentry, etc. abound throughout our members. Fortunately water is abundant and the fishing is good. Our group is organizing communal food preparation areas and serving all. People are beginning to live with more in one home to conserve heating efforts and chores so that fewer can do for more. Everyone still has their personal space. This seems to be the beginning stages of communal living.

While some were undertaking the centralization of cooking and eating, a wonderful ritual began to take hold. After eating the evening meal, many would stay and play music and sing. They would do this around a campfire. Then, some began to put on plays and skits. Much laughter, joking, and good cheer was had by all. The most amazing part of this shift from the way life is now to this new time is that no one gets angry or upset. Everyone makes the most of the hard work that faces them and all are grateful for what they have no matter how small. Everyone shares whatever they have. Meditation and prayer groups begin to form; there is a new energy present that is uplifting. Harmony and peace is the new order of life.

Simplicity returns and people are awakening to a new and beautiful reality. They are relaxed and not stressed out over unimportant things. They now have the time to focus on loving relationships while contributing whatever they can to the whole. The inner opens inside of people – like the blooming of an inner flower. They realize they have been waiting for this and smile. They are becoming aware of the truth of who they really are - beautiful spirits who are all interconnected to one another. These spirits are connected to the pure joy of being. We are creating union, community and happiness. No hustle and bustle, rather there is an air of calm and contentment."

This woman found this community an amazing answer to her question regarding this crossroads in her life. Her guide explained to her that part of awakening humankind needs to be going back to the basics, to simplicity. The current complexity of human society is pulling most away from what is important and into competition, greed and violence. It has become too easy to justify harming others and the planet.

The current level of technology contains the ability to destroy the planet. This new time in the future will bring a movement away from the individual to the importance of community and kindness. The spirit guide told her that the only way to prepare was to meditate so that the mind learned to be and appreciate calm and quiet. In this state, the mind can remain present with adversity and guard against emotional reactivity in difficult situations. She left this regression with a new commitment to her meditation practice.

In mid-2009, another client, in his late 30's, wanted to do a life-between-lives regression to ask his spirit guide if he had missed the line of work he was supposed to do. He had an unsettling feeling that he was supposed to make an important contribution through his work, but had instead chosen a "mundane paper pushing position", to quote his own words. He was not deriving any personal satisfaction or meaning out of his current career, even though it was a "good" job. That meant he made good money. This is not necessarily everyone's goal in life. He felt he had missed his calling. As the regression moved forward and he was with his Council of Elders, he asked them about his current job and if he should be doing something else. He explained to them that the job did not feel meaningful. Their response mystified him at first until they provided an explanation that took him into a future community that bore no resemblance to anything he had ever known. The following three paragraphs were written by GHE in 2009.

"Standing before my Council of Elders, I asked them about my job and if I was supposed to be doing something else. They responded that I would not be doing my current job much longer. When I questioned them further as to what I would be doing after this job, they told me that I would be a great teacher of the children; that I would teach them to be loving and compassionate. Speechless, I asked how this was possible because I had no skills in that area at all. With this question a large screen behind the council opened and started to show me a future scene of a community in the area where I currently live that was vastly different from its current state. This community had no power and there was no electricity. We were growing our own food in huge gardens along the river and hunting deer and elk for meat. The climate had changed; there was no longer any snow. The winter at its worst was like November is now. Plus, the growing season was longer but there were still pine trees. We used candles to light our homes. Three or four years after the shift, there is no more need for firewood to heat the dwellings due to the climate changes. In this community, there were no stores or monetary system. It was a tight knit community and everyone worked hard at whatever it was they could do to contribute. Those that could not contribute were cared for by the others. We lived in modest huts. There was no transportation except for walking, a few bikes, horses, wagons, canoes and row boats. But then there was nowhere to go. Our community was self-sufficient and sustainable. There was lots of water. My council told me I will be helpful in bringing these people together and organizing this new community when it initially forms. They say I will help give the people spiritual tools at the outset.

The children did go to school of a sort. They learned to read and write. Someone else taught them that. But I was there teaching them empathy and understanding. I knew about these topics. In fact, I was not the person I am today. Something had happened between now and then. Also, these children were different. They seemed to exemplify everything I was teaching them. They were like little glowing lights of loving energy. This energy was present all over the community, not just in the people but in the plants and animals. This community was a place where humanity seemed to have been remade and reborn. Harmony and contentment was all there was. There was no conflict and no anger. Yes, life was difficult, but not really, because the attitude toward all of the various tasks at hand was one of joyful doing. Everyone was smiling happily as they worked. Where was this place? I felt like I had landed in utopia. I started quizzing my council in disbelief. How is this possible? They assured me that it was going to come into being, and not very far from now.

I asked them how I should get ready for this time. They told me that I need to let go of fear and remain calm. They also told me I needed to learn and practice repentance and forgiveness. This did not set well with me at all. My council told me I was "to meditate and seek spiritual guidance; to lean into love and peace; to study and strive for these and to learn self-love and love for all others. When faced with adversity do not be adverse. These are the lessons you are working on in this life. Learn them well. This future community is coming. You will succeed in your learning."

As they said this, I remember thinking, "Well, maybe with a lot of help from someone!"

This man remained in an unsettled state for weeks, trying to decide if what he had been told by his council and saw on the big screen could be true. After much soul searching, he arrived at a place of acceptance that it was true. As time passed he settled into a calm understanding that this had to be the truth. He told me that in his opinion, the current state of human society could not continue unchecked. He believed that if it did, the greed and violence on the planet would destroy the earth. It was clear to him that there needed to be some sort of divine intervention. The community that he had witnessed was, by his admission, a wonderful place. He began to be excited at the possibility of living in that seemingly divine place.

"How do the people change from the way they are now to the way I saw them in that community? I mean, they glowed, as if somehow their level of consciousness had taken a dramatic leap upward." GHE asked during a subsequent session.

I smiled in response because I had been asking myself this very question for five years. How does this happen? Every progression that has happened in my office to date had contained that very quality – an obvious increase in the level of spiritual awareness in human beings. It is as if our vibrational level, the frequency at which we resonate, radically increases. But how?

As the spirit world would have it, the answer to this question walked into my office one day in mid-2009 in the form of a woman who wanted to do regression work. Carla's goal was to find out what it was she was to do at this point in her life. She was almost 50 and felt deeply that her work here on the planet was done. She was unable to get away from this feeling, even when doing the work that she loved. There was no apparent reason why she should have this prevailing feeling. As per my usual request, she had brought a list of ten questions that she would like to have answered when in the spirit world. We went over this list just before her regression. As the facilitator of life-between-lives regressions, I knock myself out to try to get my client's questions answered. Carla had the typical list regarding people, events, etc. At the top of her list was the question about why she had this feeling that her work here on earth was done.

She went into trance state easily and went to a brief past life where she died at age three of a stray bullet in a war zone. There seemed to be no reason for her to see this particular past life. Carla rose rapidly to the spirit world. Half way there she was met by a spirit guide, but not her guide. This guide led her to a place in the spirit world where she was handed off to another guide that was not her guide either. This new guide took her to another location where, yet again, she was handed off to a third guide that was not her guide either.

By now I was in a quandary. I have never had a client not met by their guide or handed off along the way. Oddly enough she thought all this was the way it should be. She was on her way to where she was supposed to be. This she was sure of. And me? Oh well! I felt that my facilitator role had been usurped by a spirit who clearly was in charge. I let go and from that point forward the entire life-between-lives was being lead by another. I did get an opportunity along the way to ask a few very important questions – but most of my questions were simply answered by the dialogue between my client and her guide. Finally, she was taken to him!

Diane: Where are you now?

Carla: I'm now with my spirit guide, his name is Oak. I have been taken to the place of the elementals. This place is like an old growth forest with huge trees that goes on forever. I work with the nature forces creating tinctures here in the spirit world that will help people heal. I work well with my fingers.

I am here to work with other nature beings. We are fixing something that was damaged with our fingers. There has been some destruction that should not have happened – we are fixing it. There is a replication of the earth here but it is in light. As I am sitting here I know how to pull the earth's light into the elements: the nature elements. I know how they are all interconnected. It is very specialized work.

D: Is this your specialty in the spirit world?

C: No, my people are on a special assignment. We are working with the grids, there is something wrong with the grids, and they are out of kilter. They are light grids. We are trying to light them up again. I can see the light and how the lines are supposed to be restructured. We are repairing the damage. It is the earth's grid. I came in for a mission. We are working on the grids. We are also building a new grid to replace the old grid. We are working on aligning the old one and the new one with some purpose. We are bringing light into the grids. There is an ancient knowing in repairing the grids. Many of my people are telepathically working on the grids. We are all interconnected somehow. We are spirits – light spirits. We work with light. This feels very normal to me.

D: Are these spirits that you are with, those that you call "your people"; do they normally incarnate on the planet earth?

C: No – I belong someplace else completely. A veil is being put over that information – I am not able to share it. I'm now weaving lights together. The vibration is not where it is sup-posed to be right now on the grid. I am a grid worker. We are working on bringing the vibration up so that a whole bunch of beings can go up to the next vibration together. It is purple now. I am turning purple now. It is bringing the consciousness up. The darkness, the hard stuff is not going to be in this next place where we are going. The physicalness is going to be transformed. It is not going to be as solid, it will be lighter. I am a bridge between these two energies, the current grid and the new higher vibration grid. I am supposed to bring beings with me into this new energy level. There is a vibrational shift out of the so solid physical. There is something happening on the earth planet that is not right. We are all going to be light beings and it feels really good. The people on the planet earth are going to have a choice to move into this new, higher vibration or they can go someplace else. There are many of us working on bringing the grids together in a specific configuration so that beings can go up into this next layer or level. It is like another dimension. I am part of a team. We all came in together. There are a bunch of us.

D: Why is this new grid beginning created?

C: Something is going to 'bang' if we don't do this. It is a sense that something is going to combust. It will destroy us if we don't help. There is a sense of timing – and if the timing is not right on we are going to lose souls. There is urgency to our work. Beings are overseeing my team. This vibration is moving up and I am part of the group that is bringing the vibration up. There is a strong energy that is starting to be with me – it is sort of silver light – that just flashed over here. There is a tone that keys us to do our work together, it is like an orchestration of forces and my people are all part of the group that helps with this toning of the new energy- it is a sound that we are working with to pitch ourselves to help with this opening to bring us through the veil into this new dimension. It is a project that has been worked on for a really long time and the time is almost here. This is the detail work of moving things that are in the way out of the way.

D: So what is in the way?

C: It is getting peaceful, we are nearing the end of the time, it is getting really quiet – there is a new dawn coming. The time is changing, and it is almost there, and there is a pitch that will hit and we are waiting for that right moment. There is a lot of light that is going to come with this. We all know it is a really good thing. There is a lot of fear that does not need to be there. And somehow we are trying to clear the fear. We are a collective here working on this grid. I am going to be leaving this place now.

D: Where are you going to be going to?

C: I am going to my council. I am already there. There are six of them. There is a being that is overseeing the whole thing. This being is up above the council. A higher level being than the council. I'm in a purple robe. There is a coming together of two forces, a blending together, like a hybrid. I am part of the group that is trying to meld the change. We are trying to bring this liquid silver light into the golden light and there is a weaving of the forces. We are trying to braid these vibrations together to create another – there is something that is cracked from this side and the light can help mend it. I am fixing it now. We are here to work for the whole. We are hard wired to do what I am doing. We are architectural designers, we build with light and we get called in to repair things that go wrong. I am welding the bridge together and when I am done I get to leave. A new matrix is being built and I am part of the team. Now I am welding with a light beam. The people will pass over to the new grid and up to the new dimension. It feels like a lot of people will be on it soon. Many of us are meant to go together. There is a transition, lots of bright light. My people work more with tones than colors. I have left the council.

D: Where are you now?

C: Floating. There is a tone, a vibration around my spirit – it is an energy that heals me, it is in the heart. There is no fighting, no polarities, and no adversity around me. My work is done here in the spirit world and on earth, I don't have to be here anymore, the grid has been weaved and is connected. There is one connection that still needs to be made on the bridge to the new grid. I see the hands of my team helping to hold the vibration to help with the connection that needs to be made between the forces – some will be left behind – all are choosing which way they want to go – leave the planet earth or stay. There is a split of the people on earth. Those that have chosen will step into the new vibration. We are all toning together and as we do the pitch will change. When the pitch and color are right we are all going to transform. And it is good. The new dimension is of more light. People chose before they incarnated which way they are going to go: back to the spirit world or to stay on earth in the higher vibrational dimension of the new grid. It is a holograph, a mandala, with sparks of light which all need to spark together. This new energy will be infused into the cells of the physical body. Then we change vibrationally and we will all light up together. But the old needs to let go. Without fear – everything is fine – and going to be better – much better! We will all integrate together. This new grid is coming in, it has a newer quality of light than the old one, it will interconnect all beings, and we will be enmeshed together. It will not be a time as we now know it here. We will be part of a new dimension. What has been going on is not going to be going on anymore on earth. It is the end of a time. It is time to get off the boat and go into the new time or return. An interdimensional shift and change will happen. Planned at a higher level for a long time, choices have been made. People will not exist the way they have anymore. When we incarnated this time we all understood this shift would be happening on a spiritual level. Souls have chosen which path is best for their learning at this point. When the shift happens those going to the new grid will feel a flood of energy filling their bodies and hear a new tone, a hum. This energy looks like crystal blue sand. Then we will be up on the new vibration level, on the new grid, which is a significantly higher vibration. This new grid is like a gateway, a portal. The new grid will expand the interdimensional family. It is more all encompassing than the current grid. The polarities will be destroyed when we step up onto the new grid. Tension is important for the shift to happen.

When this regression was over I brought Carla back from the spirit world and into my consultation room. She was exhausted. But she said, "Wow, that makes my entire life make sense. I thought I was just an earthling that didn't fit in anywhere! Everything fits together now –

everything!! No wonder I am so uncomfortable here on earth!" So in a very real way, all of the questions on her list were answered, just in a different way. She was very grateful for her new understanding about herself.

After Carla left my office, I felt like I was in a place of suspended animation; in a space of deep contemplation of the mechanics of this upward shift in our level of consciousness. This was the answer to my five year old question. A new energy grid with a significantly higher vibration! A brilliant answer to the out-of-control problems present on planet earth! And coupled with this increased vibrational level would include the collapse of the polarities – this meant no more good versus evil; no more love versus anger; no more peace versus conflict. How wonderful. This explained what was related in other progressions about the communities after the shift from what is now into this new reality. We are being ushered into this new time – painful because it is like giving birth. But we are being assisted in the process of moving out of the darkness and into the light. And this plan has been in the making in the spirit world for a long time. It is an opportunity for souls to step into their fullness. It is sort of like we are all in a huge arena now, playing out the final moves of a failing game. What is in front of us is a portal through which we will pass into a renewed earth – a renewed earth with no more game playing - where all the pieces fall into place on one side of the polarity, where we will all become one in purpose, in love. No more fear. We will awaken to the truth of who we really are – loving beings. I was left with an amazing feeling that at all times help is here and on its way. This information affirmed my unending faith in the divine that somehow all will be alright. Whereas I have never given up hope for the future of humankind, it feels good to know that we are indeed headed into a time of peace and harmony. It is such a gift to know this now, so that as our situations intensify and adversities increase, we will know that it is all for the good and beautiful future of people on this grand planet.

Carla returned one month later for a second life-between-lives regression. Needless to say, I was prepared with my list of questions for her spirit guide. I don't think she was as excited as I to continue this exploration into the potentials of this future reality. She moved into trance easily and went straight to the spirit world.

Diane: Where are you now?

Carla: I see the crystal grid. I hear the tone, the hum. We are moving into the time of the breaking of the heart. There is going to be a break in the consciousness as we know it. It is hitting me in the heart and the ears. The hum is not harmonic now. The times are not harmonious now. There is no honoring and no loyalty. It hurts me to be in disharmony.

D: Is there anyone with you now?

C: Yes, I have just been ushered into my council, into a great hall. There is like an overseer here. I see a four pointed star. I am humbled by their presence. It is majestic here. They are showing me a portal; it is an opening for us, like a birthing. It has to break before the birth can happen. Then there are two pathways – and I see the ones I will be working with. There is quiet and a peaceful calm energy around them. It is a contemplative energy. On the other path there is a gray energy that is not lit up. They want me to hold the tension for the next piece. Tension is needed for growth. The disharmony on the planet is the tension. This tension is like a contraction in the birthing process. It is something to push against. We need to tighten ourselves up so we can push ourselves through the portal. This tension is beginning to be felt as grief; as pain in the heart. It is necessary to push this new creation through, which is full of light.

D: What will it be like here on earth after the shift?

C: The new time on earth after the shift will be calm; there will be a reverence and gratitude for what is there. There is a linking of the hands together between the people. I am in a canoe now, it is peaceful, and there is a lot of water around me. It is sort of like after a storm when there is calm. There is a forest where I am. We are fed from the land. It feels like things are back the way they were when the Native Americans lived on the land. The community where I live is in a forest. We are helping each other but in quiet. There is a reverence to it. We are all spiritually working together. It feels like a powwow circle. We are all working together and staying calm. We know our duties and are doing them. It is a planter and agricultural based community. Things are very simple. We get around in canoes and walk in the forests. It feels very right for the time. We live off the land. There is wholeness on the planet. The forest is what I resonate with. The grid has tightened a lot, it is now cellular. The light is tight. There is an elder in charge of the community; he is an overseer of how the people are working together. And the people are working very peacefully with the plant world. It feels very different from where we are now. Things are more pure; the vibration level is much higher than it is now; there is no pollution; there is a crystal clear energy around that feels very healing. The level of consciousness in the people is significantly higher. People are doing what they need to do but there is not the disharmony in the hearts. There is a common purpose. People know their path and live their path; there is not the confusion like I feel now. People are in harmony with their spirit, because of that we are in harmony with the nature elements. We are all one: the consciousness of the beings and the consciousness of the plant world and the animal spirits all understand each other and we do not create harm to each other like we do now. It is like we are all in our own little bubble and the bubbles all connect up. The new grid integrates onto the physical; it has become 3D and moves through the physical and sparkles. The people and animals are integrated into the grid, they are lit up and it feels like a 3D light thing but it actually embodies all of the physical. Our current reality feels flat compared to this new reality which feels saturated with light and there is a tone to the colors, a resonance that is very palpable. It feels like a fantasy kingdom! We are all in harmony. You can't pull one thing out without ruining everything else. All is one, but there is a placement for everything. We all are in harmony because we are in line with the spirit within the physical. There are not the polarities here. The guides here in the spirit world are very careful as to what they are letting me see. We are mid-whiffing this reality; a birthing that will pull us through a portal into this new reality. There is an energy burst forward that jumps us onto the new grid. There is a huge amount of energy that has not been available before that is pumped into our bodies. The body I am in now feels like a shell in comparison. There is a lot of help for us from the spirit world as this shift takes place. This energy feels very healing to me.

D: When will we jump onto this new grid?

C: This is all mapped out by us already; we just need to finish out the plan. These cards have been set in place. The rest will open up. The timing needs to be right. We are nearing that moment. We are in the birthing now. The actual timing is unpredictable because there is no time in the spirit world. We are moving into the alignment – when we hit the light we will move through the light and the shift will happen. When we move into this moment it will be like a switch is tripped, it will feel like a huge burst, with a flash of light. It feels like an atomic bomb as we jump onto the new grid. We will feel the quality of the moment as a vibration in our being that will resonate and we will be attracted to what we need. And this attraction will fuse us into this peaceful place that I see filled with beautiful trees and waters, all are pure again. It feels like a collective energy. It is a time of purification. A toning will come from above into our planet. A hum will permeate all.

Of all of my clients who experienced progressions, Carla was the only one who had no fear about the changes that are coming. For her, it all seemed like the normal flow and movement of the universe. She sees this as just the current reality which is birthing a new time. For Carla, change is just change.

But change is feared by most people because they do not know what the future will hold. Frightened humans will describe this transitional time with terms like "disasters" and "chaos". This attitude will cause emotional suffering added to the actual adversity these times will bring. In addition, most people do not handle difficulty well; they become emotionally reactive when faced with any sort of pain which in turn causes them untold suffering. Carla's two regressions, when seen together, show us clearly that the current difficulties are ushering in a new era that seems worth the almost certain increase in difficulties that will happen prior to the shift. Her guide also shows us how human consciousness will jump upward into a higher frequency. This higher level of consciousness will create new communities based on peace and union. Loving kindness will be the order of the day, leaving behind anger and violence. This feels like a blessing worth any difficulty that might precede the new enlightened time.

The next question is how to prepare for the difficult times before the shift, during the transition, and for the enlightened times to come.

It is clear that there are times of trouble in front of us that will bring with them intense and deep fear. The guides are aware and care deeply about humankind. They have shared methods to deal with this fear to keep us centered and focused on hope for the future.

Chapter Nineteen

Preparations: Start Now!

"Enlighten the people generally, and tyranny and oppressions of body and mind will vanish like evil spirits in the dawn of day."

Thomas Jefferson

"If you don't know where you're going, any road will get you there."

Lewis Carroll

As the unsettling factors increase in intensity, a deepening concern follows that may evolve into panic. We have choices, and the fork in the road may be approaching at warp speed. Was it planned prior to our birth? Did we know then what approach we will take when our choices narrow to survive or die, benefit others or only ourselves? This adversity presents an opportunity for individuals to accept the situation as a steep learning curve...which they will accept or deny.

Open, trusting, prepared souls will move through these times of turmoil by being present moment to moment – taking one step at a time, with a minimum of fear and doubt. Take time to develop a deep trust and faith in the spirit world and know that their plan is for the good of all. Any other information is miss-informed at best, or mis-truths based on greed and hatred. We must stand focused on the truth of our reality: we are divine loving spirits.

Some people have the luxury of time and money to work on increasing their level of consciousness. Others are focused on the day to day realities of surviving in these difficult economic and political times. Aware or not of the desire to increase our level of consciousness, it is time to align ourselves with our spiritual agenda, not our human agenda.

Identify with spirit, as all things material may not be what they seem and are colored by the fear we bring to the table. Those fears are already strong; look at the headlines, listen to the evening news, watch the talking heads on cable. When you identify with your spirit you will be able to keep to your path, focused on the truth of who you are and make your way through the swirling misperceptions. Tall order? Of course, but it's time to learn how to accomplish this balance amid the fear and chaos.

Through life-between-lives regressions, my clients' spirit guides have shared a three step process to support your journey. It begins with nourishing the body, mind, emotions, and the spirit. Meditation is emphasized in order to discipline the mind and develop an ongoing relationship with our spiritual center. Meditation nourishes the spirit by bringing us to a place of peace and harmony within ourselves. This is the natural state of our mind.

The second element emphasizes self care of the physical body. Because it is a container for our spiritual self, the physical body needs our respect and devotion to maintaining health and well-being in order to support us during the upcoming adversity. Beginning with the breath, expanding to the diet, and finally movement and rest, we have control over the choices we make with regard to our body.

The third element asks us to cultivate now the qualities of the future enlightened communities. Before the rebirth, we must choose to become part of the solution, not part of the problem that polluted our planet in the first place. Express love, perform kindnesses, and exercise a generosity of spirit daily. Extend a hand to another, express sincere concern, walk your talk. Be the golden rule.

Imagine for a moment everyone striving for this behavior in every moment... our world improves...measurably. Our hope for the future exists right now...the spirit guides challenge us to be that now. Acting in this way will bring you joy and happiness in your heart immediately. Be the person you want to become!

Meditation...

Meditation is an ancient practice present in all of the world's wisdom traditions. Meditation is a technique used to tame and train the mind toward single focus. The human mind is like a bucking bronco that is constantly chattering and commonly creating fearful negative story lines that lead us down the well-worn path of self-created misery and suffering.

Meditation quiets the mind and brings it into the positive service of its owner. Meditation is the best known technique for getting rid of stress. When we quiet our mind, the story lines that cause fear fade away as we focus. Meditation enables us to remain in the present moment. This makes it possible to direct our energy into positive caring places. Meditation opens the heart to compassion. It naturally causes us to be concerned about others, regardless of our differences. As our attention moves inward through meditation we directly encounter the divine wisdom center. This inner point of guidance enables us to make better choices. This ability dramatically increases the quality of our lives.

Meditation is practiced by putting your attention on the breath: the in-breath and the out-breath. You do not think about the breath; just put your attention on it. Also, just breathe normally. I like to meditate with my eyes closed so that there is one less distraction. The distractions during meditation are hearing noises, feeling body sensations like an itch on your face, and thinking about something. The goal while meditating is to quiet the mind. Whenever we become aware that our attention is no longer on our breath we simply and gently bring our attention back to the breath, and let go of any thoughts that we are having.

It is important to sit in a comfortable position and keep that position for the duration of your practice. Also, make sure the place where you are going to meditate has no unnatural noise, no TV, no music. Put your pets in another room, and choose a time when the people you live with will not interrupt your quiet space. Ensure respect and space for this important part of your life.

This simple description makes meditation sound easy. If it was, everyone would do it, and there would not be thousands of books, blogs, e-books, and CDs on the subject. The mind is constantly active at first. As time passes, we begin to notice a decrease in the number of thoughts that arise, and an increased ability to notice that our attention is not on the breath. Over time we begin to experience the peace and harmony that meditation brings.

To establish the practice, I recommend a minimum amount of three times per week for twenty minutes per sitting. If you do this, you will notice after a few months that the incessant mind chatter slows down. Another benefit within a relatively short time is a reduction in your emotional reactivity when something is going on in your life that you wish was not happening. When not meditating, you will notice that you are much more able to remain present with what is – including the fearful and the bad. This increased ability to remain in the moment without emotional reactivity enables you to make better choices, choices motivated by love, not fear.

My intention is not to teach meditation, but to give a brief understanding of what the practice entails. There are many myths around meditation in our culture. Just as aerobic exercise is good for cardiovascular health, meditation is good for our mental and spiritual health. Rather than be the victim of the fearful negative story lines your mind imagines, get in touch with the loving energy in the heart by quieting the mind through meditation. This shift in consciousness from the fearful mind to the loving mind will create an amazing life for you in an otherwise chaotic world.

Meditation is worth the time you put into it.
Meditation returns benefits beyond the value
of the time spent practicing it.
Meditation's rewards?
Priceless.

Physical Health…

The second part of this threefold path to well-being and preparedness, as outlined by the spirit guides, entails taking good care of your body. Exercise, eat nutritionally healthful foods, and keep your body weight within the healthy range. Daily aerobic exercise helps prevent various health problems. Working out with weights also increases our muscle mass and therefore our energy.

The human body is the only machine on the planet that improves with use. Not using our body makes us feel tired, and causes us to procrastinate, succumbing to laziness. Healthy foods, free of toxins like insecticides, pesticides, and growth hormones, will maintain our energy at a higher level. Toxins stored in the body cause illness.

Refrain from mind-altering drugs, alcohol, and tobacco products. It is not healthy to be underweight or overweight. Carrying extra body weight is one of the largest contributors to various health problems. Being overweight also causes us to be less mobile, less able to walk long distances, and decreases our response time.

Physical health contributes to our self esteem, mental health, and emotional well-being. Unhealthiness in the body contributes to negative thoughts in our mind. The mind and body are constantly interacting, an instant simultaneous communication. So if we do not keep our body healthy, we are less likely to set aside the time to train our minds.

As we move into the future, it is imperative that our body is healthy. A healthy body responds quickly, capably, and effectively. The spirit guides indicate a life-style change that includes more physical activity: walking more, lifting more, moving more. Our culture is full of items that help our work to be easier, everything from can openers to chain saws. None of these handy contraptions will be available in the future if they require electrical power or gas...personal preparation benefits all of us.

The End of Inertia
"When you get to the end of your rope, tie a knot and hang on."
Franklin D. Roosevelt

Not only do healthy people get sick less frequently, but healthy people feel better all of the time. Many of us are challenged by the discipline required to maintain a healthy body. One spirit guide in a life-between-lives session showed my client a prayer group in the spirit world that is constantly meeting – they never stop. This group is praying for the end of human inertia. Because humanity seems unconcerned, this prayer group prays for this disregard to stop and enlightened awareness to take hold. Unfortunately, many on our planet are not willing to take any steps to improve their situation, or to put any energy into the issues challenging our planet. Apathy, powerlessness, boredom, and lethargy are unacceptable excuses to allow the decline of bodies, minds, and spirits.

The message is clear; as we move into the increasing troubles of the immediate future, our ability to deal with adversity will be greatly enhanced if we now attend to improving the physical health of our body.

Emotional Health...
The third part of this threefold path is emotional health. The spirit guides suggest this process is about taking on now the emotional qualities of the enlightened communities of the future. They urge us to be, right now, the change we want to see in the world.

- This world needs more caring and helpful people.
- This world needs more people that will have a positive attitude toward their daily chores.

- This world needs more people who are committed to their community rather than their own personal gain.
- This world needs more people who will celebrate differences, not judge them.
- This world needs more people who will be happy for another's success, not envy others.
- This world needs people who will promote the well-being of all on the planet.

The biggest problem on the earth contributing to the downfall of the human race is hatred and violence, which is spreading. Between nations, between neighbors, and within families, violence is on the rise as stress and fear increase. We take our frustrations out on our loved ones, those we are closest to, because we trust them to take it. Child and spousal abuse destroy the emotional integrity of people as much as famine and warfare. Gangs, drug trafficking, bullying, and stalking affect not only the intended victims, but also innocent bystanders.

Re-scripting...Restoring Civility Among People...

Peace and loving kindness begin at home. Working on getting rid of our negative emotions is a difficult task. Begin by observing them and their effect on others and ourselves. Every time we express one of these emotions we need to step back and ask ourselves how we could have expressed our feeling or opinion in a more positive way. This is what I call 're-scripting': rewriting what did not work. If we do this diligently and are honest with ourselves we will see a shift happen quickly.

We will notice that we allow ourselves to indulge in negative emotions at the expense of others. If we choose our words carefully, we can say what we need to say without harming others. It is a skill that we need to develop so that our homes, workplaces, and communities will be kinder and more caring places. The hope for the future is held in this present moment. Express only positive emotions to promote a loving community now.

During a life-between-lives regression, the spirit world has us look at various negative emotions with the intent of transforming them into loving emotions. Every difficult emotion has its positive counter-part. Many of us have chosen lessons to work on in this life that have to do with negative emotions. This lesson may involve a difficult relation-ship, a phobia, or a painful body part that causes us to regularly express a negative emotion. If we lean into working on negative emotions we invariably will also be working on the lesson we chose in this life. Many of these lessons involve letting go of fear and doubt and moving toward unconditional love toward ourselves, toward another in an important relationship, and from there out into the world. This emotional work that we do in our own area of the planet positively affects the energy field of the entire planet.

When we begin to work on our emotional health we all will face the negative emotions of fear, anger, pride, deceit, envy, greed, lust, and laziness, to name a few. Fear seems to trigger most negative emotions. It seems to be the driving force behind most difficult moments. Anger is a secondary emotion and is most often used to cover up hurt, or fear of rejection, *and is always used to try to control others.*

When we get angry it is because we want others to do it our way. Anger is unfortunately easy for most of us to express and is a knee-jerk reaction. Deceit, on the other hand, is usually not obvious and is used to get away with something. Lying may or may not be known by the other at the time, but when discovered the damage is much more harmful.

Envy is the opposite of being happy for another's success. Sometimes we are envious of another's career, or maybe their home, or car. Envy causes us to feel bad about ourselves, that we are not capable of doing or getting something for ourselves. Envy can cause greed. Greed can be about money, power, or possessions. Greed comes from a position of scarcity – wanting as much as you can get – it is like gluttony – constantly wanting more.

Lust most often refers to sexual lust. This causes the one lusting to take advantage of the other. Those working on the issue of lust will find themselves using others as objects. This negates the spirit. Laziness causes us to let life pass us by. It shows up in our not working on our issues and not seeming to care about the quality of our life. Laziness causes us to put off what may be important opportunities for creating good in our life. Our lessons will not be learned if we cave in to laziness.

Working on our emotional health is a continuous process. Preparing for both the difficult times to come, and for an easier transition into the enlightened communities of the future, calls for us to work diligently on our emotions in every waking moment. Our work is to overcome negative emotions and express loving feelings as frequently as possible. As we make this commitment and take on the task of this process with time we will find that love and joy are more constant in our lives. We will notice that when we slip into old habits of negative emotions that are harmful to ourselves and others, we will quickly catch ourselves, correct the error, and move forward. This process will enable us to summon helpful emotions when adversity arises.

Summary...

The threefold path prepares us for adversity in the future. It includes developing a meditation practice, taking care of the physical body, and creating emotional health by transforming negative emotions into helpful loving thoughts, words, and deeds. If we work to keep our body strong, our mind clear, be with our spirit, feel its truth through meditation, and project this out into the world, we then will be ready for whatever arises. These three parts together enable each of us to bring optimal health to our mind, body, emotions and our spirit. Embracing this threefold path will put us in the best possible position now and for the future. This path gives us hope for the future, which otherwise would look like an increasingly dismal picture. If we take on this path diligently we will come to understand that the enlightened times are available in this very moment. Where love is, so is the awakened mind. Be truly present in the moment and you will experience the light of love eternal.

Spiritual Warrior...

To undertake this threefold path is to become a spiritual warrior. Commitment and courage will be required along the way. Many spiritual teachers have walked the earth for eons. They have shown us the way of love and harmony. Their lives have demonstrated the level of caring for humankind that is necessary for enlightened times to unfold and overtake the planet as a way of life.

One who wrote clearly about how to care for others was an 8th century monk named Shantideva. His name means 'the god of peace'. He writes of a level of compassion that, if practiced, would transform our world. His words remind me of the messages received from those highly evolved spirits in the spirit world, who work so hard to help us accomplish our spiritual agenda here on earth. They are always patient with us. Their words are always encouraging and non-judgmental. They want only love and kindness to exist here on earth. They will be there for us and will help us find the strength to carry on when all seems lost and we have come to our darkest moment. This is the same flavor that Shantideva carries throughout his writings. His words clearly state the level of commitment that we can create for ourselves that will change our world and create enlightenment in this very moment. He said:

"May I become at all times, both now and forever

A protector for those without protection

A guide for those who have lost their way

A ship for those with oceans to cross

A bridge for those with rivers to cross

A sanctuary for those in danger

A lamp for those without light

A place of refuge for those who lack shelter

And a servant to all in need."

Shantideva